LET'S STICK TOGETHER

AN APPRECIATION OF KITMASTER and AIRFIX RAILWAY KITS

By Stephen Knight

To my wife Claire, for her patience.

Copyright IRWELL PRESS & STEPHEN KNIGHT
ISBN 1-871608-90-2

Biographies

The Author

Stephen Knight was born in Kingston, Surrey in 1961. From a young age, he was fascinated by railways and witnessed the closing years of Southern steam from the family home in Basingstoke. In 1987, he discovered a built-up Kitmaster 'Pug' in a box of second-hand model railway items he had purchased. It was love at first sight. From then on, he determined to find out as much as possible about these fascinating models, culminating in the publication of this book In 1990 Steve founded the Kitmaster Collectors Club, which now has more than 200 members.. He is married, with two young sons and a cat, and lives in Essex.

The Model Maker

Marcus Archer was born in Chester in 1959, the year Kitmaster appeared in the shops. He attended a school in Chester with a railway line at the bottom of the playground. His father is a commercial artist and Marcus has inherited his love of painting and his endless patience. He started building kits as a boy and even then paid special attention to correct painting and lining. Today, he enjoys building the occasional Kitmaster and Airfix model and as Exhibition Officer of the Kitmaster Collectors Club he has regular opportunities to put them on public display.

Acknowledgements

The Author would like to thank the following people for their invaluable assistance with this project:

Stephen Alexander (Companies House), Dennis Andrews, Keith and Patricia Anthony, Marcus Archer, Ken Bancroft, Mrs. Rose Barker, David Boyle (Dapol Model Railways), David Brown (British Railway Modelling), Lee Buckingham, Andrew Burford, R.D.Bushby, Michael Catalani, Linda Cuthbertson, Joe Chubbock, Ray Clarke, Peter Corley (Grafar Circle), Roy Cross, Mrs W Crozier, Howard Corn and David Gould (The Eagle Society), James Day, Roger Dent, Merl Evans, Mr Fergusson, The late Cyril Ferry, Tom Freeman, Nick Gillman, Caroline Goodfellow, (V and A), Bruce Gregory (Top Shed Models), Peter Hilton, David Howarth (Northants Herald and Post), Graham Howe, David Jinks (Model Railway Enthusiast), Tony Kendall, Geoff Killick (Braintree Model Railways), John Law, Corinne Lawrence (RPC Containers), Maj. W.S.Lee, Pat Lewarne (CollectaKit), Richard Lines (Hornby Hobbies), Joe Lock, Luciano Luppi, David Luesby, Chris March, Rod Moore (Cumberland Toy and Model Museum), Joseph Moss, Bob Murchison, George Nixon, Liz Oliver (Northants Newspapers Ltd), D.C.Owens, Robert and Janet Parker, John Rimmer, Kenneth Rush, Kathleen Shaw, Graham Short, Milan Simek, Tony Palm, Terry McAvoy, Peter Skinner, Nick Smith (3 mm Soc.), Mr S. Smith, Hazel Smith and T. Eric Smith CBE (Rosebud), David Stocks, Mrs. W Sweeting, June Thompson, Trevor Tremethick, Dixon Upcott (TTRCA), Neil Walker, John Wells (Airfix Collectors Club), Andy Wright, Stephen Wheatcroft (SNCFS), David Winpress, Pollock's Dolls Museum, Robert Opie Museum of Packaging, RPC Containers Ltd.,Cereal Partners UK Ltd., Ordnance Survey Publications, Hunting Aerofilms Ltd., RFWW Publications/ British Railway Modelling, Peco/The Railway Modeller, Model Railway Enthusiast, Model Railways, Northants Herald and Post, Chronicle and Echo, Northamptonshire Newspapers Ltd, the staff of the Northamptonshire Museums and Information Service, and the members of the Airfix and Kitmaster Collectors Clubs and the Braintree and Halstead Model Railway Club. Special thanks are due to the photographers Tim Shackleton and Tony Wright and the Irwell Press team, Chris Hawkins and George Reeve for their enthusiastic support of this project.

Grateful thanks for permission to reprint material is extended as follows:

For articles from *'Railway Modeller'*- Peco Publications and Publicity Ltd.
For articles from *'Model Railway News'*- *'Model Railways'*/Argus Publications Ltd.
For articles from *'Model Railways Constructor'*- Ian Allan Ltd.

CONTACT THE KITMASTER COLLECTORS' CLUB AT HTTP://WWW.KITMASTER.MCMAIL.COM
OR WRITE TO THE SECRETARY, 109, HEAD STREET, HALSTEAD, ESSEX CO9 2AZ

First published in the United Kingdom in 1999
by Irwell Press
59A, High Street, Clophill,
Bedfordshire MK45 4BE
Printed By DPI Printers Luton, England

CONTENTS

Preface to the First Edition.

In 1962, the precariously balanced finances of the Rosebud organisation finally tipped against Kitmaster and the company was sold outright to Airfix. I was too young at that time to remember anything of the brightly coloured Kitmaster boxes which had rapidly established themselves as favourites in model shops throughout the land. I first came across Kitmaster models in a box of old locomotives purchased from a jumble sale many years later. Where does the fascination with these models lie?

Could it be a yearning for the brash kitsch of a bygone age, or the wonderfully eccentric planning behind the Kitmaster concept; or perhaps enthusiasm born from a realisation that these were, and still are, some of the finest scale railway kits ever produced? They are certainly varied and interesting, to the point of becoming idiosyncratic. In an attempt to provide something for everyone, we are faced with a range of kits that lines up a diminutive L&Y Pug next to a towering Hudson locomotive; models that are geographically and historically in two different worlds.

Here lies the magic: the unanswered questions, the enigmas lost in the mists of time, submerged under a mountain of dusty paperwork. My research over the last eight years has taken me far and wide in search of the answers. I hope you will enjoy the fruits of my labour, for this is truly the story of a remarkable company with a remarkable product. At the time advanced and innovative, Kitmaster and Airfix models are today cherished collectors' pieces in their own right.

Wherever they are, Kitmaster models always manage to create a sense of excitement in people. The older ones fondly remember them from their heyday, saving their pocket money to buy the latest model. Younger observers are fascinated by the wealth of detail in these vintage "toys", which once used to keep their fathers and uncles very creatively occupied on a Saturday evening!

For me, they will always hold a certain magic, as through the pages of this book I hope to bring Rosebud Kitmaster to life for a whole new generation of modelmakers. Whilst space constrains the amount of detail it is possible to provide in a work of this nature, you will find a series of essays on particular models in the range. I apologise whole-heartedly and in advance for the choice of models. If your particular favourite is not covered, it is only because I chose them in no particular order and wrote them over a period of years. I do hope that you will not be too disappointed!

Stephen Knight, Halstead 1998.

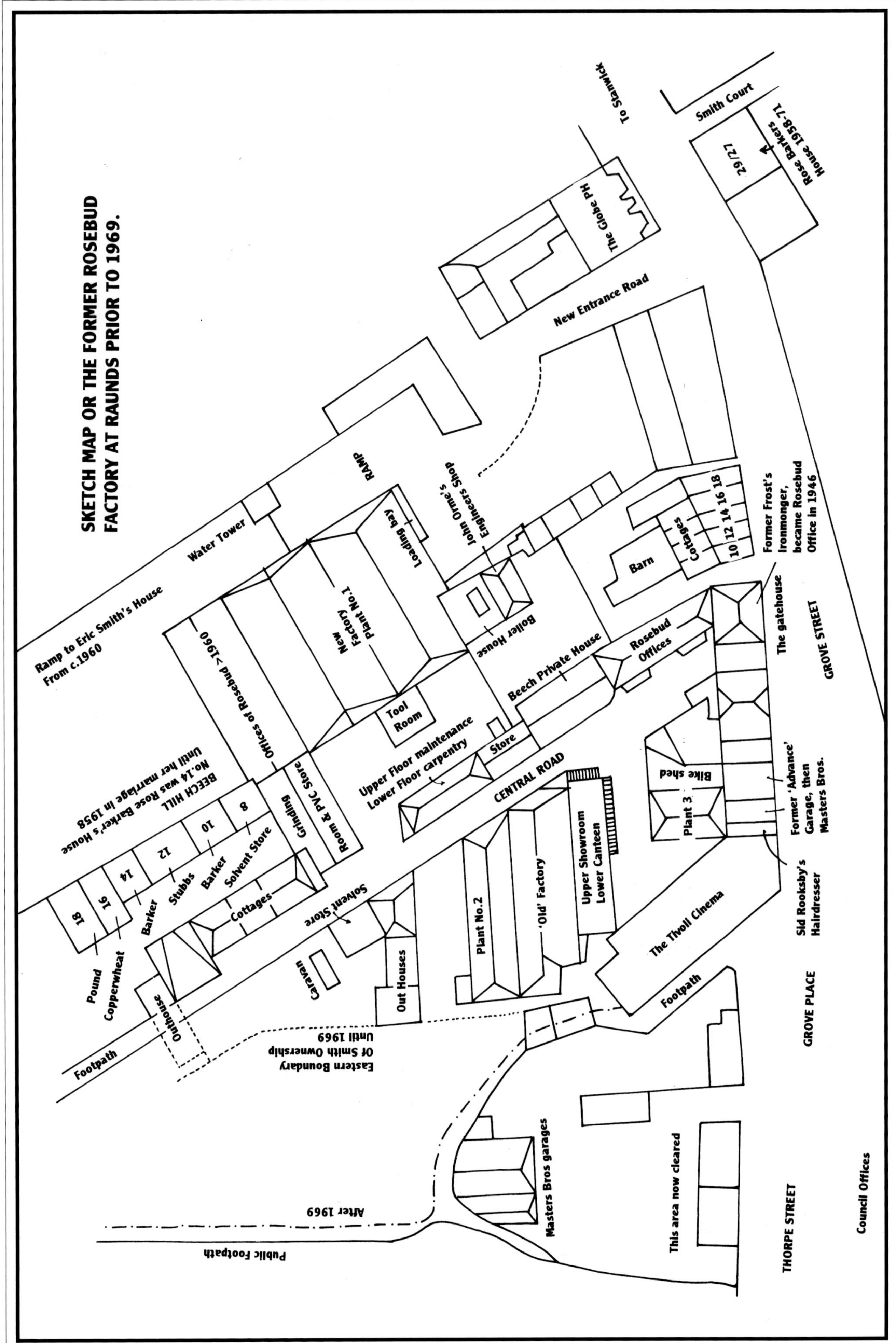

This map of the Rosebud site in Raunds was compiled from aerial photographs and notes from interviews with former workers. It is based on the 1929 Ordnance Survey 1:2500 scale map.

An Introduction to Rosebud Kitmaster

A Rose by any other name...

Who Were Rosebud?

The story of Rosebud is really the story of one remarkable businessman. The Managing Director of the Rosebud group of companies was Thomas Eric Smith, always known as T. Eric Smith. He was born on 22nd April 1916 in the East End of London, where his father and mother had their own business making and selling toys. Eric spent his formative years learning the toy trade and left school at just 13 years of age. He was immediately set to work for the family business, but his father proved a hard taskmaster. He put Eric to work in his first week cleaning out the loos, much to the annoyance of his mother. So one might say that he learned the business from the bottom!

When Eric was fifteen, his father died and from 1931 he had to support his mother, himself and the business. The family had two factories in east London making beech horses, dolls houses and forts.

By the outbreak of war in 1939, the family business, Masks Ltd, was mostly producing heads for soft fabric dolls. The old factories were heavily bombed over a three-day period in 1940. The first factory was hit on a Sunday night, followed by the second factory on the following Monday lunchtime and, just to make things worse, the Smith family house was hit that very same Monday night. With nowhere to live, nowhere to work and no possessions to speak of, Eric and his mother were forced to leave London.

Sheltering from the blitz in a temporary shelter away from the bombing in Northamptonshire, Eric and his mother took stock of their situation. The war was at its height. London was taking a regular pounding from the Luftwaffe. There was little point in trying to set up their business in the capital again. But life in the Salvation Army hostel in Rothwell was grim and soul destroying. Eventually, they decided to move back to London and to start again.

Having set off on the long journey down the A6 back to London, Eric began to have second thoughts. In Kettering, he stopped the car, went into a newsagent to buy some tobacco and casually asked the proprietor if he knew of any vacant factories thereabouts. He was told of one near Rushden, further down the A6. When he reached Rushden, he asked again in a similar shop. This time it was a customer who answered: "Go to Raunds and ask for Alderman Corby OBE". Eric had never heard of Raunds in his life, but soon located it. "I drove into town and

NORTHAMPTONSHIRE

VYNOLAY

J. A. Watts & Co. Ltd

Evening Telegraph

Every Weekday since 1897 TUESDAY, JUNE 16, 1964 Price 3d.

EXPRESS DRY CLEANERS

ALL GARMENTS ARE NOW HAND PRESSED

RECEIVER APPOINTED FOR ROSEBUD DOLLS

Work to continue while affairs are being investigated

A Receiver has been appointed for the Raunds and Wellingborough firm of toy manufacturers, Rosebud Dolls Ltd., about whose affairs there has been speculation in recent weeks. The announcement was made in a brief statement issued to the "Evening Telegraph" today.

It stated: "In order to safeguard the position generally, the debenture holders of Rosebud Dolls Ltd., have appointed Mr. E. C. Baillie, chartered accountant, as Receiver from June 15, 1964.

In dealing with the company's affairs, the Receiver intends to ensure continuation of employment while the matters of the company are being investigated, and supplies to customers will continue as before."

AT LEAST 18 KILLED BY JAPANESE EARTHQUAKE

At least 18 people are known to have died and more than sixty were injured in an earthquake which rocked northern and central Japan this afternoon.

RIVER

Contd. on Page 2

Weather

TRAIN CRASH AT HARBOROUGH BLOCKS MAIN LINES

Sharing the front page with a train crash was the financial crash at Rosebud. Dig that groovy BR standard A container!

Rosebud News **was first published in September 1953 and ceased publication at the end of 1955. It was highly regarded by the workers and management alike.**

ROSEBUD DOLLS LIMITED

RAUNDS, NORTHAMPTONSHIRE

TELEPHONE: RAUNDS 2141 (10 LINES) TELEGRAMS: ROSEBUD, RAUNDS: CABLES: ROSEBUD, RAUND

K. Shaw

I have now had an opportunity of looking into certain aspects of the business and have arranged increased schedules for the factory.

Following my appointment as Receiver I now confirm that I have taken over responsibility for your employment on the same terms you had with Rosebud Dolls Limited, with immediate effect.

Yours faithfully,

E. C. BAILLIE
Receiver.

DIRECTORS: T. E. SMITH, J. R. ASHBY, D. H. BIRCH

This letter was sent to all staff at Rosebud Dolls by the Receiver Mr.Baillie, following his appointment in June 1964.

The British Industries Fair was held at Olympia each year and showcased all that was best from Britain's exporting industries. This 1955 display was re-erected by carpenter Wally Thomas in Rosebud's own 'shop window' on Grove Street.

stopped the first man I saw in the street" he recalls. "I told him I was looking for Alderman Corby OBE. He drew himself up to a full six feet and said "I am Alderman Corby OBE". I said that I'd been told he could help me find a vacant factory site. He looked over his shoulder and said "See that building there? That's it. Do you want to look around it?" We had stopped right outside Frost's the Ironmongers in Grove Street. Well, we looked it over and I agreed a three-year let at an annual rent of £100 per year." So they never did make it back to London, but settled in Raunds, even bringing some of their East End girls up to Raunds to help them. The girls didn't stay long: they hated the countryside, the quiet and slow pace of life in Raunds, and soon pined for London.

No sooner had Masks Ltd been relocated, during October 1940, in the former William Nicholls' Boot factory in Grove Street than Eric Smith was called up for active service. He joined the RAF and was posted abroad, not returning until 1946. Mrs A.R. Smith had set up business in the shop and former mechanics workshop of the Advance Garage, also part of the former boot factory in Grove Street. During his service career, Eric had conceived some new and exciting ideas for toys which he now wanted to put into practice. His best ideas involved the low cost construction of dolls using glues and sawdust, known as composites. Some of his early experiments were conducted in the kitchen ovens of the family and their friends in the Raunds area. Before the Second World War, most dolls were made in Germany with heads of porcelain. These expensive dolls were effectively made extinct by the War, thereby creating a market opportunity. When Eric returned to the UK, he resumed working for Masks Ltd, where he was a Director. However, hungry for new success, T. Eric Smith founded his own toy making company, Nene Plastics Ltd, on a new site in the former boot factory in Grove Street. The new company was set up with £10,000 of authorised share capital, of which Eric owned 7,248 shares each of £1, and registered at Companies House, No. 424125, on 21st November 1946 with Eric as the first Director and Beatrice Cole as Company Secretary. He was soon joined by his new wife Hazel Lillie Smith, whom he appointed a Director of Nene Plastics with a further £1,000 of shares. They had married on 12th June 1946.

Nene Plastics' first range of dolls was branded Starlight Dolls, although this name does not appear to have been registered. Following a successful mortgage application to TMF Ltd for £846, submitted on 18th December 1946, the area behind his mother's business was purchased and used for production and offices. This proved inadequate very quickly and a further mortgage was secured on the 7th April, enabling Eric to purchase more of the former boot factory from Kirkstall Estates, who owned it. This new deal for £6,000 bought land and property around the site, which included cottages 8-16 in Beech Hill and 8-12 in Grove Street, together with *'All of that barn situate at the rear of 14 Grove Street, all of those two shop fronts situate on Grove Street, 5.6 acres of land and paddocks and all of that band hall of the Raunds Temperance Band.'* Although underwritten initially by Eric together with Edward J Moran, Works Manager, this loan was transferred in 1949 to the Halifax Building Society and extended by a further £1,200 to facilitate the purchase of remaining property

A critical day in the history of Rosebud was 20th June 1967, in the Mattel Inc. boardroom, Los Angeles, USA. L to R: Hazel Smith, Eric Smith (with ubiquitous pipe), Ruth and Elliot Handler. The Rosebud Directors sign the deal to merge with Mattel Inc.

Rosebud maintained showcases for their dolls in a showroom above the Canteen at Grove St. Later this area also contained a model railway layout populated by Kitmaster.

on the site from Kirkstall Estates. This gave Nene Plastics most parts of the former boot and shoe factory, together with the frontages on Grove Street that had been Frost's Ironmongery and several other businesses, including a hairdresser. These buildings were eventually designated Plant Two (Doll final assembly) and Plant Three (Doll head/wig production).

There were plenty of local women who were very pleased to work for the new enterprise, Nene Plastics Ltd, making its premier doll range, Starlight Dolls. At about that time in 1946, British Overseas Airways Corporation began a new air service to South America and called it *'The Starlight Service'*. Eric liked the name and used it for his new doll making venture. By May of 1947, Eric had secured orders form the USA for $100,000 worth of dolls and adopted the slogan 'Dollars for Dolls' to spearhead his export drive. The new 7' high composite dolls were shown at the British Industries Fair at Olympia, a fixture which became a regular event in the Rosebud year, together with the Harrogate and Brighton Toy Fairs. These dolls were immensely popular with British audiences and remained in production, albeit made of PVC, for many years.

Eric soon settled into his newly adopted home town. He became a town councillor and with his new wife, moved into an imposing house called Ashfields Hall. This Victorian property had been constructed for a former partner in the Nicholls Boot factory, also called Smith, who had left and started his own successful footware company.

At the beginning of 1946, Nene Plastics employed 39 people in the Raunds factory. On 20th March 1947, Eric registered the trademark "Rosebud" for dolls, No. 657461. The name 'Rosebud' was originally coined when a young girl, who was visiting the factory, was presented with a choice of dolls from the factory display cabinet by T. Eric Smith. The girl chose a new design which Hazel Smith had only just dressed and placed on display. The girl thanked 'Uncle Eric' and then her mother asked her why she had chosen that doll and what she liked best about it. "She has lovely rosebud lips" said the girl. Eric adopted it as the name for that design of doll. 'Miss Rosebud', as the doll was known, was very successful. Soon, all the other dolls were being given Rosebud names in line with the new trademark.

With the retirement of his mother, T. Eric Smith acquired her business, Masks Ltd., together with the parts of the Grove Street site which had been used by that company. On 16th February 1949, Eric and his fellow Directors increased the Authorised Share capital of the company from £10,000 to £20,000, thereby raising some much needed cash. More Directors were appointed, so that by 1950 there were seven:

T. Eric Smith	**Chairman and Managing Director**
Hazel Smith	**described as "Married Woman"**
R.F. Ruff	**Company Secretary**
R.W. Shaw	**Manager**
Sid Wilding	**Maintenance Engineer**
F.W.Burton	**Accountant**
A.F. Palmer	**Accountant**

The last two held just one share each, which was the minimum required to qualify as a Director.

During 1950, T. Eric Smith registered two important patents, on the subject of 'Improvements in the design and construction of dolls', which were duly granted in 1953, as Nos. 667091 and 667906. By the beginning of 1953, a new PVC plant, making beachballs (!), had come on stream. In September 1953, a 10,000 sq. ft. site, to the west of the existing plant, was cleared for construction of a new injection moulding plant which would boast 25 moulding machines turning out 25,000 dolls per day at peak production. Constructed to the design of Philip Loaring, Rosebud's chief draughtsman, by Smith and Son builders (no relation) under the direction of site foreman Tom Sanders, the new factory was completed ahead of schedule.

The new facilities, formally designated

Gaily coloured Point of Sale displays were supplied to the Trade during 1959. They combine a made up model, a 10s 6d kit and a handful of '59 catalogues.

Plant One and often referred to as the 'New' factory, initially went on-line on 1st February 1955. Boasting a full suite of offices, toilets, rest areas and a loading bay, it was the epitome of modern manufacturing and a big improvement on the improvised facilities of the 100-year-old former boot factory. Plant One was commissioned to set about making the injection moulded parts for Nene Plastics' two main product lines: 'Rosebud' dolls and 'Neneware' kitchenware. However, by the summer of 1955, doll production was far outstripping everything else. At the end of that year, with doll sales soaring 63% to top 5,000,000 units, Eric decided to drop 'Neneware' and 'Masks' and to concentrate on Miss Rosebud - the premier Nene Plastics Ltd doll. To reflect this change of emphasis, the Board of Directors agreed at an Extraordinary General Meeting of the company on 27th January 1955 to change the name of the company to Rosebud Dolls Ltd. The change was approved by the Board of Trade on 15th February 1955.Eric also took his first steps away from the Raunds site about this time. A lease on premises in Rock Street, Wellingborough was acquired. This was formerly C.E. and H.B. Groome, leather suppliers. Although it was initially used for doll production, to alleviate pressure on space in Raunds, Rock St was eventually converted into a warehouse. It was managed by Bill Crozier and despatched Rosebud Dolls as finished products direct to Millwall docks for shipment abroad, as well as to the UK market.

Polymer	*Product Range*
Polyethylene	**Children's Buckets**
	'Neneware'
	Pails
	Washing-up Bowls
	Sink-tidies
	Measuring jugs
	Beakers
	Soap Dish
	Egg Tray
	'Aquatoys'
	Swimming fish for the bathtub
Polyvinyl chloride	**Children's inflatable balls**
	Rosebud Dolls - parts
	Rotary cast toys such as the 'puppy'
Cellulose Acetate	**'Teddy Bear' doll**
	'Miss Rosebud' dolls

In 1955, the shareholding of Nene Plastics was as follows:

T. Eric Smith	**81.5%**	**(Managing Director)**
Hazel Smith	**15%**	**(Eric's wife and chief dress designer)**
R.F.Ruff	**2.5%**	**(Company Secretary)**
W.S.Lee	**1%**	**(Major Lee, Works Manager)**

The company had an impressive portfolio of products at this time: according to Eric, the plastic bucket was the first product to be advertised on a full half-page and in colour in the *Daily Express* newspaper. Eric and his management team travelled down to Fleet Street to see the paper being 'put to bed' and printed with their ground-breaking advertisement in it. A later introduction (c. 1958) in polystyrene was a birdbath and bird feeder, which according to the women who worked on them, were extremely monotonous to make.

Rosebud's site chemist, Mr Robert Parker, had trained at ICI in Welwyn Garden City and by 1955 was living with his wife Janet, Rosebud's Personnel Officer, in a caravan on the Rosebud site, there being still an acute housing shortage following the War. His skill enabled Rosebud to capitalise on all the latest polymer developments and he was instrumental in the later switch to polystyrene needed for Easi-Build and Kitmaster products. T. Eric Smith says that Easi-Build and Kitmaster were not the first polystyrene products they made. Bob and Dennis Franklin seem to remember a pull-along dog toy that had a polystyrene base which may well have been the first use of the material by Rosebud. Certainly, Rosebud was one of the first British companies to make full use of injection moulding machines.

Hazel Smith was Rosebud's chief dress designer for the dolls' costumes and went to great lengths to research the very latest styles around the world, always keeping abreast of the latest trends and fashions. Eric attributes much of Rosebud's success to Hazel's skill as a designer, rating her second only to her contemporary designer at Ideal Toys in New York at the time. Even the *Evening Telegraph* attributed most of Rosebud Dolls' success to 'the great demand for the Rosebud series because of their originality of dress.'

From an early point in the business, the sole sales concessionaire for Rosebud Dolls was L. Rees and Co. Ltd, of 32-35 Wilson Street, London EC2, an association which lasted from 1947 to 1958. In the very first edition of the house newsletter, *Rosebud News*, in 1953, Mr Sydney Myers, a Director of L. Rees and Co. Ltd, wrote an excellent article detailing how the dolls were marketed and sold around the world. A major change occurred towards the end of 1963, when the sales policy was switched from distribution via wholesalers to direct supply to retailers, a move that has become more popular in recent years.

In 1958, Rosebud Kitmaster was formed to make plastic construction kits by the injection method, using excess capacity in the Rosebud Dolls Ltd. injection room. This technology was well understood by Rosebud, there being a number of injection moulded products and parts in their catalogue. T. Eric Smith says that they decided to move into kit manufacturing "because at the time it was a growing industry. We went into the train side because it was different." T.E. Smith was Managing Director, whilst J. R. Ashby acted as the Finance Director. John Raymond Ashby, who had replaced R. H. Ruff on his retirement in 1954 as Company Secretary, was formerly with W. J. Thompson and Co. Ltd, the firm of chartered accountants which audited the books of Nene Plastics Ltd., and was consequently familiar with their operations. He later became a Director. By 1962, there were two more named directors of Rosebud Kitmaster Ltd., Douglas Howard Birch and Charles Arthur Green. Mr Green was Works Manager and later became Works Manager at Rosebud-Mattel and eventually at Smith's Containers, whilst Mr. Birch was the Sales Manager at Rosebud.

The Company Secretary of Rosebud Dolls was Mr J. R. Ashby, but Rosebud Kitmaster Ltd. had its own Company Secretary to comply with the Companies Act. For some unexplained reason, there are no records of a limited company called Rosebud Kitmaster Ltd at Companies House. With the recent death of John Ashby, it is not now possible to say why this should be. One can only suppose that Rosebud Kitmaster was a private trading partnership with no issued share capital. However, the Company Secretary was Mr.P. G. Minney, who held the post from 1958 until 1960. Philip Minney was the General Office Manager for Rosebud Dolls Ltd. from 1951 until 1960 and oversaw a team of four workers in that capacity. His role was rather low-key in the Kitmaster organisation. Ashby was a much

Baby Rosebud was a very popular pocket-money doll which sold by the thousand.

A selection of Rosebud's non-railway products. Larger Miss Rosebud dolls and another Baby Rosebud sit together with a plastic squeaky dog!

more powerful figure, and it seems as though Philip was appointed very much 'on paper' only. His job expanded rapidly when Rosebud wound up their long partnership with L. Rees and Co. Rees had been responsible for representing Rosebud products to the trade. However, their long association came to an end in 1958 and Rosebud had to recruit its own sales force. This required a trebling, to twelve people, in the size of the General Office staff and immediately wiped out any cost savings over the previous arrangement. Kitmaster had an entirely separate sales force, since the distribution network used very different types of shops to the main doll business. Philip Minney left Rosebud in 1960 and went to Basset-Lowke, where he remained until 1969. He is now retired and lives in Worcestershire.

Rosebud Kitmaster Ltd. had no premises of its own, but part of the 'New' factory, known as Plant One or just 'P1', at Raunds was converted for use by Kitmaster (*see site plan*). In December 1959, T. Eric Smith disclosed to the press that main doll production would be relocated to Wellingborough. New premises were found in Westfield Road, which had been a former Co-Operative Wholesale Society corset factory. It proved spacious and ideally suited to Rosebud's needs. Initially, a bank loan facility was used to purchase the premises, but on 8th September 1960 this was converted to a £20,000 mortgage provided by Credit For Industry Ltd. Production was transferred there in spring 1960, leaving Raunds to concentrate on Kitmaster and a wide range of vinyl toys. The Wellingborough Rock St. site became the main warehouse at this time.

During the 1960's, Rosebud issued a number of interesting doll-related toys, including a Red Devils parachutist kit, hand-launched, with figure and 'chute. These were a source of amusement to the workers on the production line who frequently 'fired' them into the air instead of packing them properly in their boxes! The company logo had been stylised by this time to remove the rose and used a more modern condensed bold typeface with white lettering on a red background. This was rather dull compared to the two original logos, both of which were designed by Hazel Smith

At this time, Rosebud Dolls Ltd. was under financial strain from the Kitmaster project. In order to finance their ambitious plans, the Rosebud board had approved on 27th November 1958 a first charge over their fixed assets with Barclays Bank Ltd. in order to clear all 'monies owing to the bank'. This was to prove one of two critical factors in the failure of Rosebud as a business. In 1959, Rosebud took powers to create up to 6 executive Directors in addition to those holding shares, but the critical step came in 1961. With the Kitmaster project damaging cash flow and draining Rosebud's reserves of cash, on 28th September 1961, the Board agreed a deal with Industrial and Commercial Finance Corporation which gave them a preferential charge over the company's fixed and floating assets ahead of the charge held by Barclays Bank. This debenture enabled Rosebud to refinance itself during a very difficult trading period. However, the result was that Rosebud Dolls Ltd. was now fully mortgaged to three separate lenders.

Although Rosebud continued to trade successfully throughout 1963, it had to lay off staff that summer due to a lack of orders. By early 1964, things were looking desperate. In spite of an upbeat press release previewing Rosebud's new products for the Toy Fair, which included children's play outfits and the Magic Dolls House, a number of junior staff left at this point. Problems with export credits and introduction of direct-to-retailer sales, with no wholesaler to act as a buffer, caused bigger and bigger problems for Eric. Eventually, on 15th June 1964, he was forced to call in the Receiver by his two main creditors, ICFC and Barclays Bank. Rosebud Dolls Ltd was put into administrative receivership and the Receiver appointed issued a short statement to the press:

'In order to safeguard the position generally, the debenture holders of Rosebud Dolls Ltd. have appointed Mr E. C. Baillie, chartered accountant, as Receiver from June 15th 1964.'

The financial situation was not insurmountable. Gross assets were stated to be £364,526, whilst gross liabilities were estimated at £379,623, giving a shortfall of just £15,097. Remarkably, the priceless moulds were valued by the Receiver at a total of only £20,000, whilst the stock in trade was estimated at £120,000.

The receiver, Ean Claude Baillie, worked for the London firm of Chartered Accountants Layton Bennett Billingham and Co. and was initially appointed for a renewable period of one year at a consideration of £5,000. Mr Baillie administered Rosebud's finances until it was brought out of receivership on 26th July 1967 by the merger with Mattel Inc.

Within a few days of coming into the company, the Receiver issued a written statement to the 240-strong workforce. It read:

'I have now had an opportunity of looking into certain aspects of the business and have arranged increased schedules for the factory. Following my appointment as Receiver, I now confirm that I have taken over responsibility for your employment on the same terms you

The plastic telephone and iron were Rosebud products, but the soap dish is pure Neneware - an ill fated experiment in household goods.

The famous articulated Walking Teddy! Injection moulded in hard polystyrene, he may well walk, but he's not very cuddly...

had with Rosebud Dolls Limited, with immediate effect. Yours faithfully, E. C. Baillie, Receiver.'

Despite being in Receivership, Rosebud Dolls Ltd. started to rebuild itself and became Europe's leading manufacturer of dolls. Sales of dolls in the first year of receivership topped £500,000 and in the second year reached over £600,000. The Receiver appears to have been satisfied with the company's performance, as his official report for the first year of his tenure stated *'I have no comments to make'*. He even allowed Eric to buy himself a Rolls Royce.

Eric was always to be seen travelling abroad to find new buyers for British-made dolls. Amongst their most popular brands were the Rosebud Talking Doll, Chatty Kathy, and a licensed Bugs Bunny. Dolls were being produced in every size from 4' up to 34' and in many different styles and colours. Rosebud even developed a smooth injection moulded articulated teddy bear that swivelled its head as it walked! T. Eric Smith made a *faux-pas* when he turned down the opportunity to produce under licence the then-new *Action Man* toys. He reasoned that boys would never play with dolls, which proves that you can't win them all! Although Rosebud had been rumoured to be a take-over target for the UK chemicals and fibres giant Courtaulds, it was eventually to fall prey to forces from the other side of the Atlantic. Although trading successfully, the company desperately needed refinancing to clear its major debts and allow retooling for new production.

Consequently during 1967, Eric was persuaded to sell Rosebud Dolls to Mattel Inc. of America, thereby forming Rosebud-Mattel Ltd., the worlds largest doll manufacturer. At that time, Mattel was run by Elliot and Ruth Handler, and was built around the success of the Barbie doll. Barbie and her boyfriend Ken were in fact based on the Handlers' own children. The deal with Mattel was concluded on 29th June 1967, when the Barclays overdraft was cleared, and at an Extraordinary General Meeting at 73 Cheapside, London EC2, a Special Resolution was passed which changed the name of the company to Rosebud-Mattel Ltd. Approval was granted by the Board of Trade on 3rd August 1967.

Rosebud Dolls Ltd. disappeared as a trading company when the lawyers acting for Mattel changed the name and registered office on 21st December 1967 to Bunker Hill Properties Ltd. However, Rosebud-Mattel was used as a trading name until 1971, when it became Mattel (UK) Ltd. J. R. Ashby and Elliot Handler remained directors of Bunker Hill Properties Ltd. until their resignation in 1971, Elliot giving his address as '2222 Avenue of the Stars, Los Angeles'. Thereafter, the company became 'closed' and no further trading took place. In September 1977, its assets were transferred to Mattel Inc. and it was officially dissolved by a notice in the *London Gazette* on 9th December 1980.

Having sold the company, Eric and Hazel went on a world cruise and tried to adapt to a new life of quiet retirement. However, it was not to be. Frustrated by the lack of telephone calls from the bank, traders and business contacts, Eric decided that he wanted another business to run. He was, in his words, 'tired of being a nobody'. Eric was also bored with life away from England. He says that, whilst sitting on a beach in Antigua, he decided to return to England for

This series of small PVC animals was designed for bath-time use.

two main reasons.

These were:-

1] *It is the only place where the grass is always green,* and

2] *It is the only country in which you can speak to a policeman!*

Whilst highly subjective, there is no doubt that the globetrotting life of a tax exile did not suit Eric or Hazel.

Eric started to look around for another suitable market opportunity. Working on a hunch, he chose the emergent field of plastic containers. In a remarkable turn of events, Eric returned to Raunds and approached Rosebud-Mattel to negotiate repurchase of the Raunds site! In 1969, he was successful and Rosebud-Mattel moved out and consolidated on their second site in Wellingborough. Both Eric and Hazel moved back into their purpose-built architect designed bungalow, *Broadfield House*, on the hill overlooking the factory. This large property, with all the latest modern conveniences, had been constructed to Eric's design during 1956 and included a plate glass window so large that it took six men to carry the single pane of glass during construction. Measuring some 9ft high by 18ft long and half an inch thick, this beautiful window gave panoramic views across the rolling Northamptonshire countryside behind Raunds. Later on, Eric also purchased the adjoining field from the farmer, Mr Groom, and had a small practice golf course constructed on it.

When they first arrived in Raunds, Eric and Hazel lived at Ashfields Hall in Raunds, another palatial residence which was used to host the Nene Plastics Christmas Party until the workforce outgrew even this grand venue. It was opportune that they should move out in August 1956, as the Hall caught fire on 4th June 1961 and was destroyed. Eric's bungalow survived up to the last reorganisation of the Reed Packaging site in 1989 when it was demolished after access was lost by further site development, the wonderful window removed by the simple, if crude, expedient of driving a bulldozer shovel through it. According to witnesses to the demolition, it exploded with a crack which could be heard all across the town.

Having reacquired the old site from Mattel, Eric set about razing the oldest parts of the dolls factory, referred to as the 'Old' factory, an ancient hotch-potch of buildings including Plant Two and Three, to the ground, keeping the part then known as the 'New' factory or Plant One. He built an entirely new factory on the site and imported a single second-hand German blow-moulding machine to work with HDPE, High Density Polyethylene, a versatile polymer made by BP. The first 13 employees were mostly former Rosebud/Mattel staff, including Mrs Rose Barker, a stalwart of Masks Ltd, Nene Plastics Ltd and Rosebud Dolls Ltd, who became Wages Clerk together with Eric's loyal handyman and chauffeur, Cyril Ferry, who was persuaded to rejoin Eric in the new company, Smith's Containers Ltd. Cyril Ferry, who always referred to T. Eric Smith as *'The Boss'*, remains a close friend, having acted as gardener, chauffeur, handyman, waiter, decorator and machine-hand in his time with Eric's companies. When Cyril's daughter announced her engagement in 1970, Eric insisted on driving her in his maroon Rolls Royce, KNV 666, on the big day, even purchasing a chauffeur's cap for the occasion! Cyril himself was a little wary of driving it, Eric came down one day and said 'Come on, we're taking the Roller out'. We went down to Stanwick and then on the back roads. Suddenly, Eric pulled over and got out. He turned to me and said "Right Cyril, it's your turn, you drive now". I told him I couldn't, not the Rolls. "Don't be so bloody stupid! How's the car going to get to the airport the next time I come back? Is it going to drive itself there? Now get in!" So I got in and drove it. It was superb. So quiet you couldn't hear the wind or the engine, just a gentle purr. I drove him everywhere in it, including up to Gleneagles and Turnberry to play golf. I loved driving it, but eventually, he changed it for a limited edition Mercedes. The Merc. was nice, but it wasn't the same. I loved that Rolls Royce." In fact, Eric had two Rolls over a period of time, the earlier one being FRP 999, which was brown in colour, but it seems Cyril drove both machines. As this book closed for press we are saddened to hear of the death of Cyril Ferry, peacefully, in Raunds.

On the 7th January 1970, with Cyril Ferry at the controls and Eric Smith watching, the first blow-moulded half-gallon plastic bottle in Britain came off the new production line at Smith's Containers, Grove Street, Raunds.

It was an instant success, new machines were installed within weeks and the product range increased at a huge rate. Now the company, which is known as RPC Containers Ltd, has seven UK sites including Halstead in Essex, where by coincidence the Collectors Club is based, and turnover exceeds some £18m per year. T. Eric Smith has really retired, and lives in the Channel Islands, from where he and Hazel maintain contact with their many friends, ex-employees and other colleagues in Raunds, the town which will always be associated with Rosebud Kitmaster.

The dawn of the Kitmaster age. A superb model of Patrick Stirling's eight foot Single locomotive was only one highlight of the first dozen kits to be announced.

A taste of things to come. The ex-WD Class J94 Saddle Tank is still sought after by today's modellers. The tool was unfortunately destroyed by the fire at Dapol's old factory in Cheshire.

1. THE ROSEBUD KITMASTER STORY

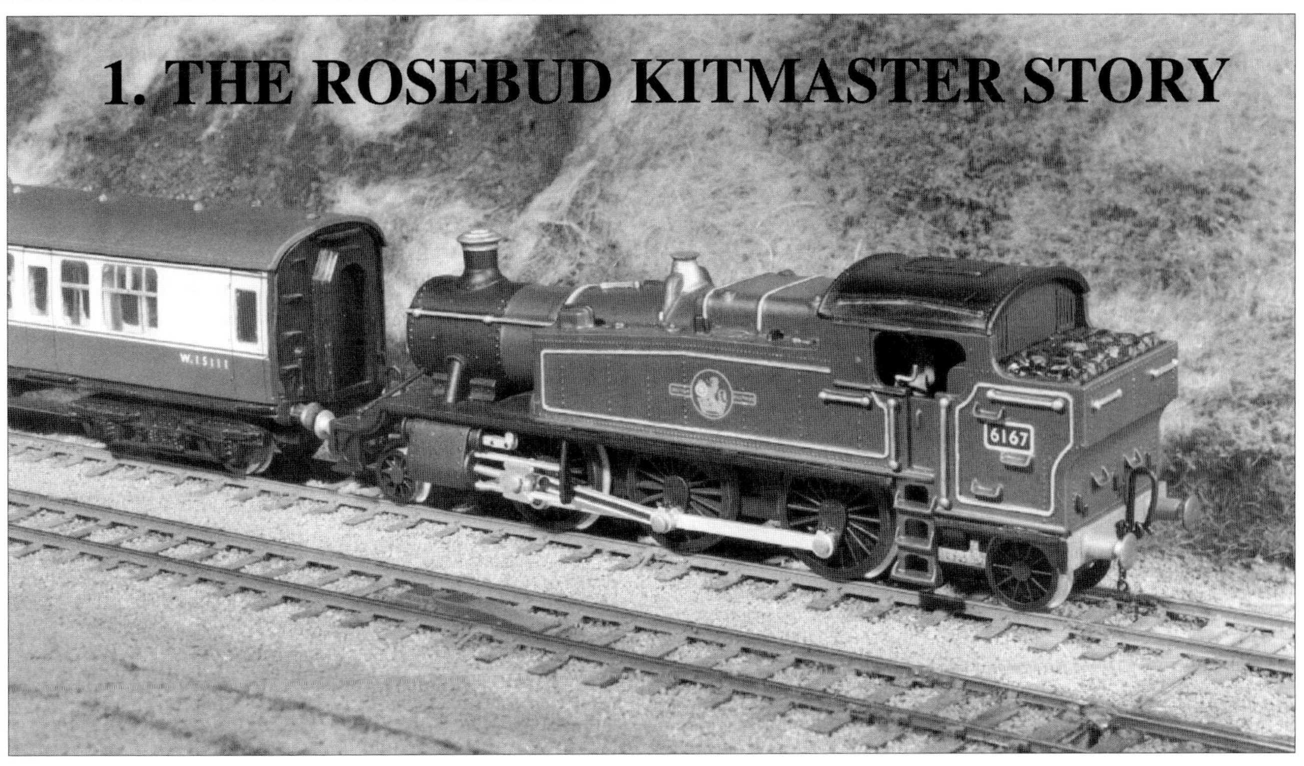

London suburban in the late 'fifties. A Churchward 61XX Prairie tank hauls a train of Kitmaster Mk1 coaches in the pleasing Chocalate and Cream livery.

The advent of the mass-produced plastic assembly kit in Britain was the celebrated Airfix Ferguson Tractor. This remarkable kit first appeared from Haldane Place in 1949 and celebrates its fiftieth anniversary as this volume closes for press. It was followed into production by a rather crude model of the Shaw Savill Line liner *'Southern Cross'*. In the USA, it was not until 1952 that toy manufacturer Gowland & Gowland started a mass production line for 1/34th scale model cars, known as *Highway Pioneers*. The Gowland & Gowland company, based in Santa Barbara, California, eventually licensed the range to Revell Inc. of Venice, California for distribution in the US and Europe.

In the UK, the *Highway Pioneer* range was made available from 1954, distributed by Bailey's Agencies (1953) Ltd. By today's standards, these early models are crude and have few detail parts, but they represent a landmark in the development of the plastic kit. Another milestone in the genesis of Kitmaster is the *Trail-Blazers* series. Launched in 1954, these kits included a 3.5mm scale model of The General, together with a variety of freight and passenger cars. It was the success in the States of these models which led directly to the introduction of the Kitmaster range just four years later.

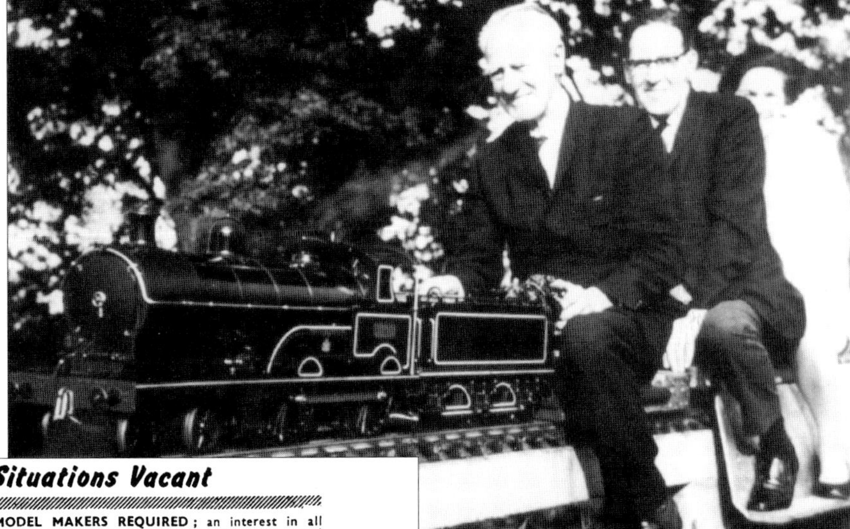

Situations Vacant

MODEL MAKERS REQUIRED; an interest in all aspects of model making an advantage; good rates of pay depending on experience; five-day week of 42 hours; canteen facilities available. Apply Rosebud Kitmaster Limited, Raunds, Northamptonshire.

Jack Gain (behind the driver) was a freelance patternmaker for Rosebud responsible for several of the later patterns. He is seen here on the Birmingham Society of Model Engineers test track circa 1960. (Inset) Rosebud advertised for modelmakers in the *Railway Modeller* Classified Advertisements during 1960.

Photograph Rose Barker

Dennis Franklin masterminded the Kitmaster project from it's inception, whilst Bob Parker (right) was Rosebud's site chemist for many years.

The Kitmaster range of plastic assembly scale kits was introduced during the period 1959 to 1962 by Rosebud Kitmaster Ltd. The revolutionary growth in UK plastic injection moulding capabilities at this time led directly to the introduction of a range of 4 mm, 3.5 mm and 3 mm scale assembly kits moulded in the then-new plastic, polystyrene. Polystyrene is much more rugged and durable than cellulose acetate, which had previously been used for trains, can be easily welded with a liquid cement and forms a rigid structure, unlike polyvinyl chloride which was the softer, more elastic compound used to make Rosebud Dolls. Two competing ranges of plastic kits were introduced in the late 1950s, the Rosebud Kitmaster series of famous locomotives and the Airfix Railway & Trackside series. Both ranges brought

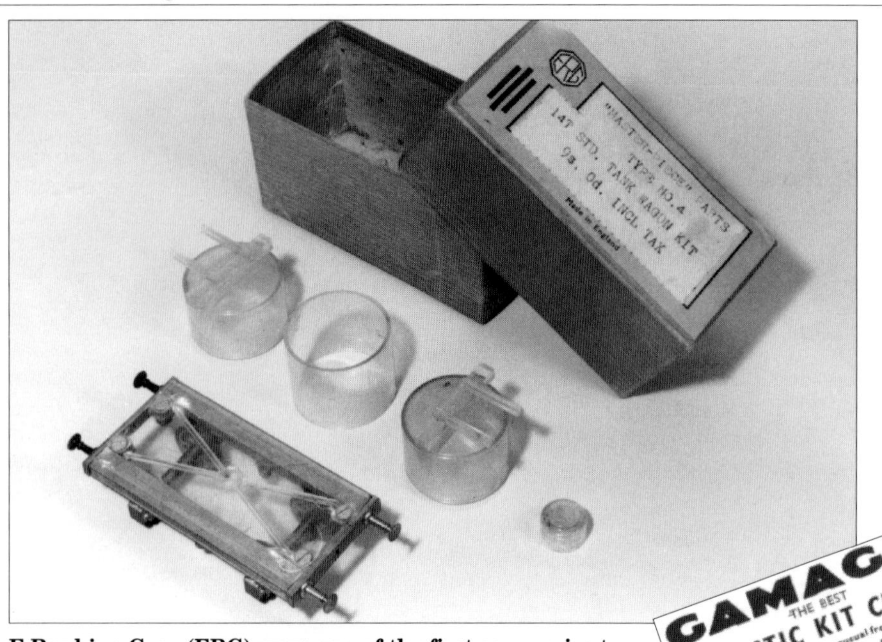

E.Rankine Grey (ERG) were one of the first companies to attempt to make plastic railway model kits. The tank wagon was a popular, if rudimentary, model.

Right. **Gamages herald the introduction of the new range.**

GAMAGES
THE BEST
PLASTIC KIT CENTRE
Always something new and unusual from home and abroad.
NEW! FOR YOUR LAYOUT
Kitmaster
Presenting for the first time something QUITE different—models of new and old locomotives (to "OO" and "HO" standards), with movable parts and full details of the real thing.
No. 2 DIESEL ELECTRIC SHUNTER 4/6
No. 3 EARLY AMERICAN GENERAL 6/6
Also available now—Kit No. 1. Stephenson's Rocket, 4/6. Kit No. 5. School's Class Harrow, 7/6.
Other interesting locomotives which will be available in 1959 are— Coronation Class Stirling Battle of Britain Class Giant Swiss Crocodile and many others.
Post and Packing 9d. if outside our van area.
GAMAGES · HOLBORN · LONDON · E.C.1. HOL 8484

unheard-of detail to contemporary modelling at an affordable price. However, Rosebud kits were always more expensive than comparable Airfix types. In fact, whenever Airfix reintroduced an extant Kitmaster kit it was invariably accompanied by a hefty price reduction in relation to the original Kitmaster price. For example, in 1959 a Kitmaster Pug cost a not insubstantial 4s 6d, but by 1965 Airfix had reissued the Pug at just two shillings! Whilst there had been attempts at using injection moulded polystyrene for railway kits before Kitmaster, these were limited to a few highly specialised manufacturers. An early example was E. Rankine Grey, or E. R. G., who, in 1956, introduced two wagon kits, one a box van and the other a 14t standard tank wagon. However, these kits used a combination of whitemetal, brass and plastic parts, and were extremely rudimentary. Rosebud really were the first company to make 100% injected plastic rolling stock kits and proudly proclaimed this as a 'World First' in their 1959 Trade catalogue. Of course, they could only say this because the *Trail-Blazers* series had used some metal parts, such as screws for bogie pivots and hand-rail wire.

AIRFIX—KITMASTER

READERS have wondered over the past few months what was happening to the popular Kitmaster range, and we are pleased to announce that the plastic moulds and stock of kits have been purchased by Airfix, who will continue to market them as at present. We understand they have plans for development and incorporation into their own series of kits later on.

Below. **Rosebud's later offerings included Easi-Build, a construction toy of little merit, and the Red Devils parachutist, beloved of bored assembly line workers.**

Rosebud Dolls Ltd employed a number of toolmakers over the years. At one point, there were twelve people working in the toolroom. Some were experienced toolmakers who came from other local companies, whilst others started their careers with Rosebud. One such was Mr Sydney Smith, who finished his National Service in 1954 and immediately joined Rosebud as an apprentice, first in the Maintenance Department and later in the toolroom. He recalls that whilst the earlier patterns were made from brass, the later ones were nickel-plated copper which could be used to die-sink the tools directly by electro-etching. Mr Smith remembers the toolmakers taking the first shots from a number of products as a perk of the job. Whilst his wife was ill at home with a cold, he brought her the very first shot of the Swiss Crocodile to while away her time!

Initially, Rosebud's Assistant Technical Manager Dennis Franklin undertook all the work on the Kitmaster project himself, but it soon got to be too much for one man. Franklin had trained as a draughtsman at the Kettering Iron & Steel Company and was with Rosebud Dolls Ltd. from 1953 to 1960, eventually becoming the Assistant Technical Manager. He was given the Rosebud Kitmaster project at a very early stage of its development by Rosebud's Managing Director, T. Eric Smith. Dennis has very fond memories of his time with Rosebud and also of the period he spent at Mettoy working on the Playcraft Railways range. He is also an accomplished model-maker in his own right and whilst at Rosebud, was a member of the Northampton Society of Model Engineers, a position he retains today.

Dennis needed help with the Kitmaster project and so, with Eric's agreement, recruited staff for the toolroom. Some of the railway patterns which were made in-house were produced by a couple of young toolmakers who had joined Rosebud from Mettoy in Northampton. However, it was Dennis Franklin above all who was responsible for the birth of Kitmaster and the selection and design of the first two series of kits. He travelled extensively to research locomotives and carriages and to secure drawings from manufacturers and railway companies alike. It was Dennis who decided that they should make all the locomotives to a single constant scale: 4 mm to the foot, irrespective of their country of origin. In the end, this proved a fatal flaw in the product range, cutting off the vast Continental European and American markets which were

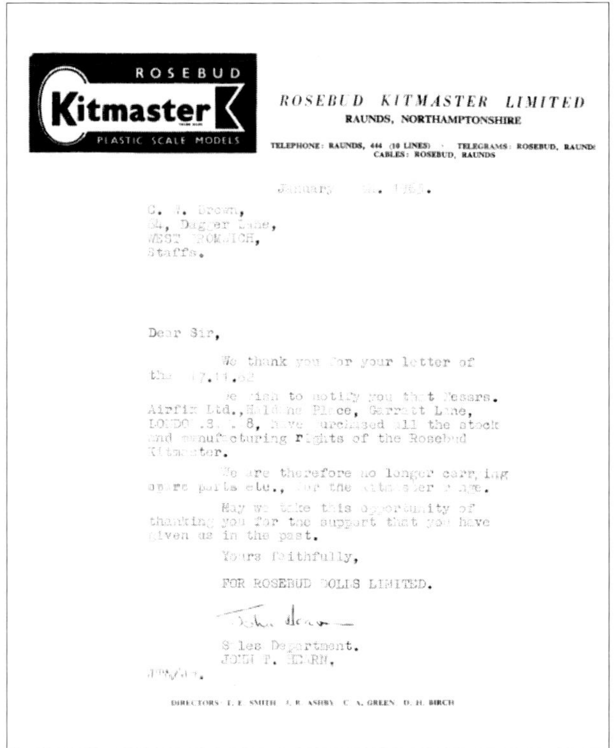

ROSEBUD Kitmaster PLASTIC SCALE MODELS

ROSEBUD KITMASTER LIMITED
RAUNDS, NORTHAMPTONSHIRE

TELEPHONE: RAUNDS, 444 (10 LINES) · TELEGRAMS: ROSEBUD, RAUNDS
CABLES: ROSEBUD, RAUNDS

January [illegible] 1963.

C. [illegible] Brown,
54, Dagger Lane,
WEST BROMWICH,
Staffs.

Dear Sir,

We thank you for your letter of the 17.11.62

We wish to notify you that Messrs. Airfix Ltd., Haldane Place, Garratt Lane, LONDON S.W.18, have purchased all the stock and manufacturing rights of the Rosebud Kitmaster.

We are therefore no longer carrying spare parts etc., for the Kitmaster range.

May we take this opportunity of thanking you for the support that you have given us in the past.

Yours faithfully,

FOR ROSEBUD DOLLS LIMITED.

Sales Department.
JOHN T. [illegible],

DIRECTORS: T. E. SMITH, J. R. ASHBY, C. A. GREEN, D. H. BIRCH

This letter informs enquirers that all the rights to Kitmaster have been sold to Airfix Ltd.

so firmly embedded in 3.5 mm scale modelling. This was pointed out in no uncertain terms by Mr Sidney Pritchard of Peco to Dennis Franklin. However, Dennis remained a staunch supporter of the 'constant scale' concept.

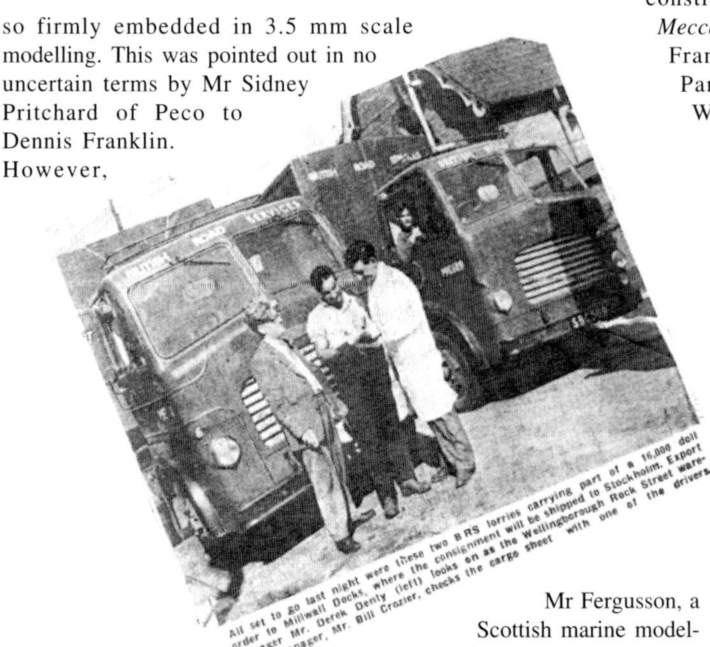

All set to go last night were these two BRS lorries carrying part of a 16,000 doll order to Millwall Docks, where the consignment will be shipped to Stockholm. Export manager Mr. Derek Denty (left) looks on as the Wellingborough Rock Street ware-house manager, Mr. Bill Crozier, checks the cargo sheet with one of the drivers.

During the period of Kitmaster production, the toolroom was attempting to turn out one new tool every month, but this was said to be impossible. Finally, T. Eric Smith came into the toolroom one Friday evening and told them all that in future, the work would be contracted out. Three of them, including Sid Smith, left immediately and within hours they were on the payroll at John Orme & Co. in Higham Ferrers. Orme had previously done work for Rosebud, including making special tools, to Rosebud's own designs, for doll assembly. Such tools included the first ever machine for stitching dolls' hair to their heads, designed at Raunds by Jack Branson, a Rosebud development engineer, after he saw a worker stow a needle by sticking it into a reject doll's head. Another Orme production for Rosebud was the first rotary casting machine for dolls and toys, the prototype of which was constructed from *Meccano* by Dennis Franklin, Robert Parker and Sid Wilding.

Eventually, a number of toolmakers left, causing a re-think in the strategy. When Mr Fergusson, a Scottish marine model-maker, joined the toolroom in 1962, all work on railway subjects had been postponed, mainly due to the resignation of the pattern makers and toolmakers. He worked on the new motorcycle range, preparing the Ariel Arrow tool and working up drawings and patterns for a Matchless racing bike which never saw the light of day. He left Rosebud in 1964. Other noted toolmakers at the time were Mr East and Mr Learing. These gentlemen shared an office at Rosebud's Grove Street premises with Dennis Franklin. Dennis and his team undertook the specialist pattern-making required for the railway subjects until he left Rosebud in 1960, just as his masterpiece, the Beyer-Garratt, was about to be released. From that point onwards, the railway pattern-making was subcontracted out to freelance modelmakers. From then on, the patterns from which the tools were developed were mostly made by one man: Jack Gain. Jack was born in Birmingham in 1911. He was a design silversmith by trade with a workshop in his garden. He worked for E. Clifford Davies & Co. in Warstone Lane, Birmingham and taught silversmithing at evening classes. He was well known as a superb LNWR modeller. He was first approached by an agent for Rosebud at a Birmingham Club exhibition in 1958. His life-long friend, and one-time Proprietor of CCW Models, Joe Moss, remembers Jack working on the tools for the third series including, specifically, a pattern for the NYC Hudson.

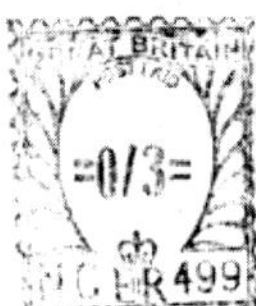

Rosebud never supplied free finished kits, but made Jack buy them at trade price! Jack Gain designed his own chassis for many of the locos in order to motorise them for his own layout. His motorised version of the Rocket subsequently became the pattern for the Tri-ang model. One pattern which was

AIRFIX PRODUCTS LTD
Manufacturers of Plastic Construction Kits and Toys

HALDANE PLACE · GARRATT LANE · LONDON - S. W. 18.

Telephone: VANdyke 7575/8/9
Telegrams: Airfixco Put, London
Code: A.B.C. 7th Edition

Our Ref. EHS/MH/HOME

Date 14th July, 1965.

Mr. R.K. Bickers,
6, Downes Court,
Winchmore Hill,
London, N.21.

Dear Sir,

In reply to your letter of the 4th July, we note that when attending at the Interplas Exhibition recently you were advised of our proposed intention to re-introduce the former Kitmaster models.

As you will be aware from the enclosed Catalogue of our range of construction kits, we have in the last year to eighteen months re-introduced several of the items which were formerly marketed by Kitmaster and whilst we cannot give you any advance information, would advise you that where these items are likely to blend suitably with our own range of rolling stock, etc., future re-introductions may be made. At the moment, however, we cannot give you any firm indication of any future models which are likely to be re-introduced.

Yours faithfully,
AIRFIX PRODUCTS LIMITED

E.H. SPALL
Sales Office Manager

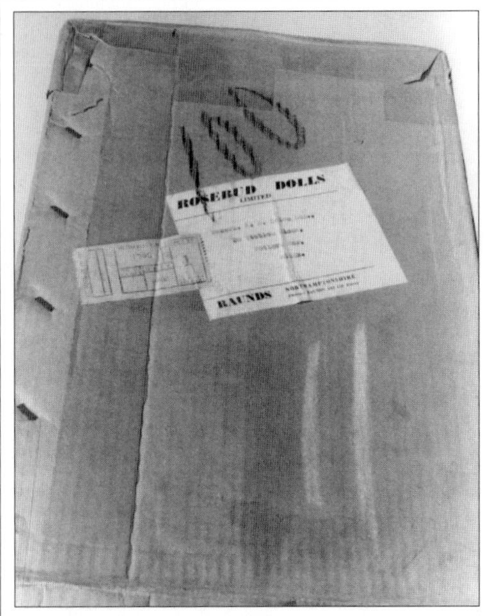

Rosebud shipped the kits in packs of 1 or 2 dozen. Here we see a dozen Pullman Parlours ready for shipment to A.A.Hales (the wholesaler) by BR Parcels service from Wellingborough.

not all Jack's work was the 'City of Truro'. Halfway through the process, Jack asked Rosebud for more money to finish the complicated pattern. Rosebud refused and tried to find another modeller to finish the pattern, even advertising in the Classified section of *Railway Modeller* in June 1960!. No modeller, when faced with the complexity of the pattern, would touch it for the money Rosebud were offering and so they had to go back to Jack with a better offer. Joe Moss is certain that Jack made patterns for the SR Class USA Tank and the LNER Class A3, but cannot remember one for the CN U-4-A Jack Gain died, of kidney failure, on 10th November 1969, aged 58.

His work has been described by fellow pattern-maker Mr Fergusson as 'beautiful, exemplary models'. He used carbon arc resistance soldering to build the brass patterns, together with techniques which were peculiar to his trade as a silversmith. This was very different to Mr Fergusson's work on the Ariel Arrow, which revolved around solder and gas blow-torch, techniques picked up from his marine model-making career.

Interestingly, the principle Design Engineer of British Trix Ltd, Michael Catalani, on the demise of the Trix factory in Northampton, briefly came to work for Rosebud in May 1960. He had been about halfway through the development work for the British Trix Mk 1 coaches at the time Dufay Ltd. (the owner of the Trix brand) decided to centralise operations in Birmingham. Michael, who was then living at Wootton in Northampton, called a number of local companies looking for work and was invited to an interview with Rosebud Kitmaster on 22nd April 1960. This turned out to be an auspicious day, being both T. Eric Smith's and Michael Catalani's birthday. How could he fail to get the job with Eric in such an ebullient mood? Michael began work almost immediately. Although he had been mid-way through the development of British Trix BR Mk 1 coaches, his input to the Kitmaster Mk 1 tooling was limited as the tools were at a very late stage by then. However, he did work on the drawings for the Pullman Cars, which were in the process of being redrawn from the Metro-Cammell master drawings, but within three weeks of leaving Trix, Dufay Ltd. had enticed him back with the promise of his own 'branch' office in Northampton and he left Rosebud's employ. T. Eric Smith was in Scotland at the time of Michael's departure, which, according to Michael, was probably just as well!

Rosebud launched their range in early 1959 with an 'exciting series of famous locomotives', whilst Airfix concentrated on the lucrative trackside accessories and freight rolling stock. Growth for both ranges was strong throughout 1960. It was not until 1961 that Airfix brought out their first locomotive, the Drewry Class 04 0-6-0 diesel shunter, and followed it with a Park Royal Railbus. Rosebud told buyers to '*Watch for a new model every month*' , '*Collect them all*' and followed up with '*Have you got them all yet?*' which is almost a motto for the Collectors Club. Remarkably, this rapid rate of introduction, one new kit each month, was initially maintained.

Dennis Franklin explained how the project got off the ground.

'Although LonScan did the basic design, we had to decide what would be the projected range of models. We didn't have the die-sinking technology ourselves, so we chose LonScan because of the cost and complexity of die-sinking the tools themselves without CAD/CAM. LonScan had the experience with tools that had cores and cavities that we needed and their General Manager, Robbie Robson, was very interested in Kitmaster as a project. We knew we had to make patterns, but we thought it would be easier if we did them at a scale of 1:1. Of course, it transpired that Eric wanted one per month. We all said 'Oh yes, we'll do it' It sounded great at the time. It's only after the first twelve months, after the trials and tribulations, that you realise it's a bit of an impossible task to some extent. But anyhow, if you don't try anything you're never going to get anywhere, are you?'

This 'can-do' attitude seems to have prevailed at Rosebud in the late 50s, when all sorts of projects were being undertaken or looked at for future years. Samples of competitors' products would be bought in and analysed to see if there was any potential for Rosebud to do something similar. Site Chemist Robert (Bob) Parker remembers seeing the prototype model ship floating in a water tank: grey and rather long. Dennis explained 'We were thinking about all sorts of things, motorcycles for example, but also ships. To get the information, I had to write to the Admiralty Office in Bath and it always used to amaze me, because I'd get the correspondence back and it would start off: 'Dear Sirs, I am commanded by my Lords Commissioners of the Admiralty to reply to your letter...' and I felt ever so important!

In ths aerial view of the redeveloped site, all that remains of the original factories is the injection shop built in 1955. This is the structure at the top right of the picture. It was where the Kitmaster kits were made and is still extant today.

Telephone Potters Bar. 2226/7

FEB 1960

A.A.HALES LTD.
26 Station Close, Potters Bar. Middlesex.

Dear Sirs,

A visit to Harrogate has shown rather clearly the trends for 1960. There were not many new plastics on view but the outstanding new development was undoubtedly the very large expansion in the Kitmaster range. Their programme for 1960 includes oo coaches and locos, TT coaches and locos, OO & TT electric bogeys and a completely motorized Box Wagon. We are obtaining some illustrated leaflets of the whole range and will forward these together with anticipated delivery dates as soon as possible.

Yours faithfully,
A.A.HALES LTD.

A .A. Hales Ltd were the first company to distribute Kitmaster kits, although they were very soon joined by E. Kiel and Co. Ltd. This letter is typical of those sent out to dealers informing them of the latest additions to the Kitmaster range.

These were water-line models. We pulled everyone else's to bits, it could have been an Airfix one or a Revell one that Bob saw, but we never actually made one.' Nevertheless, they did start on the motorcycle range, with the Ariel Arrow in production and the Matchless Racing bike in pattern making before the Kitmaster project was abandoned. At the time, the Kitmaster project was viewed by the industry as at the leading edge in toy production.

'We also received great help from British Railways, who were very interested in the project. They sent us drawings of the locos, some of which were over twenty feet long! Also, they sent us details and specifications of painting and logos. Mr Wilson at Euston, the Publicity Division, I think was very helpful. I can't remember if it was him or Sid Pritchard of Peco who told us about the logo. It should only be facing one way - we were told about that. We thought in actual fact that the lion would always face the front of the loco, so we did it that way. But Mr Wilson came back and said 'You've got the British Railways lion wrong' What do you mean wrong? I said. He said 'It should be facing to the left, there's only one design which is registered and that's the lion facing left' Another slap on the wrist!'

The foreign prototypes presented Dennis with more of a problem. 'We would approach the Commercial Section of the relevant embassy saying that we wanted to do these locos. They would put us in touch with the overseas railway, but can I say this: Marklin and Fleischmann came in very handy! They're very good models.'

Help also came from another direction. Mettoy employed another great train man as a pattern-maker. His name - Frank Roche. 'Frank and I have known each other for years. We would meet and have great discussions about things. I used his drawings a lot in the Kitmaster designs. When we were choosing the initial designs, Eric really left it up to me. He wasn't interested in locos or what ones we would model. I would talk to lots of people, model railway enthusiasts. We would get a lot of letters in about what we should make, because you can imagine the interest that was generated at the time. Also Sid Pritchard advised us. He'd say 'It wouldn't be a bad idea if you did one like this'. He had to be a bit tactful, but Sid Pritchard really was quite helpful. I'm an LMS man myself. There's no doubt about it, we do have our prejudices. We relied on the trade to tell us, plus feedback from the model railway fans themselves. We got a lot of positive criticism from modellers which was very useful. I wanted to include a big Great Western prototype such as a Castle or King.'

In spite of the help from Sid Pritchard, Dennis decided not to adopt the Peco Simplex coupling. The Rosebud coupling was designed to fit the Tri-ang coupling, according to Dennis. 'I thought the simpler

Rosebud transported their outlying workers to Raunds in this natty little Morris minibus. Their fleet included the Dodge Q pantechnican HBD 729, booked for speeding at 24 mph!

The "New" factory building encompassed a suite of offices (on left in picture) and abutted straight on to the old cottages in Beech Hill, the nearest of which was used as a solvent store for many years.

The main centre for doll production was Plant 2, seen here on the right hand side. This view is looking up Central Road from the gate house.

This rear view of Plant 1 (The New Factory) was taken, like the others on this page in 1969, prior to demolition of the older buildings on the site. It clearly shows the boiler house and loading bay at the rear of the injection shop. Eric Smith appears to be lurking inside...

the coupling, the more robust it would be. It was as simple as that. In fact, when I was at Playcraft, we went over to the Hornby-Dublo style coupling for the same reason. We talked about an alternative coupling, but never did it.' Each of the larger tools, such as the Duchess and Battle of Britain cost £10,000 to make. They were created from original patterns supplied by Rosebud at the London & Scandinavian Metallurgical Company in Wimbledon, south-west London. The tool-making process was long and complex, but is summed up here by Dennis Franklin. 'First, I did a breakdown of the loco into individual piece part drawings, which I then handed over to Gordon and John, our two modelmakers. They made the master patterns. What happened to those, I don't know. I wish to God we'd got our hands on them. They might have gone to Airfix, or they might have remained at London & Scan. Then London & Scan would mount them onto perspex and take a silicone rubber cast. From the cast, they took a positive in epoxy resin. At that time, we carried out inspection and then detailing, such as rivets. The cavity epoxy male was then sprayed with a microns-thick active metal silver layer to excite the surface. It could then be electroplated with nickel, then backed up with copper to the thickness we wanted, normally 0.25in. The cores could be cut directly out of steel or plated, depending on their complexity.

'The sideframes, wheels and motion would all be machined from solid. It's a damn sight easier than trying to make wheels that fine with all the spokes at that size. We also machined all the gates and runners into the finished tool. The amount of plating done determined the cost of the tools. Some of them would be in the vats for weeks. Smaller locos were running at about £6-7,000, but something like a Duchess cost us £10,000. That was a huge amount of money in 1959. After laying out and balancing, the steel tool was then spark-eroded from the plated masters. Finally, they were case-hardened for durability. We wanted the tools to last and to have a useful life of more than one million shots. We were shifting up to 100,000 units per year of the more popular kits, I should think. You only damaged the tools if they were put up on the press wrongly.

'I personally found the laying-out and balancing of the tools the most interesting part, and I learned a lot during my time on the Kitmaster project. We had to balance up dead sizes and run sizes. We had to lay out, in conjunction with LonScan, the position of the relevant parts and where the runners would be machined in. We had to work out the projected area of each part and then balance it up so that the top half of the tool had the same projected area as the bottom half and the left hand side had the same projected area as the right half. Next, we had to put the runners and gates in so that it all filled at the same time. Technically, that is what you wanted to do, to get the same pressure on each tie-bar. You can do it by altering the size of the gates or the size of the runner to get it to fill pretty evenly. You will always get one part that fills last. To ease the operator's task, he was instructed always to look at that last part. If that part was full, he could put it in the box, if it wasn't full, the whole thing was rejected.

'For obvious reasons, I was on tenterhooks when a new tool came in. The number of times I would go through the parts list and

This classic view down Central Road from the Plant Two showroom shows the administrative offices over the archway and T.Eric Smith's office in the house on the left. Through the arch is Grove Street.

then when the first shots were off. I heaved a big sigh of relief.

Airfix reduced the diameter of the sprues, which in the original Kitmaster kits are rather thick. Dennis commented 'Hydraulic pressure on the end of the ram and therefore on the leading material could be as much as 20,000 psi, but because of the tremendous pressure drop across the ram, cylinder, gates and runners, by the time you get to the other end of the tool you might only have 5 or 10 psi! We had worked with polystyrene before, for bases of push-along toys. They had wheels in polythene for toughness. We also experimented with high density polystyrene for dolls, before we settled on blow-moulded H.D. polyethylene for dolls' arms and legs. With Kitmaster, we were working exclusively with polystyrene. The sprue diameter is judged in various ways. If the material was too hot in the tool, it would blister, and if it was too cold, it would freeze solid in a narrow runner. You have to get the right combination of sprue size and temperature profile across the tool. When we started, we were using a Windsor 1044 twin interlocked screw machine. You couldn't get a lot of pressure on it. Then we got a Windsor SH1 and an SH4. They were very modern and ran at higher pressures, but Airfix may have been using an Ankhewerk or something else. If you're producing 200,000 per year and you can save 5 g of material by reducing the sprue sizes, it counts. We decided to use larger runners and to hell with the expense!'

However, by the end of 1960, delays were setting in, and promised introduction dates began to slip, by up to six months in some cases. The ever-expanding Kitmaster stable had reached some thirty models when things started to go wrong. The problem was mostly a cash flow crisis: tooling up for a different kit each month had financially drained Rosebud by the end of 1961. It had taken too long for Rosebud to get their distribution and marketing strategy sorted out and the projected growth in plastics modelling had not materialised. Consequently, revenues were not enough to fund the ambitious launch programme and market conditions were also far from ideal. Compounding the difficulty, the production area for Rosebud Dolls was being compromised by the expanding tools and stock of Rosebud Kitmaster. Eric Smith took the decision to look at a buyer for the Kitmaster business. At the end of 1962, he successfully negotiated the sale of all tools and remaining stock to Airfix Ltd. In October 1962, Christopher Brown of West Bromwich purchased a Kitmaster Battle of Britain kit. On inspection, he found that one side of the front bogie was missing and the left-hand coupling rod was badly moulded and unusable. He wrote to Rosebud for a replacement part, but on hearing nothing by mid-November, wrote again. This time his letter was answered, by John Hearn (Sales Manager of Rosebud Dolls Ltd.) to inform him '...that Messrs Airfix Ltd., Haldane

***Middle.* Factory assembled models were exported all over the world by Rosebud. This Stirling went to Vancouver, British Columbia**

***Left.* The beautifully symmetrical tool for the Deltic, now at the Dapol factory in Llangollen.**

Place, Garratt Lane, London SW18, have purchased all the stock and manufacturing rights of the (sic) Rosebud Kitmaster.'

At this point, it is worth considering the British outline model scene at that time. The growth of OO scale model railways between 1950 and 1960 had been truly astonishing. Nearly all the models which are today thought of as the 'classic' core of railway modelling were introduced during this period. These include the Jinty Tank, Electra, 3MT and Britannia from Tri-ang, the Standard Class 4MT tank, MetroVick Co-Bo and Bulleid Pacific from Hornby-Dublo, and the Trix Britannia and Standard Class 5MT.

Vast sums of money were being invested in new tooling and new models by a far larger number of manufacturers than one finds today. Firms such as Meccano (Hornby-Dublo) and Lines Bros. (Tri-ang) were releasing upwards of a dozen new models each year during the decade. Add to that ready-to-run releases from Graham Farish, Playcraft and British Trix, and you begin to appreciate the scale of this expansion.

Unfortunately for Rosebud, the year 1961 saw a sharp decline in revenues for all these manufacturers as the OO gauge market became saturated. Too many new releases meant that fragmentation was occurring. No single company was receiving enough income to fund ambitious product development programmes. An editorial in the *Model Railway Constructor* of January 1962 noted that many companies, including Kitmaster and Hornby-Dublo, had been forced to cancel or curtail new product introductions planned for 1962. In fact, the March 1962 issue, in an editorial report from the Toy Fair, specifically mentions the suspension of issue of the SR Tank, LNER A3 and Canadian National 4-8-4. The same article also noted that 'Kitmaster have, however, introduced the first in a series of large scale motorcycle kits.' This was, of course, the Ariel Arrow Super Sports in 1:16th scale.

Sometime after 1961, Rosebud introduced a set of Lego-like construction sets known as Rosebud Easi-Build. These were simple injection moulded construction kits. There were two Easi-Build sets, known as A and B. Each set comprised a single sprue of parts which interlocked to make simple toys, rather like a stripped-down plastic Meccano. They were not toy bricks like Airfix Betta Builda or Lego, but were designed as constructional toys. Although one kit would make several simple models illustrated on the card, the best results were obtained by combining sets A and B, or preferably numerous sets of each type!

Easi-Build appears to have been moulded in several colours, including yellow, green, red and blue, and came packed in a clear plastic bag with an instructional header (253 x 213 mm) showing exploded diagrams on one side and made-up toys on the other. Priced at a premium 2s 6d, they featured the same Rosebud logo as the famous dolls. These kits can sometimes be found unopened even today and do not appear to have sold well.

1962 was not only a bad year for Kitmaster. Hornby-Dublo cut its programme in half and struggled on for a further two years, the end finally coming in 1964 with a Lines Brothers agreed takeover to form Tri-ang-Hornby. As has been noted above, the agreed takeover by Airfix went ahead at the end of the 1963 season.

An interesting twist in the story then occurred. The Hermes Supply Company of Ravensbury Terrace, Wandsworth, London SW18, a fully-owned subsidiary of Airfix Products Ltd., secured a contract to supply certain kits from the excess stock of Kitmaster on behalf of Nabisco Foods Ltd. Nabisco at that time manufactured Shredded Wheat breakfast cereal and ran a promotion which enabled collectors to obtain free or reduced price Kitmaster models. This promotion ran throughout 1962 and 1963, after the sale of Kitmaster to Airfix Ltd. Airfix and Hermes together continued to supply Nabisco promotional kits until January 1964. More information can be found in the separate section on Nabisco.

As for the other players, British Trix, which had been sold in 1957, was again sold in 1962 and survived long enough to be taken over by the Swiss Liliput company in 1970, whilst Graham Farish, who had ceased all production for a while during 1957, stopped all OO production in 1976 in favour of concentrating efforts on the growing N gauge market.

When Kitmaster was sold, the moulds and all remaining stock in the UK were acquired by Airfix. Importers in each country disposed of residual overseas stocks. This led to some kits being available for a prolonged period after liquidation. Indeed, some distributors had tremendous problems clearing their warehouses. The Italian importer rediscovered a warehouse full of Kitmaster products in 1969 and, despite prolonged advertising, could not shift them. Eventually, they were given to local children's homes. A similar fate is said to have befallen a large number of kits imported into Sweden. After years of storage, they were circulated to the Occupational Therapy departments of several big Swedish hospitals, where long-stay patients were encouraged to make them up!

TT 3

Kaufen Sie diese TT-3-Modelle bei Ihrem normalen Eisenbahnhändler!

Die Kitmaster HO-Serie wird von Modelleisenbahn-Freunden in aller Welt gesammelt. Nun führt Kitmaster die TT-3-Serie vor ... fünf Plastikeisenbahnmodelle, die Sie selbst bauen und auf TT-Spuren laufen lassen können. Mit TT 3 erhalten Sie ganz genaue, originalgetreue Modelle von Englands berühmter Rebuilt „Royal Scot"-Lokomotive und vier Korridorwaggons der British Railways. Lassen Sie sich noch heute Englands populärste TT- und HO-Eisenbahnmodelle zeigen!

TT 3 Neubau „Royal Scot" Nr. 16	**DM 5,10**
TT 3 Normal-Durchgangs-bremswagen Zweiter Nr. 17	**DM 4,40**
TT 3 Normal-Durchgangs-wagen Zweiklassen Nr. 18	**DM 4,40**
TT 3 Normal Durchgangs-wagen Zweiter Nr. 20	**DM 4,40**
TT 3 Normal-Restaurant-wagen Erster Nr. 21	**DM 4,80**

(Preise gelten nur für Deutschland)

16 HO-Modelle sind erhältlich, die berühmte „Baureihe 23" eingeschlossen.

It is hard to believe that this model is forty years old. The Kitmaster "Schools" in all her glory.

During 1967, W&H were able to offer most of the original series of twelve models which had been reimported.

Airfix originally planned to incorporate at least some of the models into the successful Airfix Rolling Stock range. However, during a period around the transition from Kitmaster to Airfix, the tools were put into storage in a warehouse near Peterborough with a leaking roof. Water coming through the holes was channelled onto tarpaulins covering only some of the tools and thus found its way into others, causing the case-hardened steel to oxidise and thereby producing tiny pits in the surface of the tools. When Joe Chubbock, toolmaker, and John Grey, MD of Airfix went to inspect their new acquisitions, they were horrified at the damage caused by the water. The rust damage to the worst affected tools was thought to be irreversible and a decision was taken to scrap those tools straight away. Although the coach tooling was rusty, a report from the 1964 Toy Fair, in Peco's trade newsletter, *News Special*, mentioned that the '...the former Kitmaster coach dies are being rebuilt and their introduction is still in the future.' The same report noted the reintroduction of the Kitmaster L&Y Pug locomotive and asserted that 'Airfix have long established the principle of saying nothing of new productions until they are actually available...' During the 1965 Interplas exhibition in London, the Airfix representatives were questioned about future Kitmaster reissues. A carefully worded letter was sent by Airfix to prospective stockists explaining that the ongoing programme of reintroductions '...over the last eighteen months...' would continue wherever the models could be '...sensibly incorporated into our own railway range.' In the end, only nine of them were reissued: the Ariel Arrow, Pug, J94, Prairie, City of Truro, Schools, Battle of Britain, Mogul, and Evening Star. The omissions from the British outline range were particularly surprising, especially when some of the tools were so new. The Beyer-Garratt, Class 08 Shunter, Duchess, Deltic and Mk 1 coaches were all omitted.

However, the greatest shock was the news that none of the Continental prototypes would be reissued. Airfix had two separate distribution companies in America - Airfix Craftmaster and USAirfix, both of whom regularly imported and repackaged Airfix kits for the huge US market. Why Airfix Products Ltd. would not let Airfix Craftmaster acquire the mould for the NYC Hudson loco or The General 4-4-0, we shall probably never know. The situation is made even more bizarre when one realises that Airfix had issued their own HO scale rolling stock kit - the Interfrigo refrigerator van. This last kit is all that remains of the HO production of Airfix and Kitmaster. All the other tools were scrapped, variously by Airfix and Palitoy in the period from 1964 to 1982, when Dapol acquired the remaining tools.

After the collapse and subsequent acquisition of Airfix in 1982, the Haldane Place factory in Wandsworth was systematically cleared. Most of the documentation, records and artwork was transferred to the Palitoy Design office, located in a converted snooker hall in Coalville. The machines were sent to France, whilst the tools were despatched to another Palitoy site at Glenfield, near Leicester. To avoid paying rates on the vacant buildings, the roof was removed. The buildings were sold and eventually demolished and replaced by a Texas DIY store. Some of the tools went to Calais, others to Glenfield. Airfix had become part of the Palitoy group, owned by the US conglomerate General Mills. The entire stock and most of the Airfix moulds were located in the warehouse at Glenfield near Leicester before production of Airfix kits was transferred to the Palitoy factory in France. During a visit to Glenfield in 1984 David Boyle, proprietor of Dapol Model Railways, whilst negotiating the purchase of Mainline Railways from Palitoy, witnessed the wholesale destruction of many priceless moulds in response to an order to 'clear the warehouse'. In order to stop the carnage, during which the Beyer-Garratt and Stirling Single moulds were opened and 'a sledgehammer put across the face of the tools...', David contacted the Palitoy management and offered to buy the Airfix trackside range, along with Mainline, from them on the spot. Dapol initially acquired eight moulds in spring 1985.

The collapse of Palitoy's European businesses, Mainline, Airfix and Action Man, was the direct result of a reorganisation of the business by the American managers in Cincinnati. They decided to abandon all European product development. Instead, subsidiary companies would be offered a 'shopping list' of US designed products, which they could repackage for sale in Europe. This was a disaster for Airfix. Palitoy UK had carefully stored the entire Airfix archive in a specially-constructed room at Coalville, but with the redundancy of the entire design team and closing of the Mainline sites in Coalville, everything went pear-shaped. Artwork, drawings, archive photographs, mock-ups and roughs were unceremoniously thrown into a skip. Even framed artwork was thrown out. Employees were offered the chance to buy any item from the site for just £5! Some material was rescued by employees, while other items were donated to the Bethnal Green Museum of Childhood. Much important historical material was destroyed, but luckily some of the railway artwork from the ex-Kitmaster kits has survived in private hands. That for the 9F, Truro, Pug and Prairie is with the Club, whilst the Bethnal Green Museum has the J94, Tank Wagon, Brake Van and Prestwin Silo Wagon. The fate of the rest is unknown.

Although eight of the ex-Kitmaster tools had arrived with the Mainline business, there were some which had disappeared. The missing tools were eventually located in the French factory at Calais, after David Boyle obtained permission from Palitoy management to search it. The tools had been marked with the name of the model when they were acquired by Airfix. In 1986, the non-railway Airfix range was sold to Humbrol, production of the famous aircraft kits remaining in France at the Heller plant in Trun. Dapol set about releasing all the Airfix trackside models in a second deal with Palitoy.

However, they were unable to agree on the Airfield Control Tower kit. Palitoy maintained that it was not a 'trackside' kit, although the 1962 advertisements and the Airfix complaint slip clearly show it as part of the 'Trackside' range! When released in 1959 as Pattern No. 4017, it was clearly a trackside kit, but upon reintroduction in the 12th Airfix catalogue it had become 03305-1 numbered in the AFV/Diorama range. Subsequently, it was listed with Series 3 Aircraft Kits! It was reissued again in 1991 in the Airfield series.

When Dapol shot the mould marked on the manifest from Palitoy as '0-4-2' they found it to be the original Kitmaster Deltic. This tool had been earmarked for scrapping by Airfix and indeed the tool for the clear parts was destroyed. The search in the Calais factory also unearthed the Rocket, Prairie, City of Truro, Pug and J94.

All of these were eventually incorporated into the Dapol range, but it was some time before the Drewry became available again. Over 2,000 Deltics were produced in the initial run. The tool was recently repaired by Chris Scott at Dapol. The initial issue of the J94 by Dapol, catalogue number C34, only ran to 2,400 kits and the tool was only engraved with the Dapol logo for the very last batch. The J94 tool became unusable before the disastrous fire at Dapol's old factory in Winsford, but during the inferno, a girder fell on it and destroyed it forever. It has recently been scrapped and the kit has been deleted from the Dapol range.

Now, after more than thirty years of continuous production, these fine kits are still giving hours of enjoyment to the young modeller and providing an invaluable source of parts for 'Kitbashers' everywhere.

The Raunds Site

The small town of Raunds in Northamptonshire, which lies between the A6 and the A1 trunk roads near Wellingborough, was for many years the home of Rosebud Dolls and Rosebud Kitmaster. Rosebud's Grove Street original premises are no longer in existence, having been redeveloped in 1970 by T. Eric Smith for the Smith's Containers site. The Rosebud factory was situated at the junction of Brook St and Grove St in buildings which started life as Nicholl's Boot Factory. After the recession of the 1930s, the boot factory was broken up into separate units, part of it becoming Frost's Ironmongery. Other parts became the Tivoli Cinema, the Advance Garage, another small boot workshop and a Barber Shop/Tobacconist run by Sid Ruxby. Sid supplied Eric Smith with a constant supply of pipe tobacco, for Eric is rarely to be seen in contemporary photographs without a pipe in his hand! When, in 1940, T. Eric Smith's mother moved the toy-making company from London to Raunds and formed

This fascinating photograph was taken in 1956, just after Rosebud's new moulding shop opened. In the foreground Keith Anthony tends one of the new machines, whilst Bert Varney and Frank Starry can also be seen. There were 25 machines in use at peak time.

Some of the more famous kits in the range were to re-emerge under the Airfix regime, but sadly many more were never to see the light of day again.

Masks Ltd., she took over the redundant Advance Garage premises. In 1946, T. Eric Smith himself acquired Frost's Ironmongery to provide offices for his new company, Nene Plastics Ltd., and the building was duly converted. Other buildings in the former boot factory were converted for use as a showroom, canteen, production area, solvent store, carpentry and maintenance workshop, and further offices.

The new office boasted five telephone lines with the number Raunds 191, but by 1960 this had been doubled to ten lines with a new number, Raunds 222. The manufacturing plant was situated in numerous outbuildings and parts of the old boot factory at the rear of the former shops. Components for the dolls passed down a chute under Central Road to reach the final assembly area. In 1954, Rosebud began construction of the so-called 'New' factory at Raunds. This was to house new doll-making injection moulding machines, but would eventually house the Rosebud Kitmaster production area. The New factory, which became Plant 1, was adjacent to the rather ramshackle Old factory, which was designated Plant 2 & 3, and contained a suite of offices along the south wall. When Rosebud-Mattel moved out to Wellingborough and sold the site back to T. Eric Smith in 1969, he demolished the Old factory and Grove Street offices, replacing them with a brand new factory for the Smith's Containers business. A 1969 Ordnance Survey aerial photograph shows the cleared site of the old factory with just the new Plant 1 left, but in a 1970 view a completely new plant has arisen, Phoenix-like, from the ashes. This adjoined the former Kitmaster New factory, which is still in existence as part of the RPC Containers site. Further building work has taken place at RPC from 1984 onwards and no trace of the original Grove St premises exists except the New Factory building.

A separate office was set up in New York by a Manufacturer's Agent called Mark Price, a personal contact of Eric Smith. He traded as the Rosebud Corporation of America Inc, but according to T. Eric Smith, the project was not a success, and the venture came to nothing. The address did appear on the rear of the 1960 trade catalogue and on certain 1959 catalogues showing the office address on Fifth Avenue, New York, but Rosebud had effectively abandoned the US market. There were no other subsidiary offices according to T. Eric Smith.

Distribution to the UK model trade was initially via A. A. Hales Ltd., who at that time, 1959, were based at 60 Station Rd. New Southgate, London N11. By 1960, A. A. Hales had relocated to 26 Station Court, Potters Bar, Hertfordshire and had been joined in distributing the kits by Messrs. E. Keil & Co. of Russell Gardens, Wick Lane, Wickford, Essex. By 1960, Harold Skinner was delivering a van-load of Kitmaster kits to KeilKraft every week.

Rosebud used two vans and drivers, the vans being a Morris Commercial, KNV 555, and a larger Dodge Q pantechnicon, HBD 729, bought in May 1952 and fitted with a Perkins P6 engine. It was overhauled at Marshalls of Cambridge and outshopped in Rosebud's colours. The livery for both vans was pale blue with pink lettering to match the style of the dolls' packaging. The second driver was Cyril Ferry. The drivers delivered the kits in bulk direct to the wholesalers' warehouses each week. They also picked up raw materials from suppliers around the country. For example, the castings for the KM1 and KM2 motor bogies came from Stalybridge. In addition, there was the daily staff pick-up shuttle from Corby and the nearby villages. The Corby run quickly outgrew the Morris van and a more suitable 29-seater Duple-bodied Bedford OB was obtained from the Westonia Garage in Northampton specially for this service. The Dodge truck was initially restricted to 20 mph on the run down to London for L. Rees & Co., but the Government decided to raise the speed limit to 30 mph. In the week before the new limit came into force, the Dodge was clocked at 24 mph on the A6 Bedford Road in Rushden and duly given a speeding ticket! During the Kitmaster period, the vans delivered kits to A. A. Hales and E. Keil & Co. on Tuesday and Thursday each week, while on Monday, Wednesday and Friday dolls were delivered to L. Rees & Co.

Both the Keil and Hales companies used self-employed Sales Representatives to travel around the model and toy shops promoting their full catalogues of products. Eric Smith had his carpenter, Jack Woods, fabricate some special travelling display cases for these salesmen. The wooden cases open to reveal shelves containing made-up examples of the locomotives. Eric still retains his own personal showcase, together with his own collection of Kitmaster locomotives constructed from some of the first test shots from each new tool.

The Kitmaster Presentation Sets are amongst the most-sought after items today. Gaily packaged and containing all you needed to build and paint the models, they were a popular gift for Christmas and birthdays in the early 1960s.

Kitmaster's foray into TT scale was less than successful, but the coaches and the Royal Scot are still sought by today's 3mm modellers.

2. THE KITMASTER CONCEPT

The idea of easily built, inexpensive scale railway kits was a good one. At the time of their introduction, ready to run rolling stock left much to be desired.

Tri-ang offered crude under-scale length coaches, many 'freelance' designs and a noticeable lack of detail in the mouldings. Indeed in the 1966 publication, the *Tri-ang Hornby Book of Trains*, Rovex describe how a new model may differ considerably from the prototype: "Some dimensional divergences are deliberately made...to make use of standard components...to hold down costs."

The alternative system, Hornby-Dublo, was also lacking in detail and attention to scale. At the time, Hornby-Dublo were just starting to introduce the so called 'Super Detail' coaching stock. Whilst it represented an improvement on the earlier all-tinplate construction, the printed tinplate sides still looked primitive in comparison with Kitmaster's highly detailed coach mouldings. Tinplate was the order of the day at British Trix, whilst Graham Farish offered a combination of tinplate and plastic.

Only Rosebud Kitmaster seized the full possibilities of plastic injection moulding with the commensurate detail it could give. An advance mention in the *Model Railway News* of March 1959 stated that 'Rosebud Kitmaster, a new name to the hobby, will introduce a model of the British Railways Class DEJ3 Shunter as a complete plastic assembly kit at the reasonable price of 4s 6d.' This was the first mention anywhere of a Kitmaster product.

'DEJ3' was the original Eastern Region designation of the 350 hp 0-6-0 diesel electric shunter designed by the LMS and built at Derby Works. However, as the article points out, what actually emerged from Grove Street was a model of the DEJ4 350 hp Class 08 locomotive, being the ubiquitous British Railways standard design constructed at Doncaster Works. Further details regarding this kit are given in the section '*The Models in Detail*'. This was the first Kitmaster model to be available in the shops, despite carrying the series number 2!

Eric Smith got the idea for plastic assembly kits from America and brought back a samples of early US kits for the wood-burning 4-4-0 locomotive 'The General' and rolling stock. Sold under the *'Trail-Blazers'* brand, it was manufactured by Advance Molding Corporation of 54 West 21 St, New York, and was to 3.5mm scale. It could be purchased separately, or as a composite kit together with two coaches, a Mail Coach and a Day Car. Freight cars were also available to model a complete 1860s train.

Eric discussed the possibilities of doing something similar with Dennis Franklin, Assistant Technical Manager. This project would be something of a 'labour of love' from Dennis as both his father and grandfather were enginemen with the Kettering Iron and Steel Company. To begin with, The General was shamelessly copied exactly from the Trailblazers kit, so, unlike other early releases, is also to correct HO scale. Dennis would have preferred to ignore this locomotive in favour of something not already covered as a kit.From the outset, the choice of locomotives was rather esoteric. This was due to the direct involvement of T. Eric Smith and Dennis Franklin in the selection of prototypes to be modelled. Eric Smith himself states that his favourite model of them all is the first one, 'The Rocket'. The first batch of four was released in April 1959, four years into the British Transport Commission's 'Modernisation Plan', which would inexorably lead to the death of British steam power. Kitmaster failed to grasp the marketing opportunity provided by the plan. The first series of 10 kits to be advertised contained only one production series diesel, no electric locomotives and no BR Standard Steam designs. The eventual inclusion of the BR Class 9F and Class 4MT designs came far too late to affect sales figures. No concessions were made to the wave of optimistic enthusiasm gripping the country at the beginning of the new decade. A sense that only steam engines would sell certainly pervaded the Rosebud camp.

The first four kits were, however, a promising start. The BR Class 08 Diesel shunter was a good choice, preceding the Tri-ang and Hornby-Dublo models by several years. The Duchess was a popular prototype, although here Hornby had stolen a march on Kitmaster, whilst Southern enthusiasts everywhere welcomed the Schools Class 4-4-0. 'The Rocket' was such a delightful and diminutive model that most people looked favourably on it, although it was difficult to incorporate into a contemporary model scene.

The original concept involved these motorised bogies driving weighted Kitmaster locomotives from behind. With the exception of the Deltic, it barely worked.

From there on, it was rather an uneven choice. Models came in every size, shape, form and livery. What was needed was a coherent plan backed up by some solid market research. But, alas, this was not to be. There were of course highlights: the Bulleid Pacific, the Pug and Prairie were all welcomed rapturously. However, the Italian tank and the Crocodile had a reception that was less than enthusiastic.

Whilst the finished Kitmaster product had most of the handrail and pipe detail moulded on, Dennis Franklin had thought hard about making it more realistic. "I thought about having spigots coming out of the sides and then using long thin wire rod like we did on 'The General' and 'The Rocket'. However, we were always conscious of price. I think you can get away with having handrails on the smokebox, but being a modeller myself, I think I would have gone at an earlier stage for the little bosses coming out with a little groove in them to take the wires. If you make it too fiddly, then young people wouldn't be able to do it. We were trying to get a foot in all sorts of camps and we were not going to succeed. It's the same about this four-millimetre scale.'

Table A summarises the design groups into which Kitmaster railway vehicles can be classified. The 1955 Modernisation Plan affected areas shown in **bold** in the table. As can be seen, these were precisely the areas Rosebud Kitmaster chose to ignore, or to treat only superficially.

Perhaps if Rosebud had concentrated more on the exciting diesel and electric prototypes of the Modernisation Plan, their sales would have continued to grow during 1961/2, the period when most of the new designs were being introduced. We shall never know.

Table A : Design Groups of Kitmaster railway vehicles

British Steam Designs			*Continental*	*Diesels*	*Coaches*
Stds.	*Pre-Grouping*	*Big Four*			
9F	Pug	Duchess	Hudson	**Shunter**	**BSK**
4MT	Rocket	Schools	General	**Deltic**	**SK**
	Truro	Bulleid	Baureihe	**Pullman**	**CK**
	Stirling	Prairie	Mountain		**FO**
		SR USA	Crocodile		A9myfi
		A3	Italian		B4yge
		J94	CN U4a		**Kitchen**
		Rb Scot			**Parlour**
		Garratt			

A Rush Job

The artwork which so characterised the Kitmaster products was commissioned through a leading London agency called Richard Lonsdale Hands and Associates, where a Mr Jeffries was responsible for the Kitmaster account. Artwork was prepared, at a scale of 2:1, many months in advance of the issue dates in some cases. The Patent Office received the first six box designs for Registration on 13th November 1958, some six months ahead of their public debut. Not all the designs were registered, only the first six, it appears. Dennis Franklin remembers 'I can tell you quite categorically that in the toy trade you would either have a design registered or you put 'Registered Design applied for' and that would put some people off copying. It was used quite a lot. And of course the logo was copyrighted.'

Dennis also had to manage the artwork side of the project. 'We had to decide what sort of view we wanted, whether a side view, a three-quarter view or anything like that. We generally tried to make it look striking. I had to go down to their office in Holborn to approve new artwork or to suggest alterations. As well as using free-lancers (like Ken Rush) they had their own team of illustrators who made final alterations. If you look at the artwork now, it's very cluttered. If you were designing them now, you wouldn't do it that way, but it was in keeping with lots of other artwork that was about at the same time.'

The box artwork varied dramatically according to which artist was given the commission. The best of this box artwork which makes these kits so attractive to collectors has been described as a 'design icon of the 60s'. It is primarily the work of Ken Rush, although other illustrators were used. Ken is a freelance illustrator who was much in demand during the early 1960s for box artwork. He left the RAF in 1950 and immediately began work illustrating books, magazines and children's comics, including *The Eagle*. He also accepted commissions for Revell, Airfix and Frog, were he was house artist from 1972-74 responsible for a large number of aircraft paintings including the *D.H. Sea Venom, Gloster Gladiator, Lockheed Neptune* and *Maryland*. In 1968, he was asked to illustrate a set of *Brooke Bond PG Tips* tea trade cards entitled *History of the Motor Car.*

Rush was a freelance, as were most of the artists illustrating kit boxes at the time, and had no particular affinity for the models he was asked to illustrate. He returned to railway subjects in the mid-70s with some work for Airfix-GMR, illustrating the first Airfix Railways catalogue. His signature may be seen on the GWR Prairie tank train set in the Trade version of this catalogue and on the Wild West 4-4-0 locomotive set in the Retail catalogue. Throughout the early years of the 1960s, his studio in Soho was crammed with commissions for Revell (Ships, including *Sinking of the Tirpitz* and *Ben Ledi*), Frog (Aircraft), Airfix (Cars and trains) and of course, Rosebud Kitmaster. Ken confirms that he painted the artwork for the majority of the early kits including the Motorised Box Van, BR Mk 1 coaches and most of the first series of 12 kits. He also did several other aircraft illustrations, including the Red Arrows display team for the front cover of the 1966 Farnborough Air Show programme.

When Ken and his wife Jean paid a visit to the Cumberland Toy & Model Museum, in Cockermouth, curator Rod Moore took the opportunity to interview them. It soon became obvious that identifying which kits Ken was responsible for would not be easy, as Rosebud had omitted the artist's name on all their boxes.

"The sky is normally pretty distinctive: Ken's work is pretty detailed" said Jean. Ken agreed "Yes, but there was lots of overhang on these boxes. I normally signed in the track, somewhere they can not cut it off, using a different colour, blue or pale brown, something like that. Rod then asked if he still had any artwork for them. "I just handed over the artwork and that was that. In those days, they would buy the copyright, now the law is different. Normally, I had to buy the kit to get an example of it: this was not an era where you got the artwork back!"

Rod was interested in Ken's path into kit illustration, "I started off doing press advertisements for Airfix. I would get a photograph of the new model and add a line drawing over it. Then Jean would take it to the lab and have a bleach-out print made. All of the photograph disappeared, leaving you with a perfect line drawing. They used them in their *Stop Press* ads, I remember. I did them for years. I had so much work in those days, the average wage was about fifteen hundred a year and we were making five hundred a week! Still, I paid for it with a nervous breakdown. That's when I met my wife, she was nursemaid to me, until gradually I could start working again. I got a lot of kits to do. I sort of got known for them. Frog paid the worst. Revell was OK. I did the *Sinking of the Tirpitz* for them."

Jean chips in: "Oh yes, your ships were beautiful weren't they? I really liked those more than the cars." Ken agrees: "I liked doing the ships. The trains were good too. Rosebud Dolls it was, near Northampton." Rod prompts him: "Raunds", "Yes that's right. There was never any credit for the artist on the box. If there's a way of masking it off, they will. It's mean, but they do it. There's no signature on any of them. It makes me seem like an impostor, but it's absolutely true. I'd just like to find it on one of them" Ken rummages through another pile of Kitmaster kits in the museum. "The *Duchess of Gloucester* was one of mine. I know the technique I used, you see. I'm fairly certain the French Mountain was one of mine, too. This sort of treatment here (he points at the box) and the highlights. They used to say to me: "Get out your pot of highlights". I did a very long box of an aerial view of a big station with lots of track, like Victoria. *(Actually, it was Waterloo on the P2 Set.)* I've got the actual box tops for that one and a long train passing a castle *(Royal Scot at Conwy Castle on the P3 set)* cut out at my home, they're too big to take anywhere.

"Sometimes I got about a hundred pounds for an image, but that was for something

The first four kits to be issued were a promising start. The Duchess, although numbered '4' in the series, came much later.

really complicated. I did the pictures about twice the size of the box. I've got one for Airfix, they're more or less the same working size. If you went up too much, in reduction it could suffer. Or on the other hand, it could sharpen it to a certain point and then you'd lose detail. So it had to be a balance of easy to work on against size.

"I don't have many left at home. I might have prints or proofs, but apart from a half finished American Old Timer I was doing for Airfix (*Jupiter or 119)*, I haven't got any of the originals. It's sad in a way. I did so many of them, if I'd kept the copyright, I'd have been a rich man by now!"

Ken still works for a living, editing and interviewing for a ballet magazine, but the days of his illustrations appearing in your local toy shop are long gone.

According to Ken, the list opposite sums up his work for Rosebud Kitmaster:

The Export Drive

Rebuilding the British economy following the Second World War was a long and painful process. As an editorial in *Rosebud News*, written by George Lindgren, MP for Wellingborough, indicated '*Sales of your dolls abroad are providing export credits to buy food and clothing for your families and friends*' and went on to ask the workforce of war-torn Britain to strive even harder to meet export targets. T. Eric Smith was very keen on exporting his products, especially to the USA, and made many trips there, including one memorable six-week visit on board R.M.S. Queen Mary, during which he took orders for more than 1 million dolls. Naturally, Rosebud Kitmaster felt it their duty to try to 'do their bit' for British exports.

As a consequence, most Kitmaster publications and kits were written in several languages. The little 1959 catalogue for example, is known in at least six different languages. Whilst the French and German translations were presumably straightforward to accomplish, the Swedish and Dutch versions seem to have caused problems! Technical translator and Kitmaster collector English-Swedish dictionary and scribbled down the first words he came across to make a 'translation'. Naturally, the results were diabolical.' Tony ends by saying that he has not had the opportunity to check the other languages used in the kits, but assumes that

Table B (1) Kits Illustrated by Ken Rush

Definitely	**Possibly**	**Certainly Not!**
Evening Star	City of Truro	BR Mogul
Prairie	Hudson	DB Coach
Crocodile	P1 Set	SNCF Coach
P2 Set	Flying Scot	Pullmans
Italian Tank		Beyer-Garratt
BR Coaches CK, SK, BSK, RFO		Motor Bogie KM1
DB Class 23		
Box Van KM2		
Duchess		
Royal Scot		
1959 and 1960 Trade and retail catalogues		
Biggin Hill		
P3 Set		

Tony Palm comments on the languages used: 'It is interesting to note that the linguistic capabilities of Rosebud Kitmaster were not the best. In fact, the quality of the language used on the box cover of the SNCF Mountain was so poor that the text had to be blocked out with a thick black stripe, presumably following reactions from French distributors. With some difficulty, one can make out the legend '*Societe National Chemin de fer Francaise*' - a grotesque rendering of '*Société Nationale des Chemins de fer Français*'. The correct version was then overprinted above the name '241P Mountain'. The quality of the Swedish text on the assembly instructions in several kits was also appalling. It seems as though someone from the factory had just bought an they are probably just as bad! Unfortunately, Rosebud's French customers had to suffer a further blow to their national pride when the instruction sheet for the SNCF A9myfi coach described it as '...forming part of the Mistral express, famous for its high speed runs between Paris and Lille...' It should, of course, have read 'Paris and Lyon', a mistake which *European Railways* called 'An obvious blunder inviting ridicule' in their review of the kit.

Happily, Genoa based collector Luciano Luppi says the Italian was of reasonable standard. The reprinted Format 2 instructions for the first twelve kits were quite good, with just one mistake: the words 'plastic cement' were translated as "plastic concrete", whilst the 1959 Italian catalogue translates "Stirling

The advent of cheap plastic kits led directly to cheap plastic kit conversions, as epitomised by this wonderful 0-8-0 Italian tank, spliced together from two of the six-coupled variety.

Single" as 'Stirling Peculiar' and 'Saddle Tank' as 'The tender can be fitted with a saddle'!

To aid their overseas distributors still further, Rosebud made available factory-assembled and finished kits. Collector Brian Kelly, who lives in Vancouver, Canada, has two such items in his collection. These are the Stirling Single and the Duchess Pacific. Each kit is properly assembled and painted according to the Rosebud painting notes in the kit. The completed models were then packed in special foam filled boxes. The foam liners are cut to shape and appear to have been made professionally. The boxes are plain cardboard constructions which do not exactly match the retail boxes for each kit. The kits were built as 'out-work' by Rosebud workers, who could earn extra money for this task. Cyril Ferry and Keith Anthony both remember making and painting the kits for these trade sample boxes. Cyril was able to complete so many that it paid for his annual summer holiday in Switzerland! Neither man enjoyed building the DB Class 23, preferring instead the Pullman cars, a much easier task which would earn them more money! Packed in their foam lined boxes, these kits were despatched worldwide to interested dealers. The Club has an interesting example of a completed Mk.1 coach which was presented to a former worker at Metropolitan-Cammell in Birmingham in recognition of help rendered in furnishing the drawings of the Midland Pullman and Met-Cam built Mk.1 coaches. It is also packed in a foam-lined shipment box.

Rosebud Kitmaster models were widely distributed abroad with residual stocks still surfacing as far apart as Brisbane, Bombay and Buenos Aires.

THE MODELS IN DETAIL - ONE

The British Railways Standard Mk 1 Coaches Nos. 13, 14, 15, 17, 18, 20, 21 and 28

Perhaps the second most famous model(s) from the Kitmaster stud, after the Beyer-Garratt, these superb OO coach kits are still much sought after today. Embodying unheard-of detail when first released in 1959, such as flush-glazed windows and correctly aligned brake gear, they soon became the coach of choice for discerning modellers. They had significant advantages over the other available proprietary brands of Mk 1, Tri-ang Railways and Hornby-Dublo.

Firstly, the Kitmaster models were designed to scale length from the BR drawings, unlike Tri-ang's 9' coaches and the Hornby-Dublo 'Super -Detail' coaches, which were only a scale 57 ft long. Although correct for the Full Brake (BG), this is too short by some 8 ft from the actual 65 ft length of the Brake Second (BSK), Full Second (SK) and the Corridor Composite (CK). All of these, together with the First Class Open Restaurant, were correctly modelled by Kitmaster at a scale 65 ft. In fact, Richard Lines has gone on record as saying that the Michael Catalani certainly investigated a flush glaze system for the Trix coaches, but it was rejected on the grounds of cost. It is strangely ironic therefore, that 30 years later, Hornby Hobbies have reintroduced the former Tri-ang Mk.1 coaches with flush-glazing that owe much to the pioneering work done by Kitmaster.

Secondly, because they came in kit form, they were easier to convert into other prototypes from the then rapidly emerging Mk 1 fleet. A 57 ft BG could be made from two BSKs, for example, far more easily than

This factory assembled BR Mk1 coach was presented to a gentleman at Metro-Cammel who helped to supply drawings for these and the later Pullman coaches.

TABLE B (2) - British Railways Standard Mk 1 Coach Codes

Common Coach types:

RSO Restaurant Second Open	BSO Open Brake Second
BG Gangwayed Brake	BSK Corridor Brake Second
SO Open Second	BCK Corridor Brake Composite
TSO Tourist Open Second	BFK Corridor Brake First
SK Corridor Second	CK Corridor Composite
FO Open First	FK Corridor First
RB/RMB Miniature Buffet	RFO Restaurant First Open
RBR Rebuilt Buffet Restaurant	RK Kitchen

Tri-ang 10' coaches owed more to Kitmaster than any of their other competitors, whilst Pat Hammond in his definitive history of Rovex, claims that the '*Completely Knocked Down*', or CKD, coach kits were introduced by Tri-ang to compete directly with Kitmaster coaches. As noted elsewhere, British Trix were developing their own series of BR Mk 1 coaches at this time as well and must have been influenced by the Rosebud design. with an early Tri-ang model, which was a one-piece moulding for sides, ends and floor. Many such conversions were described in the model press at the time and subsequently, an index is provided in the appendices.Two interesting examples appeared in MRC July and August 1962 describing a catering

OO gauge First Class Restaurant Car by Kitmaster. It has no catering accomodation and differs from early Open Firsts only in branding.

Perhaps the greatest asset of the Kitmaster Mk1 was the ease of conversion to other diagrams. This 4-BEP set was converted during 1962 and formed a series of articles in the *Model Railway Constructor*. Afterwards, it was exported to Canada, but repatriation came in 1996. Now fully restored and running with modern 'adjustaride' bogies.

vehicle and an open brake second conversion. The catering vehicle was actually needed to run with the Kitmaster restaurant coach, which had no accommodation for kitchen facilities of its own. These coaches ran as a three-set with a diagram 700 or 701 RK and a full Restaurant Second Open RSO. It was perhaps a strange choice of vehicle from that point of view. Finally, the extra weight provided by full length ballast and the overall appearance of the flush glazing produced coaches which ran smoothly and looked accurate.

The only drawback to the Kitmaster Mk 1s, up to the release of the RFO, was the lack of any interior detail. The Tri-ang and Dublo models at least had optional rudimentary interiors, whilst the Kitmaster coaches offered none. For the 4 mm scale coaches, this was solved by the enterprising Pritchard Patent Product Co.(Peco) who rapidly introduced a range of cardboard interior kits to fit the OO Kitmaster coaches. These fine kits included all interior partitions, tables, mirror, doors, pictures and even a selection of passengers!

Scale length, detailed underframes and correct bogies, fully flushglazed. No wonder the modelling public went crazy for them when first issued during 1960.

Notes on the Diagrams and Decals
The maroon versions of all these coaches are described as E.R., W.R. and L.M. Regions on the box, whilst the green version is shown as Southern Region on the box.

BSK Corridor Brake Second OO [15] TT [17]
Maroon version has transfers for:
Diagram 181 M34090/105/671 E34422/590/35157
Diagram 182 W34152/297/763
Green version has transfers for:
Diagram 182 S34256/621/158/945/279/35020
The body shell is also common to the following diagrams:
Diagram 181 Three-a-side seating with folding armrests
Diagram 182 Four-a-side seats without armrests

CK Corridor Composite OO [13] TT [18]
Maroon version has transfers for:
Diagram 126 M15627/019/243 E15307/144/16017
Diagram 128 W15111/598/430
Green version has transfers for:
Diagram 128 S15042/573/888/903/580/873
The body shell is also common to the following diagrams:
Diagram 126 Three-a-side seating with folding armrests
Diagram 128 Four-a-side seats without armrests

SK Corridor Compartment Second OO [14] TT [20]
Maroon version has transfers for:
Diagram 146 M24133/405/861 E24222/531/25027
Diagram 147 W24165/341/719
Green version has transfers for:
Diagram 147 S24320/305/169/326/318/311
The body shell is also common to the following diagrams:
Diagram 146 Three-a-side seating with folding armrests
Diagram 147 Four-a-side seats without armrests

TSO Corridor Open Second
Peco manufactured an interior kit for a diagram 89/93 TSO with 2+2 seating , which shares a common body shell with the SK kits listed above.
The body shell is also common to the following diagrams:
Dia 94 SO Open Second with 2+1 seating
Dia 60 RS Second Class Restaurant with 2+1 loose seats Nos. Sc1014-17
Dia 61 RU Unclassified Restaurants with 2+1 loose seats Nos. E1018-57
Dia 149 SK Gloucester RC&W prototype M25456 (Many differences)
Dia 150 (Later AA204) SK Metro-Schlieren bogies M25283-5

RFO Open Restaurant First Class OO [28] TT [21]
Maroon and Green versions both have transfers for:
Diagram 36 M4/5/6/S9/W7/8/E1/2/3/10/11
The body shell is also common to the following diagrams:
Dia 71 FO Open First with 2+1 fixed seating Nos. M3000-2

Peco realised that the Standard Corridor 2nd could be built in two variants, as an Open Second (SO) or as a Corridor Compartment Second (SK). Accordingly, both interior kits were produced, along with those for the Corridor Brake Second (BSK) and the Corridor Composite (CK). No kit was needed for the Restaurant car, since a detailed plastic interior was provided when the kit was finally introduced in summer 1961.

There is also, unusually for Kitmaster, a continuous flaw in the Composite coaches. In both TT and OO scales, the spacing of the First class windows is uneven, giving a smaller end compartment than in the prototype. Whether this was due to a drawing inaccuracy on the part of BR or Rosebud, we shall probably never know.

Although the coach tools were eventually scrapped by Airfix, an interesting report from the 1964 Toy Fair, carried in the Peco trade journal *News Special* No. 3 of March 1964, indicated that '... the former Kitmaster coach dies are being rebuilt and their introduction is still in the future.' How much work was done is not known, but these tools were amongst those said to be heavily pitted after storage in the warehouse near Peterborough with a leaking roof. The decision to scrap them entirely was made even easier by the arrival of Tri-ang's 'CKD' kits for Mk.1 coaches of similar pattern at competitive prices.

THE MODELS IN DETAIL - TWO

Nos. 31, 32 and 33: The Metropolitan-Cammell Pullman Cars

Diesel Multiple Units are not, perhaps, the most glamorous of subjects for modelling, but the famous Blue Pullman trains introduced in 1959 were certainly stylish and striking as they snaked through the craggy gorges of the Derbyshire Peak District and threaded the rolling Wiltshire countryside.

From their inception, the model railway manufacturers were relatively quick to add Blue Pullmans to their range, both Tri-ang Railways and Rosebud Kitmaster making forays into this area. However, the task for modellers trying to put together complete sets for either the Midland Pullman or the South Wales Pullman was made quite difficult because not all the vehicles were available in proprietary form and a certain amount of confusion still persists.

Introduced into service on 4th July 1960, the prototype Metropolitan-Cammell diesel-electric multiple units rapidly established an image and identity for the British Transport Commission's Modernisation Plan. They were the blue-streak flag bearers of a new age of ultra-modern, ultra-comfortable and ultra-stylish rail travel. 'Britain's Most Modern Train' proclaimed the 1961 Kitmaster Catalogue, and so they were. A heavy promotional campaign by British Railways, Metro-Cammell and the Pullman Car Company had ensured that the 'Blue Pullman' became a household name by the end of 1961 and consequently the three kits of the Midland Pullman were very well received. Coming as they did towards the end of the Kitmaster programme, the Midland Pullmans embodied many refinements, including a common sprue for bogie parts in all three kits. However, they also suffered from deteriorating quality control in the mouldings and a lack of attention to accuracy in the tooling stage, some parts being mis-numbered, or even omitted completely! Even with these shortcomings, they are still fondly remembered and have accrued considerable value in recent years.

The Kitmaster Pullman Cars were modelled strictly on the Midland Pullman sets as running between St. Pancras and

NEWS SPECIAL
CANDID, UNBIASED, UP-TO-THE-MINUTE NEWS
THE STOP PRESS OF THE MODEL RAILWAY WORLD
PERFECTA No. 2 KIT
PERFECTA'S LATEST
KITMASTER COACHES

Table C BTC Type Designation of Metropolitan-Cammell Pullman Cars

TYPE	CODE	Description	Set	Modelled by & nos	
1	DMBS	Driving Motor Brake Second	WR	Tri-ang	R.555
2	DMBF	Driving Motor Brake First	MR	Kitmaster	KM31
3	TKF	Trailer Kitchen First	WR	Not Modelled	
4	MKF	Motor Kitchen First	MR	Kitmaster	KM32
5	MPS	Motor Parlour Second	WR	Not Modelled	
6	TPF	Trailer Parlour First	MR	Kitmaster	KM33
6	TPF	Trailer Parlour First	WR	Tri-ang	R.426

Table D : Arrangement of Vehicles and Allocations

Midland Pullman (St. Pancras to Manchester and Leicester)*

Car	A	B	C	D	E	F
	DMBF	MKF	TPF	TPF	MKF	DMBF
Type	1	4	6	6	4	1
Set No	M60090	M60730	M60740	M60741	M60731	M60091
	M60092	M60732	M60742	M60743	M60733	M60093
Model	KM31	KM32	KM33	KM33	KM32	KM31
1st	12	18	36	36	18	12
First Class Seating					Total 132	

South Wales Pullman (Paddington to Cardiff, Bristol, Birmingham)

Car	A	B	C	D	E	F	G	H
	DMBS	MPS	TKF	TPF	TPF	TKF	MPS	DMBS
Type	2	3	5	6	6	5	3	2
Set No	W60094	W60644	W60734	W60744	W60745	W60735	W60645	W60095
	W60096	W60646	W60736	W60746	W60747	W60737	W60647	W60097
	W60098	W60648	W60738	W60748	W60749	W60739	W60649	W60099
Model	R.555	—	—	R.426	R.426	—	—	R.555
1st	-	-	18	36	36	18	-	-
2st	18	42	-	-	-	-	42	18
First Class Seating					Total 108			
Second Class Seating					Total 120			

* Reallocated in 1972 to the Western Region, for use on the South Wales Pullman, usually as a 12 - car formation (2 x 6). The six car sets were then fitted with multiple-unit control cables.

Key:		
	DMBF Motor Brake First	MKF Motor Kitchen First
	TPF Trailer Parlour First	TKF Trailer Kitchen First
	DMBS Motor Brake Second	MPS Motor Parlour Second

Manchester Central, although the 1961 catalogue artwork clearly shows a Western Region power car, lettered 'Midland Pullman'. The WR units had tell-tale route indicator blinds on the power car sides as they operated over several different routes.

The Kitmaster models are easily distinguished from the later Tri-ang 'Blue Pullman' cars by the extra fine detail on the body mouldings, the air conditioning motors and Kitmaster logo on the underside of the floor, and the fact that they have the correct pattern Metro-Schlieren bogies. The Tri-ang units have incorrect BR coach bogies.

In fact, two patterns of Metro-Schlieren bogie were employed, the larger heavy duty one is the power bogie supporting the traction motors, whilst the smaller one is the 'standard' version. Metropolitan-Cammell had obtained UK rights for the bogie from its German manufacturer in the mid-1950s and persuaded the BTC to experiment with the design for possible widespread use on the expanding fleet of Mark 1 coaches. Three Mk 1 corridor second coaches (M24281-3), under construction by Metro-Cammell, were thus duly fitted with Schlieren bogies for the trial. After 150,000 miles of running on the London Midland Region, the wear characteristics of the Schlieren pattern were pronounced good enough to equip the new diesel Pullmans then in the design stage at Metro-Cammell. The eventual ride quality when in service with the Blue Pullman was not as good, however, and as a consequence, the more advanced Commonwealth bogie design was adopted for all future coaching stock requirements.

When examining motorised models of the Blue Pullmans, it should be noted that the Tri-ang Power Bogie fitted to their power car is virtually identical to the Kitmaster KM1 Power Bogie, often found fitted to Kitmaster power cars, since both were modelled on the BR1 Bogie. K's also produced a motor bogie for the Pullman in 1962. Priced at £2.2s.9d, there were optional correct pattern sideframes at 1s.6d per pair. These gave a much more authentic look to the models. The complete arrangement of power and trailer cars for these sets when introduced was as shown in the tables above.

For their 1963 catalogue, Tri-ang chose to model the South Wales Pullman 8-car sets which were a mixture of First and Second Class. The Tri-ang power car units are therefore Second Class (DMPS), and their Parlour cars are the Western Region First Class Parlours (TPF). The Kitmaster power cars were correctly modelled from all First Class Midland sets together with Midland First Class Kitchen and Parlour cars, so it is impossible to create an authentic Western Region composite set with first and second class, since Western Region Second Class Motor Parlour cars (MPS) do not exist.

Only Kitmaster produced a catering vehicle of any sort, which was, as noted above, a Motor Kitchen First (MKF). These are the only catering vehicles ever produced for Blue Pullmans. Consequently, anyone wishing to put together a complete South Wales set will also need a pair of Midland Kitchen cars to convert to Trailer Kitchen Firsts.

As can be seen from Table D, there are six different types of coach for these trains, of which only four have been modelled. The major differences between Midland and Western sets is in the positioning of the power bogies on the parlour and kitchen cars, and the addition of narrower second class seating bays to the two extra coaches of Western sets, together with destination route indicator blinds on the sides of the power cars.

When running, the motor bogie ends of the power cars were adjacent to each other.

Pullmans under construction, a typical 1961 table-top scene.

A dozen Pullmans in one box. This haul was retrieved from a North London shopkeeper as recently as 1997. The shop had been closed for 35 years, but still had a full stock room... model collectors' heaven?

This image clearly shows the difference between the Parlour First (top) and the Parlour Second (Bottom) with much narrower seating bays and windows. It has to be converted or built from scratch as no proprietary model exists.

For example, on a Midland set the motor kitchens and driving motor brake firsts were coupled with their power bogies together. Likewise on Western sets, the DMBS and MPS power bogies were adjacent. The Kitmaster models each contain sufficient parts to make up three bogies, either motor or trailing, which is very useful if you need sideframes to convert Tri-ang units!

Therefore, to produce a complete South Wales 8-Car set, some conversions will be necessary. These can be summarised as follows:

Trailer Kitchen First -
A simple conversion from the Kitmaster Motor Kitchen first. The powered bogie is exchanged for a second trailing bogie.

Motor Parlour Second -
This is more complex. The best way to approach it is by conversion of a Parlour First using either the Kitmaster or Tri-ang version. The major problem is the rearrangement of the seating to give seven bays instead of six. I have seen this done with a Kitmaster Mk 1 RFO interior, which gives good results and has the appropriate 1 + 2 spacing across the aisle and also the correct spacing for the new window bays. The drawback is that all glazing must be cut and respaced.

It is also possible to approach this conversion by cutting up the seating bays of a Tri-ang second class driving car and splicing them together, although you will need to destroy five dummy driving trailers for each pair of Parlour Seconds, and that could be expensive! The finished coach body will then require the addition of the power bogie and exhaust pipe removed from the Kitchen car above. A trailing bogie can then be fitted at the other end.

Multiple Unit Working-
The original Midland sets were eventually reallocated, as noted above, to the Western Region. In order to operate together as a twelve-car set, the power cars were modified

Ken Rush depicted the departing Atlantic Coast Express rather well for the second Presentation set. However, closer inspection reveals BR Mk1 coaches with Bulleid roofs and a Battle of Britain loco which has a Merchant Navy tender. Pretty dodgy trackwork too!

for Multiple Unit control. This involved cutting away the front skirt, thereby revealing the conventional buffer beam and coupling used for shunting 'dead' units. Also added were multiple unit control jumper cables on either side of the cab front. This conversion would be quite straightforward should you be contemplating a twelve-car formation!

Perhaps the best book on the subject is Ian Allan Profile Series No. 10, '*The Blue Pullmans*', issued in 1985. Sadly, it is long out of print, but can often be found on Preservation Society bookstalls.

Complete numbering and logos for both sets are available from Fox Transfers. Cast whitemetal sideframes from original Kitmaster items can be obtained from Chris Leigh via good model shops, whilst Railmatch make the correct Nanking Blue paint for these units.

THE MODELS IN DETAIL - THREE P1, P2 and P3:

The Presentation Boxed Sets

Perhaps some of the most attractively packaged and rarest items in the Kitmaster portfolio are the Presentation sets. These large, brightly coloured boxes contained groups of kits at a bargain price and often included special tools and paint.

Boxed Presentation Sets were introduced very early in the Kitmaster range. There are three boxed sets in existence, two in OO and one for TT. The 1960 Retail catalogue did not mention them, but the 1960 Trade catalogue actually had colour pictures of the boxes, previewing them for release throughout 1960. In fact, the planned introduction dates were shown as: P1 Current, P2:4.60, P3:8.60. In reality, the P2 set did not appear until 10.60, when W&H and H. A. Blunt began advertising it. All three were noted in the 1961 catalogue at prices of 27s 6d (P1) and 37s 6d (P2/P3).

The first of these to be issued was the set entitled *'One Hundred Years of British Steam Locomotive History'*. Issued in 1960, it contains three kits which are illustrated on the specially produced box cover.

Although these sets had specially commissioned artwork for their box lids, they contain the lower halves of each individual kit box, together with a small box for the paint, tweezers etc., but not the original kit box tops. In this early set, the kits were not individually wrapped. This set, with its striking painting of the three famous locomotives lined up together, was very well received and many were sold. Consequently, they are the most common among collectors today. However, very few retain their copy of *'The Steam Locomotive'* booklet and these have now become very valuable as a consequence.

The second set brought together the Bulleid Light Pacific with three BR Mk 1 coaches in a most attractive boxed set, again with a special cover, which proclaims it to be a '*Complete Train Kit*'. The truly superb Ken Rush painting on the lid captures the excitement of the unrebuilt Pacific 34057 Biggin Hill pulling out of Waterloo Station with a rake of green coaches on a West of England express. Unfortunately, the painting appears to have been based on a standard issue BR photograph of the scene, as the locomotive is clearly a 'Merchant Navy', with a curved tender rave, and the coaches are Bulleid steam stock, complete with roof tanks and double rain strip, rather than the Mark 1 Standard coaches included in the kit!

The loco kit is moulded in black plastic, any green ones you may see are Airfix productions.

From this set onwards, the kits were supplied in plastic bags, so that parts were not lost. At the same time, acetate wrappers were added to protect the outside of the sets. All instructions were multilingual from Set P2 onwards.

The final release in the series was for TT modellers. Scheduled for August 1960 release, it actually saw the light of day just in time for Christmas 1960. It represented good value for money, bringing together five kits in one box! Once again, specially commissioned artwork, by Ken Rush adorns the lid, this time featuring the Royal Scot locomotive with a rake of maroon coaches passing Conwy Castle on the North Wales Coast line of the LMR.

All these kits were supplied in protective plastic bags in open box trays, with no lids. As has been mentioned above, the distinctive

The grandaddy of them all. The P1 set contains everything you need, tweezers, files, paintbrush, even Wrenn track.

Build World Famous locomotives. This unique advertisement was carried inside 'The Steam Locomotive' booklet, together with one for the dolls range.

Set P2 'Battle of Britain Complete Train Kit'
Contents:
No. 11 Battle of Britain Class locomotive
No. 13 Green BR Mk 1 CK
No. 14 Green BR Mk 1 SK
No. 15 Green BR Mk 1 BSK
'The Steam Locomotive' Booklet
1/2 oz capsule of Humbrole/Kitmaster polystyrene cement
8 Capsules of Humbrol brand paint
Paintbrush
Emery File
Pair of Tweezers (Marked 'Sheffield')
Kitmaster 1960 Catalogue

Set P1
'One Hundred Years of British Steam Locomotive History'
Contents:
No. 1 Rocket
No. 4 Coronation Class
No. 9 Stirling 8ft Single
'The Steam Locomotive' Booklet
Capsule of polystyrene cement
8 Capsules of paint
Paintbrush
Emery File
Pair of Tweezers (Marked 'Sheffield')
3 Pieces of Wrenn straight track, 3.5", 9"and 12" each with card label red on blue G. and R. Wrenn
Kitmaster 1959 or 1960 Catalogue

feature of these sets was the artwork and the elusive copy of *'The Steam Locomotive'*. This informative booklet was written by the contemporary railway journalist, J. N. Maskelyne, Assoc. I. Loco. E, who had a regular column in *Model Railway News* at the time. 'JNM' was paid the princely sum of £50 for his notes on the early history of the steam locomotive in Britain. The booklet measures approximately 6' x 4½" and is printed in black on white. The cover shows the Britannia Pacific locomotive 70012 'John O'Gaunt' emerging from Audley End tunnel on the Cambridge-Liverpool St. line.

The booklet was specially commissioned by Kitmaster for the P1 Presentation Set *'100 Years of British Steam Locomotive History'*, issued in 1960. It includes two advertisements, one for Kitmaster locomotives which features the official BR shot of the Schools Class locomotive, and the other for Rosebud Dolls with the *original* Rosebud logo - the one that includes a rose!

Although written for and about the first presentation set, it was later included with the other two sets and is referred to on the box covers. The author J. N. Maskelyne unfortunately died during 1960 and many advertisements refer to 'the late author'. The book deals with the development of the steam locomotive between 1829 and 1937, and appears to have been written during 1959, the last year of the author's life. He was a distinguished technical journalist and engineer as well as a regular contributor to *Model Railway News*. He also had several of his books about locomotive practice and operation published by Percival Marshall and Co., the parent group of MRN.

AIRFIX PRESENTATION SET No.1
Airfix also produced four Presentation Sets during the late 1950s. These are *Galleons, Sports Cars, Aircraft* and starting in 1957 with No. 1, *Trackside Presentation Set.* This was originally a very nice red and yellow Type 1 box with special artwork, but later a more general Presentation Box was used, distinguished from the other three by a simple adhesive label. The set originally

Set P3 'Royal Scot Complete Train Kit'
Contents:
No. 16 Rebuilt Royal Scot Locomotive
No. 17 BR Standard Corridor Brake 2nd Maroon
No. 18 BR Standard Corridor Composite Maroon
No. 20 BR Standard Corridor Second Maroon
No. 21 BR Standard Restaurant 1st Maroon
'The Steam Locomotive' Booklet
1/2 oz Capsule of Humbrol/Kitmaster polystyrene cement
8 Capsules of paint
Paintbrush
Emery File
Pair of Tweezers (Marked 'Sheffield')
Pieces of Wrenn straight track
Kitmaster 1960 Catalogue

The Stirling makes a fine sight as it gently glides down the main line. A popular kit which formed one third of the first Presentation Set.

The Duchess Pacific, though welcomed by the Press, contained significant errors. For the most part these were copied directly from the Roche drawing, but the finished model still manages to impress.

contained all Type 1 kits:
1 x Pattern No. 4005 Signal Box
2 x Pattern No. 4007 Platform Section
1 x Pattern No. 4009 Booking Hall
1 x Pattern No. 4012 Platform Fittings
1 x Pattern No. 4013 Station Accessories
Set of Airfix Enamel Paints
Paintbrush
Tube of Airfix Polystyrene Cement

However, when it was reissued, the Signal Box was replaced by a pattern No. 4014 Footbridge. Early reissues retain Type 1 kit packaging, but later all kits were in Type 2 packaging, whilst the paints were now a standard set of intermixable Airfix enamels which could also be bought separately. All the Airfix presentation sets from this period are extremely rare indeed.

THE MODELS IN DETAIL - FOUR

No. 10: The Prototype Deltic Diesel

This much sought-after kit has a chequered history. The English Electric Deltic prototype was running trials throughout Britain in 1958/59 and was an obvious choice for a kit. The striking blue livery with those distinctive 'speed whiskers' (possibly the first 'Go Faster' stripes?) on the nose combine with the sheer size of the original to produce a most pleasing model. Combined with Ken Rush's highly individual style of artwork and a box art where he surpassed himself for excitement with bold sweeps of line and colour, you can see why this is a favourite kit for many people.

The Deltic was unique at the time in being the only Kitmaster locomotive model without any motion or connecting rods. The Kitmaster principle of unpowered locos driven from behind by a motorised coach or van did not work well. This is because the loco valve gear was often too stiff to turn freely when propelled. The Deltic did not have this problem and acted just like a twelve-wheel coach in practice. It could easily be driven by the KM1 motor bogie running in a coach behind it. It is necessary to weight the loco correctly to make it adhere to the track in this configuration. The officially recommended weight was 4 oz evenly distributed. However, an entry in *Railway Modeller* quotes this as being insufficient and recommends 7 oz evenly distributed above the bogies as being more useful. The problem was entirely solved by K's, who produced a six-wheel power bogie specially designed to fit the Deltic. Priced at £2.3s.6d, it could be fitted with cast sideframes to match at an additional cost of 3s.6d. This bogie is based on that company's successful design for tender drive units, but is fitted with disc rather than spoked wheels. The sideframes fit onto stretchers which, whilst white-metal, are equivalent to the plastic stretchers in size and position. Thus, the kit sideframes can be used with equal ease. Interestingly, there are significant detail differences between the Kitmaster and K's sideframes.

When Kitmaster's tooling was acquired by Airfix in 1962, it included the Deltic. However, by this time, production series Deltic deliveries had commenced to British Railways. The Class 55 Deltics were sufficiently different from the prototype to

Photograph L Luppi

The second issue by Airfix of a Presentation set used a standard box for all subjects. A set specific label was then glued to the lid.

Photograph G Short

The original issue of Trackside Presentation Set No.1 contained a full suite of Type 1 header bags and makes a fine sight. Highly prized today.

***Below.* Brian Waite of Kidderminster was midway through construction of his 5" gauge Deltic when he took time out to build a Kitmaster Deltic as well.**

make a conversion difficult. The cab detail and window patterns were wrong, a new bogie sideframe was needed and the length was reduced. Additionally, Kitmaster had moulded the 'speed whiskers' onto the sides. Perhaps this explains why Airfix never released the model. Nevertheless, an item appeared in *Mixed Freight* in *Railway Modeller* of August 1961, showing a Kitmaster Deltic painted in the new two-tone green livery as delivered to Eastern Region!

Airfix did continue to supply Deltics, via the Hermes Supply Co., to fulfil the Shredded Wheat promotion throughout 1963 and into late January 1964.

The tooling passed to Dapol at the time they acquired all the other Airfix railway kit tools. It is said that David Boyle did not intend to release the kit at first. However, when Dapol shot the mould marked 'Drewry Shunter' they found it to be the original Kitmaster Deltic. This tool had been earmarked for scrapping by Airfix due to the poor state of the central cores, and indeed the tool for the clear parts was destroyed. On the original manifest of tools acquired by Dapol, this item was shown as '0-4-2', being the body mould for the Airfix ready-to-run GWR 14XX 0-4-2T tank engine. Only later was its true identity discovered. The mould was sent to Hong Kong and one thousand kits were run off as an experiment. Because it was not intended to be released as such, the kit retained the Rosebud Kitmaster logo, whereas all the other kits were re-engraved with the Dapol logo. Early Dapol kits do not include the transparent window components, any instructions or the decal, whilst later issues lack only the glazing parts. The model can be completed using proprietary Prototype Deltic Flushglaze kit and, if required, the Deltic decal from Replica Railways.

The Dapol-produced Kitmaster Deltic retains the Rosebud Kitmaster logo on the underside of the floor. This version of the kit can only be distinguished from the original by the colour of the plastic: Kitmaster originally shot the mould in ultramarine blue plastic, whilst early Dapol issues used light grey plastic. Later Dapol issues used ultramarine plastic, but of a lighter colour density than the original. Interestingly, early examples of the Deltic did not have the logo on the underside, but it was added during the early lifetime of the Rosebud kit. The tool, although once stated by Dapol to be 'beyond economic repair', has now been refurbished and with assistance from the Kitmaster Collectors Club, has reappeared with a proper instructional header card and waterslide decal. In addition, South Eastern Finecast have introduced a Flushglaze kit, No. 99, for the prototype loco in connection with this kit.

'Deltic' enthusiast Brian Waite of Kidderminster is building the prototype Deltic in 5" gauge. Constructing the Deltic in such a large scale (1/11.3) required frequent visits to *Deltic's* former home at the

Marcus Archer's Deltic descends Stoke Bank on the East Coast Main Line with a rake of maroon Mk 1s.

Tony Wright built this Kitmaster Deltic on a motorised Lima chassis. It is seen here in latest running condition with works plates.

Tony Wright's Deltic again, this time without works plates. There is much argument amongst modellers about what the correct colouring should be. Contemporary photographs show a very pale shade of blue, but others prefer a darker shade.

Detail of the Deltic tool showing the Kitmaster logo. This tool is the only one to retain the original logo, all the others that survive were re-engraved by Airfix.

Science Museum. During one such visit, Mr Waite observed that the Museum's data panel incorrectly showed the length as 69' 6' when it should be 67' 9'. The Kitmaster model is accurate at 271mm long and after measuring the real thing, the Museum's Rail Transport curator conceded the mistake. It is hoped that *Deltic*'s new home in the NRM will be able to display it with the correct technical data. Perhaps a copy of the Kitmaster instruction sheet would help!

Motorising of the Deltic kit is best attempted with either a Class 31 or 37 chassis, both of which have the correct axle spacing, although, as Tony Wright's photograph of the motorised model shows, it is possible to achieve a good result on a Class 55 chassis. A finishing touch is the addition of EE works plates from Jackson-Evans. Coupled to your favourite rake of Maroon Kitmaster Mk 1 Coaches, this makes a very impressive model.

THE MODELS IN DETAIL - FIVE

No. 16: The TT3 Rebuilt 'Royal Scot' Class Locomotive

This rather pleasing model was the only locomotive in the ill-fated TT range. TT3 scale was introduced by Tri-ang in 1956 to take advantage of new, smaller motors and to exploit the smaller space required by the 3 mm scale.

In spite of heavy promotion and an even heavier catalogue, Tri-ang TT never really caught on in the UK and was finally withdrawn in 1966. The Kitmaster models were, as usual, accurate scale models. They did not, however, enjoy the same competitive advantages over Tri-ang as their OO big sisters. This was because Tri-ang pioneered their new standards for track, locomotives and coaches right from the beginning of TT. The coaches were scale length, unlike the OO types, and they were significantly cheaper than Kitmaster.

Kitmaster chose the Rebuilt Royal Scot for their sole TT scale model, but the example shown here hauling a rake of Kitmaster Mk 1 coaches is actually OO scale. It is converted entirely from Kitmaster parts, except for the smoke deflectors and bell, which are ex-Mainline.

The Royal Scot was therefore a risky step for Rosebud. A large amount of effort went into tooling-up for a comparatively small market. It is ironic to reflect that, had they tooled it up for 4 mm scale, it would have been an instant best seller: the first commercial model for 4 mm scale was produced by Mainline and released in the 1980s. With the demise of Mainline, there is currently no model of the type in proprietary ranges.

The decision, in 1961, not to produce the KM3 Motor Bogie was another major blow for the scale. Without it, the Royal Scot became virtually redundant, there being no locomotive motorising kit available for it at the time. This understandable decision, however, reflected the generally poor sales of TT items in the early years of production. The only power bogie made for TT was by Ks, and was not really suitable for the BSK. Subsequently, an etched nickel silver chassis by Chris Thane has been derived from Comet patterns and this does fit the kit. However, the 3SMR chassis No. 620 is not the correct wheelbase for this loco, although it claims to be so. Immediately after the initial release, Mike Bryant motorised one for the *Model Railway Constructor* using a spare Tri-ang A1A-A1A motor bogie. It was apparently successful, but Tri-ang Class 31s in TT are a bit too thin on the ground today to contemplate such butchery! Because the connecting rods are so fine in 3 mm scale, Kitmaster took the unusual step of including two sets of valve gear. The instructions note that for static display purposes, the scale size plastic valve gear and rods give the best appearance, whilst for running on a TT layout, slightly larger metal coupling rods and pistons are supplied for added strength.

The 'Royal Scot' locomotive was featured on the cover of the P3 Presentation Set, together with the four TT coaches also included in the set. The model has transfers and nameplates for three 'Royal Scot' class locos: 46100 *Royal Scot*, 46110 *Grenadier Guardsman* and 46169 *The Boy Scout*.

Also illustrated here is a specially converted 4 mm scale Scot constructed from many parts of the *Duchess of Gloucester* and *Evening Star* kits which was acquired some years ago by the Collectors Club and has now been completed by Marcus Archer. The smoke deflectors and bell are from a scrapped Mainline body, but the model is largely fabricated from Kitmaster parts.

THE MODELS IN DETAIL - SIX

No. 11 : Bulleid 'Battle of Britain' Class Pacific

The Bulleid Pacific kit, No. 11, was amongst the first batch of kits to be introduced. First making an appearance in early 1960, it rapidly established a position of fame amongst kit constructors. It preceded the Tri-ang version by several years and as a consequence, became extremely popular with Southern Region (Railway) modellers. Many photographs of Club and Exhibition layouts of the time show motorised Kitmaster Battle of Britain locos.

Airfix also had considerable success with this loco and it continues as a mainstay of

The TT Scot was available with a choice of three names; Royal Scot herself, Grenadier Guardsman and The Boy Scout; the clever OO conversion below it makes a nice comparison.

the Dapol kit fleet. It is impossible to estimate how many have been produced over the years, but it must be approaching 30,000 kits.

The model portrays the locomotive 34057 *Biggin Hill,* as running in 1958 in original condition. This locomotive was never rebuilt and the air-smoothed casing remained to the end of Southern steam in July 1967. The high-sided 5,500 gallon tender of the kit was often 'cut down' on other locomotives of the class in order to reduce axle loading on the lightly laid West of England routes, where Bulleid's Light Pacifics were regular performers. The kit has the original unorthodox BR(SR) style lining moulded onto the boiler, cab and tank sides. This livery did not follow the 'standard' BR lining pattern with a boxed-in running number. Instead, the lines were continued straight across the cab sides and onto the tender. The resulting 'sleek' appearance of the unrebuilt locos contrasted sharply with the 'stocky' look of the rebuilt version, which more closely resembled a Britannia Pacific in appearance.

The lining can be easily removed from the kit parts with a sharp knife and replaced with a suitable modern alternative: Kemco Waterslide BR/SR lining is best, but standard BR (GWR) lining from PC Pressfix, although incorrect, can also be used if preferred.

The original Kitmaster tool had no brake gear and front steps for the loco, these were added by Airfix in a major retooling which replaced the symbolic vacuum pipe with a scale example and added an NMRA buckeye coupling to the tender drawbar. For some unexplained reason, the front bogie retained the original Kitmaster coupling.

The Battle of Britain was a popular choice for motorising, as has been noted, but this was made considerably easier by the issue of Arby Perfecta Kit No. 4 in November 1960. This utilised the Tri-ang XT60 motor (originally developed for use in TT and Lord of the Isles locos) to provide traction. Pick-up was by nickel silver strips brushing the surface of steel rim tyres fitted over the plastic Boxpok wheels. The plastic axles were covered by metal sleeves running in brass frame bushes to improve the free-running performance of the chassis. To provide adhesion, a large custom casting was placed between the frames with the motor bolted straight onto it. By all accounts, it was quite a successful conversion, and many can still be found today. Only one article on motorising this loco ever appeared in the railway press, despite the popularity of the kit. Since the proposed conversion involved butchering a Hornby-Dublo A4 , it was not very practical. However, in 1969 Ray Simmons wrote three excellent articles for *Airfix Magazine* covering detailing and motorising of the kit.

Although basically a good model, and generally engineered to scale, there are many areas where Kitmaster compromised or deviated from the prototype to simplify production. The appearance of the finished model can therefore be considerably enhanced by the addition of detail parts, obtainable mostly from the workshop of famed Bulleid 'Guru' Albert Goodall. Detailing the Kitmaster/Dapol Battle of Britain Locomotive involves a fair amount of handy work with a craft knife and file, but the result is a most pleasing model at a modest cost. Marginally less work is required on an Airfix or Dapol kit because of the extra parts added when the kit was reissued in 1968. The best source for the parts is Albert Goodall, 20 Kingswood Road, Dunton Green, Sevenoaks Kent TN13 2XE. Send 40p + SAE for his list.

THE MODELS IN DETAIL - SEVEN

No. 60: The Ariel Arrow Super Sports Model

The Ariel Arrow is perhaps the most elusive of the Kitmaster models. In production for just five months from March 1962, it was a big risk for Rosebud. When the locomotive range was suddenly curtailed, before the last three advertised models had been released, announcing a large scale motorcycle kit was indeed brave. Rosebud had no experience of this market as no British motorcycle kits then existed. The decision to produce this kit can possibly be attributed to the 'Suggestion' scheme run by Rosebud. Since two of their employees were stalwarts of the Wellingborough Motorcycle Touring Club and one of them had owned an ex-WD Ariel cycle, it may have been at their instigation that the *1960 Motorcycle of the Year* was chosen as the next subject for a Kitmaster kit. In fact, there was to have been a whole series of these kits. The second kit, No. 61, was in the pattern-making stage when the company was sold to Airfix. It would have been a Matchless circuit racing machine. Drawings and some patterns were made, but

The air-smoothed grace of Bulleid's most numerous locomotive design was effectively portrayed by Kitmaster. This kit and the later, improved, Airfix version (suitably detailed) are still the best basis of a scale model of the type.

KITMASTER "BATTLE OF BRITAIN"

THE Kitmaster "Battle of Britain" appears to have preceded the "Deltic" in production. However, we doubt if any of the many Kitmaster fans will quibble about the order!

As can be seen from our illustration, the Bulleid Pacific fully maintains the high standards set by its predecessors, though the air-smoothed casing leaves little opportunity for the intricate detail of some of the other models. As can be seen, the full character of the prototype has been captured, the B.F.B. wheel, the massive motion and the relatively high-pitched cylinders.

As readers will know, there is little basic difference, other than the name and number, between the "Battle of Britain" and West Country classes; in point of fact there are more variations between individual locomotives than between the nominal classes. Therefore we have two classes to select from, while one could stretch a point and give this model a Merchant Navy name and number. Here, of course, there are slight differences of size, but we doubt if they are sufficient to be noticeable on a layout.

Once again this is an excellent model of a popular prototype, and should be as well received by enthusiasts as previous items in this range. It retails at 10/6.

***Railway Modeller* review**

The three boxed issues of the Battle of Britain nicely illustrate the difference between the highly stylised Ken Rush artwork and the detailed photo-realism of Roy Cross on the Airfix boxes.

the project was never completed by Kitmaster or, indeed, resurrected by Airfix. The Ariel Arrow Super Sports Model, to give it its proper name, was produced in a standard, but dimensionally unique, Kitmaster card box. It was numbered out of sequence as No. 60. This was meant to be the first number in a new series of kits, allowing the Railway range to continue using the 1-59 block of numbers.

The introduction was noted in an editorial from the 1962 Toy Fair by *Model Railway Constructor* at the same time as it was announced that kits 35, 36 and 37 had been suspended.

The large scale, 1:16, meant changes to the normal assembly method, with both the main superstructure and chassis being assembled as separate parts. In order to produce this kit, Kitmaster worked from a real Ariel Arrow which was taken into the Design Office and meticulously studied and drawn. These were in addition to the manufacturer's drawings, which were also made available to the pattern maker, Mr Fergusson of Kettering.

Perhaps the most interesting feature was the wheels. To enable the spokes to appear as fine as possible, Rosebud elected to mould the wheels in clear plastic. One simply painted carefully over the spokes to obtain the desired effect. When the tooling was acquired by Airfix, they retooled these parts in the same opaque yellow plastic used for the rest of the bike. Consequently, the two kits are easily distinguished.

In fact, the Rosebud Kitmaster logo does not appear on the model at all, but on the stand. This was duly re-engraved by Airfix. Airfix do not seem to have changed the thick Kitmaster mould sprues on this model. The lack of a coupling to retool led directly to the incorporation of this kit into the Airfix range as early as July 1963. In fact, the early reintroduction date would indicate that very few changes were made. However, Airfix did think it worth changing the registration number in the artwork from ONV 989, which is a

When first re-issued by Airfix, the Ariel Arrow sported this smart Type 2 header. It was later replaced by a full colour Roy Cross painting.

Northamptonshire number, to 697 AOH, which is a Birmingham number. The Rosebud factory was, of course, in Northamptonshire. Airfix chose not to use a Wandsworth number, but the area registration covering the Ariel Motorcycles factory in Birmingham. The original Kitmaster kit has ONV 989 on the box, whilst the decals are for 697 AOH.

Additionally, the price was reduced dramatically at the same time, coming down from 5s 11d as a Kitmaster model to the meagre 2s of an Airfix Series 1 kit. Later, the kit was reissued as Series 2 and finally ceased production in 1980. An interesting kit issued in 1964, pattern No. 311, was 'Ton-up Tony'. This was described by Airfix as a 'Weird-ohs' kit and formed part of a series of three kits, the others being "Flame-Out Freddie" (monstrous T33C pilot) and "Toilway Daddy" (barely humanoid dragster driver!) the other two being licensed directly from Hawk plastic models of America. The Airfix contribution to the extensive Hawk 'Weird-ohs' range involved the addition of a grotesque caricature of a demented biker astride the aforementioned Ariel Arrow! It is actually quite a sought-after kit for Airfix collectors, mainly, one suspects, because not many people bought it!

THE MODELS IN DETAIL - EIGHT

KM1 and KM2 - The Motorised Bogies

The motorising of Kitmaster models was made infinitely easier by the introduction, in 1960, of two ready-to-run motor bogie units. These are the KM1 Motorised BR1 Bogie for passenger stock and the KM2 Motorised Box Van for freight stock.

The original Kitmaster design was for a series of static models, but Dennis Franklin, Assistant Technical Manager in charge of the project, had plans for motorising them. 'Of course, there was the bogie and the box van. It was a helluva strain to get these out as well as one new model a month. We should

The original Kitmaster Ariel Arrow showed a 'bike registered ONV 989, although the transfers always read 697 AOH. Dig those groovy winkle pickers!

have bought those parts in. In the Rosebud showroom, I had a working layout built. I had motorised units there which would push the locomotives round. It worked well, but I would have liked to do a motorising kit of our own. Perhaps a diecast metal block predrilled for the stretchers and the axles to give weight low down, where you need it.'

The Kitmaster power bogies were designed to fit inside a Standard BR Mk 1 BSK coach. The appropriate Kitmaster coach number is shown on the box panel of each motor bogie, KM1 fits Coach No. 15 (OO BSK) and KM3 would have fitted Coach No. 17 (TT BSK). The KM3 power bogie was shown in the 1960 and 1961 catalogues, but was never actually commercially produced.

This was documented in an official press statement in *Railway Modeller* of July 1961. Interestingly, the *Airfix Magazine* of November 1960 described a test run of a TT motor bogie sample they had received. This was presumably a limited factory built coach fitted with a prototype bogie to promote the Royal Scot and TT Coach range.

Earlier, an advertisement in *Model Railway News* June 1960 from Southgate Hobby Shop had offered a 'motorised Utility Van to drive your Kitmaster Locomotives'. The unit was said to be available in 'red or green', presumably maroon and SR green, and cost 45s. It was heralded as a 'Southgate Speciality'. Any further details would be appreciated.

Occasionally, KM1 power bogies are found fitted to Kit No. 31 (Pullman Power Car), which has the fitting to take it and the instruction showing how to fit it. A lot of work is involved in replacing the cast metal sideframes of BR1 pattern with the driving bogie Metro-Schlieren pattern sideframes. Fitting it to the BSK involves considerable modification to the coach, including bending up the existing steel ballast weight and fitting a plastic yoke supplied in the kit.

The Motorised Box Van was designed to run behind a Kitmaster locomotive, which it pushed along. The principle was first demonstrated at the 1961 Brighton Toy Fair, using a standard KM1 motor bogie inside an RB3 Refrigerator Van. It was highly acclaimed at the time, especially by the *Model Railway Constructor* who thought it 'an economical way to motorise your Kitmaster fleet.' The construction is very similar to the KM1 motor bogie, except that the ballast weight is different and the sideframes are not diecast. Instead, black plastic sideframes are fitted to the bogie, whilst the body is a separate one-piece moulding in brown bauxite-coloured plastic. The body moulding is almost identical to the Hornby-Dublo ventilated van, even down to the tool marks on the inside, but conspicuously carries the Rosebud Kitmaster logo on the underside. The unit comes with a choice of couplings: a separate enclosure contains parts to enable the fitting of either Peco Simplex or Tri-ang Tension Lock couplings as an alternative to the standard Kitmaster hook and eye coupling.

Despite their superficial similarity to the Tri-ang designed motor bogie used in their Diesel Multiple Unit, it is certain that Tri-ang did not produce them, as Richard Lines emphatically stated in a letter to the Club. Cyril Ferry, a former Rosebud employee, used to drive up to Stalybridge to collect the raw castings for these and also remembered an armature winding machine being installed in the Design and Development Dept at Grove Street. Although former employees and out-workers can remember making assemblies, such as the choke, or assembling and packing them, most metallic parts seem to have been subcontracted to outside manufacturers and the designer remains a mystery.

A complete parts list for the KM1 and KM2 Motor bogies was recently unearthed in the 1959 diary of Kathleen Shaw, one of the women who assembled these units at Raunds. Kathleen says that they had a test track leading back from the end of the production line to the packing stage. Each completed bogie was simply popped onto this track and allowed to run under power direct to the packing station. In this way, every bogie could be quickly tested and any faults rectified before being packed into its respective box. Kathleen's entry is for August 1959, but the bogie did not actually reach the shops until July 1960.

Parts list for KM1 and KM2 from Kathleen Shaw's diary.

Part	Qty	Description
845	1	Insulator
846	2	Worm
847	3	Armature Segment
848	1	Commutator
851	2	Magnet extrusion
853	1	Magnet
854	2	Axle
855	4	Wheel
895	1	Magnet screw
896	1	Brush plate
897	1	Brush spring
898	1	Retaining plate
900	2	Felt pad
901	2	Bearing retainer
902	1	Spring
903	1	Pick-up spring
904	2	Bearing
905	4	Retaining plate screw
912	1	Bogie frame KM1
913	1	Bogie frame KM2
972	2	Bearing, small
981	2	Brush, contact
1116	1	Shaft
1117	1	Commutator insulator
1121	2	Carbon brush
Wire		0.0048' diameter
	1	Suppressor
	1	Choke
?	2	Sideframe moulding (KM2 only)
?	2	Coupling plates
?	2	10BA screws
?	1	Maintenance Sheet
?	1	Instruction sheet (KM1 only)
?	2	Couplings

These last parts with a ? are not in Kathleen's list, but are included here for completeness.

Made in-house to their own specifications, the Kitmaster power bogies are uncannily like their contemporaries from Margate. Interestingly, the box van body was also shamelessly copied; this time from a Hornby Dublo RB3 van body!

THE MODELS IN DETAIL - NINE

No. 2: The 350 hp Diesel Electric Shunter

Whether nestling behind the shed, lurking in the bay platform or simply pottering about in the yard, the humble diesel-electric shunter has become a ubiquitous sight throughout Britain's railway network. In this appreciation of the famous Kitmaster model, we turn the spotlight on the Diesel Electric Shunter and note also the five other proprietary models of this type which have been available at one time or another.

The Diesel Electric Shunter was one of the first of the new series designs for the emergent British Railways and it is therefore not surprising that several reclassifications have been made during their lifetime. Consequently, we must start by considering the various designations which have been given to these locos under British Railways ownership. Altogether, these locos have been reclassified four times since construction. Originally, they were designated into classes and sub-classes by the Eastern Region. This was followed by two sets of general BR designation in the late 1950s and early 1960s, culminating in the advent of the computerised TOPS numbering system in October 1968.

'DEJ3' was the original Eastern Region designation of the 350 hp 0-6-0 diesel electric shunter designed by the LMS and built at Derby Works. In October 1968, under the TOPS numbering system, this would become Class 11, of which over 100 were constructed between 1948 and 1952. The designation DEJ3 was arrived at as follows: DE for diesel electric, J indicating the wheel arrangement 0 6 0, design number 3 of this type. 'DEJ4' is the 350 hp 0-6-0 Class 08 locomotive, being the ubiquitous British Railways standard diesel-electric design constructed at Doncaster Works. Originally, the DEJ4 designation applied to both machines fitted with English Electric power and traction equipment and those fitted with Blackstone engines. This was soon changed, however, to allow two sub-classes depending on variant of prime mover, the Blackstone powered machines becoming D3/3 (later 3/1B), whilst EE examples became D3/2 (later 3/1A) .

Two more variants, which were powered by Crossley engines, had initially been given the design numbers DEJ5 and DEJ6, although externally they were identical to DEJ4 locos. The DEJ5 machines were powered by Blackstone, but had GEC traction motors, whilst DEJ6 had Blackstone engines driving BTH motors. DEJ5 was then reclassified as D3/4 (later 3/1C), whilst DEJ6 was allocated D3/5, followed by 3/1D. These two groups were eventually amalgamated to form a separate TOPS class: Class 10. All surviving EE and Blackstone machines at the

ASSEMBLY INSTRUCTIONS FOR YOUR DIESEL ELECTRIC SHUNTER

ROSEBUD Kitmaster PLASTIC SCALE MODELS

The instruction sheet for the 350HP diesel shunter clearly shows it to have only two marker lights.

As Marcus' model shows well, regular production examples had a full set of four marker lights at each end.

INSTRUCTIONS

In order to make this model work correctly, the following points should be observed.

(a) Notice that most parts are identified with a number or letter which is either stamped on the back, or in the case of small pins, on the ends.
(b) Examine pieces and remove any excess plastic with a special knife or razor blade.
(c) Use only Polystyrene cement when building the model, and apply only to the inside surfaces. Do not get cement on the hands, as you may smear and spoil the outer surface of the model.
(d) Special care must be taken when cementing pins into position, for no cement must be allowed to get on to the moving parts. To overcome this problem we recommend the following be adopted.
1. Deposit a small drop of cement on the end of a piece of wire or pin.
2. Push the end of the wire into the hole in which the pin must be fixed. This will leave a small deposit inside the hole when the wire is withdrawn again.
3. Place pin through the hole of moving part, and then push into cemented hole.
4. Study assembly instructions carefully to check which hole to cement.

(e) It is best to have a "dry run", so that you become familiar with the location of all parts before cementing together.
(f) Study the painting instructions before assembly as certain parts are easier to paint before cementing.
(g) Allow cemented parts ample time to dry. This will result in maximum strength of finished model.

ASSEMBLY INSTRUCTIONS

1. Cement wheels together, note that driving wheel pin halves (1) fit into driving wheel socket halves (2). Check that wheels run true.
2. Cement the two stretcher pins (3) into the stretcher pin housings on side (4).
3. Cement side of cab front (5) into its location point on side (4).
4. Insert wheels into axle holes on side (4).
5. Apply cement to other side of cab front and to each of the stretcher pins. Press the two sides of locomotive together making certain that the wheels rotate freely.
6. Apply cement to the sides of coupling housings on the front end of the locomotive (6), where the coupling plate (7) locates; see fig. 1 of assembly drawing.
7. Insert pivot end of coupling (8) through the housing below the front buffer beam. Note that the pin on the other end is pointing downwards.
8. Place the pin on underside of coupling plate (7) through the hole of pivot end of coupling and press into position. See that coupling pivots freely.
9. Repeat operations 6, 7 and 8 on rear end (9).
10. Cement top (10) to locomotive.
11. Cement rear end to locomotive.
12. Cement front end to locomotive.
13. Assemble cranks (11) coupling rods (12) and crank pins (0) as shown in fig. 2, taking care only to cement the hole in the crank.
14. Cement cranks into the end of driving wheel axles, note that cranks should point away from balance weights on the driving wheels, as shown in fig. 3. As soon as both sets of cranks have been cemented turn the wheels to see that they run freely.
15. Cement front steps (13) to locomotive.
16. Cement rear steps (14) to locomotive.
17. Cement buffers (15) to locomotive.
18. Cement vacuum pipes (16) to locomotive.
19. Apply transfers. First cut the sheet into separate subjects, then dip each in warm water for a few minutes, slide off backing into position shown on illustration. Note that the Lion on the British Railways Totem applied to either side of the body, faces towards the front of the locomotive. The numbers are applied to either side of the cab, forward of the door.

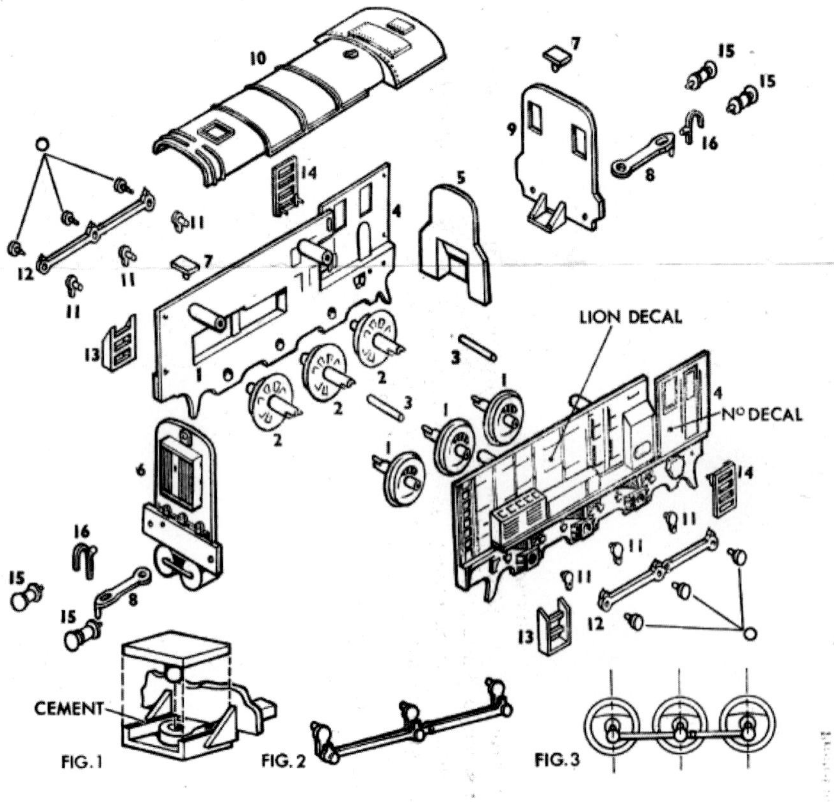

LION DECAL
N° DECAL
CEMENT
FIG. 1
FIG. 2
FIG. 3

The Nabisco kits had new instruction sheets prepared by the Airfix drawing office, as can be seen here.

1968 reorganisation of the capital fleet were grouped together within Class 08, whilst the Crossley engined examples were designated Class 10. No Class 10 machines survived long enough to carry the 10.xxx designation. all the Class 08 locomotives which survived long enough to carry their full TOPS number eventually received the English Electric 6KT 6-cylinder engine, developing 261 kW to give a top speed of 20 mph. Many of the non-standard locomotives were used in industry and, indeed, numerous examples of both TOPS classes were exported. Although built with vacuum braking alone, many of the survivors have now received air braking or, in some cases, dual braking systems.

The final development of the basic English Electric 0-6-0 Diesel Electric Shunter design is the Class 09 locomotive. Utilising the same EE 6KT power plant as Class 08, but uprated to 298 kW (400 hp) these engines are all air-braked and are regeared for a top speed of 27 mph, to match the specific requirements of the Southern Region. Only thirty were built and all were initially allocated to the SR. In recent years, however, they have become widely dispersed, one at least being allocated to Sheffield Tinsley!

Tinsley itself was home to Britain's most unlikely shunter design, the three-strong fleet of Class 13 Hump Shunters. These were formed from specially ballasted and modified Class 08 shunters adapted to work in pairs as Master and Slave units. The Slave locomotives had the entire upper section of their cabs removed and were then permanently connected to the suitably modified Master units. All were withdrawn with the end of hump shunting in 1985.

The models compared

Hamblings

This earliest model of the 350 hp shunter adhered to the basic LMS design. This single white-metal casting is now extremely rare and collectable .

Kirdon Electric

This model was extensively advertised by Kirdon during 1956 and when a factory search was carried out after Kirdon Electric was liquidated, many boxes for their model of the DEJ3 shunter were found. The proposed Kirdon Electric model was never actually put into production according to Kitmaster collector and model historian Peter Corley, 'They certainly had the boxes printed up,

Tim Shackleton's 08 is an epic conversion involving Kitmaster, Hornby-Dublo and bits of Crownline. It runs on a beam-compensated Impetus chassis and is powered by a Sagami motor.

For 4s 6d. you can now buy a "OO" gauge class DEJ4, diesel-electric shunter. This has been made available as the first of an eye-opening schedule of kits produced by a new manufacturer to our hobby, **Rosebud Kitmaster Ltd,** Northamptonshire. The complete kit is made from plastic components, and this includes driving wheels! The model is intended as an unmotorised model in the first instance, but there will be many who will do the necessary for themselves. Despite the large plastic bearings, our model ran remarkably smoothly when pushed by hand. In fact, there are many so-called scale models that fall short of this standard. A magnificent instruction and general data sheet is provided, including an offer to replace missing parts, free of charge. One small point comes to mind; it is that the model is stated as being a copy of the 350 b.h.p. locomotive (DEJ3) built by B.R.; in actual fact it is the DEJ4 class, which is 400 b.h.p. This will not matter to the enthusiast, as such variants as wheels are correct for the latter class. The moulding of this kit is to a very good standard.

It is with impatience that we await other locomotives on the 1959 schedule as these include such diverse prototypes as Patrick Stirling's 8 ft single-wheeler (price 7s 6d.) and the English Electric "Deltic" (price 10s 6d.). Others include a "Schools," "Coronation," "Battle of Britain"—in original form, G.W. "Prairie," a Swiss "crocodile" and still more!

The two different versions of Kitmaster's Class 08. The production model (left) has four marker lights, whilst the pre-production model next to it has only two, just like the instructions.

but when the factory was cleared it was a Hamblings diecast model which was inside the factory test box. There is no evidence that a tool was ever made for the body moulding.' . So this particular version can be ruled out. This loco would also have carried the number 13005, just like the 1956 Tri-ang model. The reason was that the official type photograph, as supplied by British Railways to all the manufacturers who were interested in modelling this type of locomotive, was of 13005.

Tri-ang Railways

Tri-ang introduced their model of the DEJ3/ Class 11 shunter in 1956, Rovex number R.152 and carrying the running number 13002. This was soon altered to 13005, however, and in this state the model sold over 60,000 examples. In 1960, the running number was altered to that of a DEJ4/Class 08 shunter - D3005, although no alterations were made to the body. It also appeared later as D3035. The body moulding was altered in 1957 to accommodate a clockwork mechanism and the requisite keyhole. This involved the addition of a totally unprototypical 'box' on the running plate in order to accommodate the keyhole. Electric locos then had a riveted "plate" over the redundant hole!. The major fault with this model is that Tri-ang used their existing 0-6-0 Jinty chassis for the new model. This considerably altered the proportions of the diesel body and led to the side frames being completely omitted! For more details, see Pat Hammond's excellent book '*The Story of Rovex,* Volume 1 1955-1965'.

Rosebud Kitmaster

This excellent scale model is extremely important in the history of British outline modelling because it was the first ever plastic assembly kit of a locomotive to be issued in the UK. An advance mention in the *Model Railway News* of March 1959 stated that 'Rosebud Kitmaster, a new name to the hobby, will introduce a model of British Railways Class DEJ3 Shunter as a complete plastic assembly kit at the reasonable price of 4s 6d.' This was the first mention anywhere of a Kitmaster product.

However, as the *Railway Modeller* news article pointed out, what actually emerged from the Kitmaster factory in Grove Street was a model of the DEJ4 350 hp Class 08 locomotive. The detail differences, if apparent externally, are not too great and the model is a good representation of a type which could eventually be seen all over the network. This was the first Kitmaster model to be available in the shops, despite carrying the series number 2! It featured in numerous

Table A -Summary of Classes:

BR Class BR1	Designations BR2	BR3	TOPS	Locomotive Running Numbers 1957 Nos.	1964 Nos.	Engine/Electrical Equipment
DEJ3	D3/8	3/8A	11	12045-12138	12045-12138	EE
DEJ4	D3/2	3/1A	08	13000-13116		
			08	13127-13136		
			08	13152-13365	D3000-4192 [1]	EE
DEJ4	D3/3	3/1B	08	13117-13126	D3117-3126	Crossley
DEJ5	D3/4	3/1C	10	13137-13151	D3137-3151	Blackstone/GEC
			10		D3439-3453, D3473-3502, D3612-3651	
DEJ6	D3/5	3/1D	10	13152-13166	D3152-3166	Blackstone/BTH
D3/13	3/9		12	15211-15236	15211-15236	EE/ SR Boxpok
Later Classes:						
			09		D3665-3671,D4099-4114	EE
			09		D3719-3721	
			13		D4500 Ex D4188 + 3698	EE
			13		D4501 Ex D4190 + 4189	
			13		D4502 Ex D4187 + 3697	

Note [1] : With exceptions for listed sub-classes.

Table B - The Models

Manufacturer	*No.*	*Type*	*Class*	*Date*	*Status*
Hamblings		DEJ3	11	1954	Deleted
Kirdon Electric		DEJ3	11	1955	Not Produced
Tri-ang-Hornby	R152	DEJ3	11	1956	Deleted, mould used for Devious Diesel
Rosebud Kitmaster	2	DEJ4	08	1959	Deleted, mould scrapped by Airfix.
Hornby-Dublo/Wrenn	2231	DEJ4	08	1961	Suspended, awaiting Dapol reintroduction
Hornby Railways	R050	DEJ4	08	1976	Current
Lima			09	1978	Current
Bachmann		DEJ4	08	1999	To be introduced

publicity and promotional pieces which produced favourable reviews in all three model railway journals of the time in the months of March and April 1959.

The Kitmaster model was notable for its superb attention to detail. Not only was it fitted with correct outside-frame cranks and scale width coupling rods, but it also possessed a pair of correct pattern vacuum tanks under the front buffer beam and a wealth of body detail. From the modeller's point of view, it is important because it is still, after thirty years, relatively common and does not command a high price second-hand. It is ideally suited, therefore, to a motorising and detailing project. This model remains a favourite amongst discerning modellers of today and many have been supplied by the Kitmaster Collectors Club for enthusiasts to motorise. One such example shown here was built by Tim Shackleton on a beam-compensated Impetus chassis using a Sagami can motor. The result is an accurate model which runs beautifully.

The only drawback to this model is the amount of moulded-on detail, all of which has to be removed if a full restoration to prototype is undertaken. This would necessitate removal of both front ladders on the bonnet sides, all handrails and the lamp brackets. Such criticism actually applies to all the models except the Hornby-Dublo/ Wrenn loco, which has individually fitted front ladders. It is interesting to note that most of the proprietary models depict the cab front with four electric marker lights, whereas locomotives in the initial batches built in 1952/3 were delivered with only two, set immediately above each buffer. Indeed, the very first Rosebud production kits, as shown in the instructional photograph, were modelled with only two marker lights, but the later production batches definitely have all four. The tool was modified very early on in its life, probably during 1959.

Hornby Railways

The replacement model for the Tri-ang-Hornby R.152 referred to above is dimensionally much better, but still lacks the correct outside cranks. The body is a good scale length representation of a Class 08 shunter. Apart from the lack of sideframes, the usual faults of undersize buffer heads and no buffer-beam detail require further work.

Hornby-Dublo

The Hornby-Dublo model appeared towards the end of 1960 and was not very well received. The *Model Railway Constructor* noted that the two-rail version supplied to them was only able to haul eight bogie coaches before the wheels began to slip and that the three-rail version issued some months later actually performed far better. Even so, neither would run satisfactorily below a scale 25-30 mph, which when you consider that the real thing is limited to 20 mph, says nothing for Meccano's choice of gearing!

The Dublo model was made in high-impact polystyrene and had a commensurately large amount of accurate detail on the body side. It even has separate roof ladders. However, the body is fixed to the chassis with a large and extremely conspicuous roof screw mounting downwards from the top of the bonnet. This is particularly difficult to disguise and mars an otherwise excellent model.

The tool was heavily cut down before being issued as an 0-4-0 shunter in the Hornby-Dublo 1964 Starter Set. This in turn led to a severe delay before George Wrenn could restore the tool to its original form and reissue the loco as a Class 08. The status of the reissued Wrenn model is in doubt following the acquisition of Wrenn by Dapol.

Lima

The Lima model is of the uprated Class 09 locomotive delivered to the Southern Region, but now widely dispersed. These locomotives were once again fitted with the correct style outside cranks, although the coupling rods are oversize, being too wide. The model is a fair representation, except that the buffers are very primitive and should be discarded, the forward vacuum cylinders under the buffer beam are missing and the cab steps are rather heavily reproduced. However, thinning down of the connecting rods (cosmetic or otherwise), plus fitting of new buffer heads and a Flushglaze kit can turn this into quite a respectable model.

Bachmann

The first indications that Bachmann would be producing a model of the Class 08 shunter came in 1995. During late 1995, Graham Hubbard, CEO of Bachmann Industries (Europe) Ltd., contacted the Kitmaster Collectors Club for the supply of three 350 hp Diesel Electric Shunter kits, together with a complete rake of BR Mk 1 coaches. These were duly supplied by the Club and formed the basis for the Bachmann proving and photographic models which appear in that company's 1998 catalogue. The models were built professionally by David Smith of Leeds and use the Branchlines chassis. At the time of writing, the final tooling has not been completed, so an accurate assessment is not possible. However, one can say that the development models shown to the public at the 1998 Warley M.R.C. exhibition looked very promising indeed. Hopes among the modelling fraternity are entitled to be high indeed, judging from the very fine ready to run models recently introduced by Bachmann.

Summary

The British model manufacturers have rightly devoted much effort to the BR Shunter classes and it is quite possible to model virtually the entire fleet of 1955-1965 prototypes. Whilst many have been available in ready-to-run form, the others are available as plastic (Class 04) or whitemetal (Class 01,02,05,07,14) kits. Special mention should be made here of the superb little Drewry diesel-mechanical (Class 04) modelled so effectively by Airfix. This plastic bodyline kit, the only "true" Airfix locomotive, is still in production at Dapol. Until the release of Bachmann's own Class 04, the Airfix kit on

The Standard Class 4 Moguls were widely distributed, but for some reason Kitmaster chose three numbers all allocated to the Scottish Region.

the Bachmann Class 03 chassis provided the only good model of a widely used type.

THE MODELS IN DETAIL - TEN

No. 30 The British Railways Standard Class 4MT Mogul

The advent of the British Railways Class 4MT Mogul was a major milestone in British outline modelling. Not since then has any other proprietary model of this locomotive been produced, but rather, a whole plethora of adapting, conversion and motorising kits have emerged to make the most of this superb design.

Favourably received at the time of initial launch, it was rapturously welcomed back on model shop shelves everywhere when Airfix announced the 1967 reintroduction of an improved and retooled model. Resplendent in a Series 4 box with full colour Roy Cross artwork, this kit became a mainstay of the Airfix Railways offering for many years. The picture depicts 76114 on a standard 70-foot turntable, but on close inspection it is noticeable that this loco has a 2-2-4-0 wheel arrangement! The forward half of the coupling rod is quite obviously 'missing' and only the rear driving wheels are actually coupled. Why Roy allowed such an obvious omission to escape his normally detailed scrutiny is hard to say. Certainly, all the other details are faithfully rendered. Mysteriously, the Mogul was dropped from the range at the time of issue in the Type 7 boxes, so it never received a new piece of artwork, unlike the Schools, Truro and Pug.

The locomotive is portrayed in amazing detail, considering the age and cost of the original Kitmaster issue. It provides a very good representation of the standard BR2A tender, which was widely utilised by modellers until the arrival of the Bachmann-produced Mainline Standard Class 4 in 1980. Because of the interchangeability of parts between Standard locos, the Mogul kit has proved a valuable source of parts for 'kitbashers' throughout the decades.

The concept of standard locomotive designs was actually very successful, the twelve classes giving excellent service from their introduction in 1951 right through to their untimely demise with the end of BR steam in 1968. R. A. Riddles and his design team envisaged the Standard Class 4 Mixed Traffic locomotives as a compromise between the 2-6-4 tank locomotive, numbered in the 80000 series, and a 2-6-0 tender locomotive numbered in the 76000 series. The former was chosen for a Hornby-Dublo model, whilst the latter forms the subject of this kit. These locomotives were widely deployed across the BR system during their lifetime and the kit was therefore well received.

The Kitmaster model of the BR Standard Class 4MT loco has much to commend it. The basic proportions of the body are a

Signed by the artist, even though he painted it as a 2-2-4-0.

Kitmaster modelled both the 241P and DB 23 in 4mm scale for some unexplained reason, but unlike the earlier Swiss Crocodile, these boxes proclaim "OO & HO Gauge".

The Italians nick-named these diminutive 0-6-0 tank engines 'Cafetierra' or Coffee Pots, due to the arrangement of dome and valves.

reasonable representation of the prototype and, whilst it lacks detail in many areas, it does succeed in capturing the flavour of these very useful locomotives. Motorising had to wait for a Wilro Models chassis kit in conjunction with a W&H Romford wheel pack. However, the kit was designed for the 1971 Airfix reissue. Mike Bryant showed how to motorise the Kitmaster original in an MRC article in November 1961. Today, an excellent etched nickel silver chassis is available from Branchlines especially for this kit, whilst Comet and Crownline have similar suitable etched chassis available.

THE MODELS IN DETAIL - ELEVEN

The Kitmaster Continental Prototypes

Only one company in the history of railway modelling has produced rolling stock in all three popular scales of the 60s - Rosebud Kitmaster. Remarkable as it may seem, Kitmaster appears to have been the only producer to dabble in 4 mm, 3.5 mm and 3 mm at the same time. Unfortunately, their vision was not shared by Airfix. After the agreed sale of Kitmaster to Airfix in 1963, there were high hopes for the new, combined range. Airfix originally planned to incorporate at least some of the models into the successful Airfix Rolling Stock range.

The Continental Prototypes

The choice of locomotives was, from the outset, rather esoteric. This was probably due to the direct involvement of T. Eric Smith in the selection of prototypes to be modelled. . As noted before, kit No. 3 was for the American old-timer "The General", a veteran 4-4-0 which did sterling service during the Civil War . This was a straight 3.5mm copy of the earlier Trail-Blazers kit. However, there were some very interesting foreign designs, including the famous Italian State Railways Class 835 'Caffettiera' tank engine and the massive Be6/8 Krokodil of the Swiss Federal Railways. Unfortunately, Kitmaster had not properly researched the export market for these kits. Both of these, together with the later kits of the SNCF 241P Mountain and the DB Class 23 2-6-2 were produced to the British scale of 4 mm/ft. Why this fundamental error was allowed to continue into the second year of production is one of the great mysteries of Rosebud Kitmaster. Even T. Eric Smith cannot now remember why it happened. Suffice it to say, these models found only limited acceptance in their intended target markets.

The Models Reviewed

Kit No. 3 - The General HO Scale

The General was a 4-4-0 wood-burning locomotive which became famous during the American Civil War. The locomotive was stolen from Big Shanty in the Confederate-held South in April 1862. After a hair-raising chase towards Chattanooga, with another engine in hot pursuit, the Union spies who had captured *The General* abandoned the locomotive, but only after having cut telegraph wires and burnt bridges and structures all along the line. The kit is a delightful model of this famous American 'Old Timer' and despite being produced in OO 4 mm scale, proved popular with the US market.

Kit No. 8 - The Italian State Railways Class 835 Tank engine OO Scale

This popular class of 0-6-0T shunting locomotive could, at one time, be seen all over the FS system and was popularly known as a 'Caffettiera' tank on account of the unusual arrangement of safety valves and domes, which somewhat resemble an Italian

Above. **The last train to emerge from Grove Street was the enormous New York Central 'Hudson'. Despite some poor moulding and a very difficult to follow instructional, it makes an impressive sight.**

The German Federal Railways Class 23 2-6-2 locomotives were a relatively modern design, being of all-welded construction. There was, of course, no suitable 4mm stock to run with them.

coffee-making machine! This 4 mm model was also a popular choice for motorising with the second of the Arby 'Perfecta' kits, which was designed specifically for this model.

Kit No. 12 - Giant Swiss Crocodile OO Scale

The only electric locomotive to be attempted by Kitmaster, the Swiss Federal Railways Class Be 6/8 'Krokodil, was a very strange choice. The cam-driven cranks and rigid outside coupling rods make this model at once unusual and impossible to assemble in a free running state. The dummy pantographs, whilst a reasonable representation of the prototype in the lowered position, did not make it easy to build a fully working model. Built from 1927 onwards, originally for use on the 1 in 40 gradients of the Gotthard main line, they were displaced in the early 1960s by newer Ae 6/6 traction units. Similar locomotives can be seen to this day operating on the Central Section of the Indian State Railways, with Bombay V.T. being a favourite haunt.

Kit No. 19 - German Class 23 Locomotive OO Scale

The Baureihe 23 (literally 'Class 23') 2-6-2
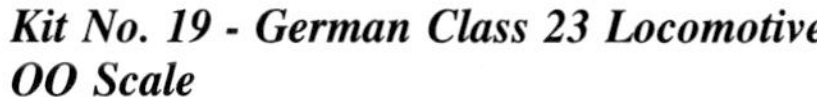
locomotives were a lightweight mixed traffic design for the Deutsche Bundesbahn. The distinctive German smoke deflectors, high running plate and articulated bogie tender made this a very distinctive model. Note that in the Kitmaster drawings the tender is shown as a rigid six-wheel construction. Introduced in 1953 as a replacement for the Prussian State Railways Class P.8, these locomotives employed novel all-welded construction to reduce weight and were one of the most successful post-war German designs. This is yet another 4 mm Kitmaster model and found little favour in its home market as a consequence. The later addition of ex-Prussian B4yge coaching stock (in 3.5 mm scale) did little to boost sales and many were remaindered after the company was sold to Airfix.

Kit No. 23 - SNCF 241P 'Mountain' Locomotive OO Scale

A monster kit of a monster locomotive. A personal favourite of the author, the elegant outlines of the Mountain contrast with its bulk and presence. It could almost be British! The last Kitmaster Continental prototype in the fatal 4 mm scale, the Mountain portrayed a popular prototype. The 35 locomotives of

The Swiss Federal Railways Class Be 6/8 Krokodil was an interesting prototype, being the only electric locomotive in the range, but the reciprocating rods meant that it was particularly difficult to assemble it free running.

The 241P Mountain Class locomotives of the SNCF were designed for the fastest and heaviest trains on the Paris Lyon-Cote d'Azur route and were Europe's most powerful steam locomotives at the time of their introduction.

this class were ordered from Le Creusot immediately after the Second World War and were delivered to the South Eastern Region of SNCF in 1948-9. They were the most powerful passenger steam locomotives operating in Europe at the time and the last steam engines to be constructed for SNCF before their headlong rush to electrification. Displaced from the crack Paris-Lyon-Nice services by electric traction, they were relegated to the Avignon-Marseille portions of such famous trains as *Le Mistral, Le Train Bleu* and the *Paris-Cote d'Azur.*

Kit No. 27 - DB type B4yge Coach HO Scale

The first of the 3.5 mm scale models. These coaches were formed by splicing ex-Prussian State Railways four-wheel bodies and building new steel underframes. Constructed during 1959-60, some 2,000 of the remaining four-wheelers were used in this project. The resulting HO scale model has a typically Teutonic rustic appearance.

Kit No. 29 - SNCF A9myfi/1958 Coach HO Scale

The latest word in air-conditioned first class luxury travel. Introduced for Paris-Lille and Paris-Lyon services, these all-steel coaches, over 82 feet long, boasted full public address systems and even radio-telephones in the vestibules! Now superseded by the superior Rivarossi model, these kits were a mainstay of SNCF modelling for many years.

Kit No. 34 - New York Central Class J.3 A 'Hudson' locomotive HO Scale

The J.3 A 4-6-4 was the culmination of a series of New York Central railroad designs. Constructed by Alco in 1937-8, these 50 locomotives had improved boilers and steaming arrangements compared with their earlier J.1 and J.2 counterparts. They are perhaps best known for their work at the head of the '*20th Century Limited*', between New York and Chicago, a train which proudly boasted an average speed of 60 mph for the journey. The model is a complex kit, reproducing a semi-working form of the intricate Baker valve gear and the intriguing Boxpok wheel design so beloved by our own O.V.S.Bulleid. These kits have long provided a source of parts for other American-outline locos and are now rather scarce. The Hudson has been a popular prototype and Kitmaster were not the first British company to contemplate such a model. That honour goes to Graham Farish, whose superb working model, tender-driven through a layshaft, is now a highly-prized collectable in its own right.

Close up of the wealth of detail embodied in the front end of the Kitmaster Hudson locomotive. The model conveys power, bulk and purposefulness to good effect.

Kit No. 37 - Canadian National U-4-A 4-8-4

Although this massive locomotive was extensively advertised on Kitmaster boxes and in their catalogues, it did not progress as far as production. Along with their proposed kits of the Flying Scotsman and the Southern Railway's 'Yankee' tanks (USA Class), it was indefinitely postponed at the Brighton Toy Fair in March 1962. The subsequent sale of the company to Airfix meant that no further development work was undertaken on this project. This is a great pity, as the giant U-4-A would, no doubt, have been a popular prototype both at home and in North America. These smartly turned out streamlined locomotives were the mainstay of express services between Toronto, Montreal and Quebec City until replaced by high-speed diesel traction. One is preserved at the CN Railroad Museum in Delson, Montreal.

THE MODELS IN DETAIL - TWELVE

The British Railways Standard Class 9F 2-10-0 'Evening Star'

Fifty years after the Nationalisation of British Railways, the introduction of Standard steam designs to a railway with 448 disparate steam locomotive classes seems eminently sensible. Under the direction of R. A. Riddles and his team, a series of twelve designs evolved to cope with the full range of B.R. traffic flows as they were in the post-war period. Many

designs 'borrowed' heavily from other successful locomotives in the constituent Big Four companies. For example, the Standard Class 3MT 2-6-2T was a rework of an Ivatt LMS design, but fitted with a standard GWR pattern boiler.

One locomotive design which was entirely new, although using many standard parts and construction techniques, was the 2-10-0 heavy freight classified as Standard Class 9, with power classification 9F. Riddles and his team excelled themselves to produce a versatile workhorse of an engine that could handle heavy block trains on the Midland and Great Central main lines at reasonable speeds or lift summer Saturday passenger expresses over the gruelling gradients of the Mendip Hills with equal ease. The 2-10-0 wheel arrangement was chosen to give maximum route availability by minimising the axle loading of these 139 ton behemoths.. The smaller wheel diameter also ensured greater traction for handling the heaviest loads.

Riddles could not have envisaged, when in January 1951 the first Standard design, Class 7F No. 70000 *"Britannia"*, was rolled out for an admiring press and public, that just nine years later one of his final Standard designs would be the last steam locomotive built in Britain for the nationalised railways. But so it was, when Keith Grand of the BTC named Class 9F No. 92220 *'Evening Star'* at Swindon Works on 18th March 1960. The British Railways Board played down the fact that she was the last steam locomotive to be built and would probably be withdrawn, along with thousands like her, after iniquitously short working lives of just over five years. The Kitmaster instruction sheet carries a quote that Reginald Hanks, Chairman of the Western Area, made at the time: *'No other machine somehow is so human and so gentle, yet, when unleashed is capable of such prodigies of strength - nothing quite so graceful in action and nothing quite so romantic. Those of us who have lived in the steam age of railways will carry with us always the most nostalgic memories.'*

Indeed, the Western Region was so embarrassed by *Evening Star* that they despatched her to that most despised and detested outpost of Paddington's new command - the former Somerset and Dorset Joint Railway from Bath to Bournemouth. If they thought that the *Star's* sojourn at Bath Green Park would guarantee her oblivion, they were sadly mistaken. Thanks to the legendary status of the S&D, the superb handling of the 9Fs by the Bath and Evercreech crews and of course the ever-watchful eyes of the myriad photographers who flocked to the line, *Evening Star* was given a broad canvas of publicity which earned her a place at the head of the preservation queue as part of the embryonic National Collection.

Altogether, 251 Class 9F locos were built, 178 at Crewe and the remaining 73 at Swindon. Although condemned to early retirement or extinction by the British Transport Commission's 1955 report *'The Modernisation of British Railways'*, the Standard Classes provided ample fodder for the contemporary model manufacturers and continue to be a source of interest today. The two major sub-classes of Class 9F are the so-called Tyne Dock locomotives, which were dual-braked and fitted with apparatus for operating the iron-ore discharge wagons and, of course, the ten locomotives adapted for trials with the Franco-Crosti feedwater preheating system. This later modification, along with three other 9Fs fitted with mechanical stokers, proved to be a dismal failure and all were reconverted by 1959.

The Kitmaster model was first shown in the 1960 catalogue. At that time, the class was in the early phases of building and the locomotive depicted in the catalogue illustration is in unlined BR black livery and fitted with a single chimney. Of course, by the time the 1961 catalogue was prepared and the kit itself was readied for release, it became apparent that the last engine to be built would be treated differently. *Evening Star*, resplendent in fully-lined BR Green livery and with the Swindon hallmark of a copper-cap to her double chimney, made a striking model. The Ken Rush portrait on the box lid does the loco no favours, but captures the essential bulk of the prototype. The later Airfix artwork is really unexceptional. Although the loco is the WR allocated *Evening Star*, it is shown hauling stylised

Tom Wright's 9F uses a modified Airfix body with Comet/Crownline chassis and valve gear. This is partnered with a Dave Alexander BR 1F tender top on the original Airfix frames. Photographed by his father, Tony Wright.

Tyne Dock - Consett iron ore discharge hoppers. There are many flaws in the painting, which is by an unknown artist. These include a running plate which is not parallel to the cab, the boiler centreline lying over one wheel and numerous other major faults. However, the image is certainly very striking and the colouration is vivid.

Evening Star was a natural choice for motorising projects, being a popular and widely used prototype found on all BR regions. There was a Wilro chassis for the Airfix version, a Bristol Models chassis for the same and, naturally, a Mike Bryant article on *Motorising the Kitmaster 9F*. Many were motorised with the Ks tender drive unit. In addition, there was a very ambitious and interesting article concerning the conversion of an Airfix 9F into the Standard Class 8 Pacific - *Duke of Gloucester*. Most articles on that subject begin with either the Tri-ang or later Hornby model of the Standard Class 7P *Britannia*, but the conversion from 9F is certainly novel.

The Airfix version of the kit was long lived and can be found in several different types of packaging. There is the original Series 4 issue, pattern number R401, which was issued in December 1964 in a Type 3 box. With the 1968 reissue of *Biggin Hill* in Series 5, the *Evening Star* kit looked out of place in Series 4 and thus was reissued in Series 5 with pattern number R502. It then stayed in that Series until its demise in 1978 when, numbered 05652-0, it was issued in a Type 7 box. This last issue is rather scarce.

The kit has been produced by Dapol in various colours and with three different header styles in the 15 years that they have had the tool. Total production of *Evening Star* kits now exceeds 100,000 pieces, making it one of the truly great kits of all time.

Tom Wright's 9F trundles out of Stoke Tunnel with a southbound parcels working.

The front 3/4 view of Marcus Archer's Beyer-Garratt shows the size of the boiler and overall length of these engines to good effect.

The 'going-away' shot provides ample detail of the rotating self-trimming coal bunker which is so distinctive on these engines.

provided number decals for the later LMS 79XX series, as befits a rotating-bunker engine, together with 47994 for the BR period.

Withdrawals began in 1955 with the introduction of BR Standard Class 9F locomotives to the Toton - Washwood Heath and Toton-Brent trains and by 1958 all thirty-three Garratts had been withdrawn and summarily cut up for scrap. Today, the only Garratts operating in this country are narrow gauge, (on the Welsh Highland Railway) whilst the sole standard gauge machine in preservation, entombed at Bressingham, is of a much smaller industrial type. However, those who have visited the Summerlands exhibition centre in Coatbridge, Scotland, will not fail to have been impressed by their repatriated North British Locomotive Company Garratt from South Africa. Whilst only 3ft 6in gauge, this beast goes some way to conveying the might and power of the Beyer-Garratt design.

In model form, there is little room for choice. Apart from the Kitmaster model with the rotating bunker, the original K's whitemetal kit is still available from Autocom UK Ltd. This depicts the locomotive is as-built condition with straight-sided bunker. Motorising originally used K's HP2M motors at each end, but clearance exists for more modern motor/gearbox combinations.

Motorising the Kitmaster model was first tackled by the celebrated Mike Bryant in the August 1961 issue of *Model Railway Constructor*. Mike reported considerable difficulty in using ready-to-run chassis for this job and in the end resorted to using a scratch-built brass framed chassis. He did comment on the Tri-ang 2-6-2T chassis and the Hornby-Dublo R1 0-6-0T, finding the former easier and cheaper to use for the conversion in this case. The Kitmaster model is generally a good representation of the prototype and was well received by the press when finally released in March 1961. It had originally been promised for November 1960.

Demand for these kits is as high today as it ever was. With the Autocom model retailing at more than £100 (without wheels etc.) and with a constant stream of modellers wishing to build a motorised Garratt, prices for the original Kitmaster model are likely to stay high for the foreseeable future.

THE MODELS IN DETAIL - THIRTEEN

The Ex-L.M.S. Beyer-Garratt 2-6-0 + 0-6-2

Long-term favourite for the most sought-after Kitmaster model, the gargantuan Beyer-Garratt locomotive of the LMSR is certainly impressive. At just over 87ft 10ins long, these monster articulated locomotives were the main power for long coal trains from the East Midland coalfields to London and Birmingham for some 30 years. Constructed in two batches, under the direction of Sir Henry Fowler, by Beyer, Peacock and Co. Ltd at Gorton Works in Manchester, these machines featured several novel patented devices. Most notable, of course, is the articulated Garratt design, whereby two similar 2-6-0 engines are harnessed to one large boiler and bunker. The resulting locomotive had a tractive effort of around 40,250 lb, as compared to the 46,800 lb generated by a pair of LMSR Moguls of the 1933 batch with which the Beyer-Garratt locomotives shared many common parts. The other remarkable design feature in these engines was the patent Beyer, Peacock self-trimming rotating coal bunker. Described as being of 'conic frustrum' shape, the bunker was itself driven by a two-cylinder steam engine.

The first three Garratt engines were built in 1927 and were not originally fitted with rotating bunkers. A second batch of thirty locomotives with minor improvements and modifications was constructed in 1930. Changes introduced with the second build included a shorter chimney and dome together with a smaller water tank, reduced from 4,700 gallons to 4,500 gallons. Since the locomotives had bi-directional water scoop apparatus fitted to the leading engine and tank, this did not cause problems in service. At the same time, coal capacity was increased from 7 tons to 9 tons, thereby increasing the duty cycle for the class and permitting return workings on the 126-mile Toton-Brent coal run. The Kitmaster instructions are erroneous in regard to water capacity, stating that the later engines have more water carrying capacity than the earlier three.

Eventually, all 33 locomotives received the conical bunker, although the first three and some of the 1930 batch were originally constructed with conventional straight-sided bunkers. In order to prevent delays to passenger services on the thirty miles of double track between Kettering and Leicester, fully loaded coal trains needed to maintain a steady 21 mph average on this section. The 5 ft 3 in driving wheels and four 18.5 x 26 in cylinders of the Beyer-Garratt gave these engines a good turn of speed in addition to plenty of traction, enabling them to handle the 1,450 ton coal trains with ease.

Only three locomotives, numbers 4997-9, were fitted with vacuum brake equipment, which would have enabled passenger train working. No heating was provided for coaching stock and the design was always intended only as a heavy freight locomotive, although they were expected to maintain 50 mph average speeds over the steeply graded Midland main line with return workings of empties. Whilst these engines were essentially a pair of LMS 8ft 0in x 8ft 6in Mogul chassis running back-to-back, the company did contemplate extending the Garratt design to a larger passenger locomotive of the 4-6-0 + 0-6-4 arrangement, similar to those constructed for African railways, but this was not pursued. The Gresley designed LNER 2-8-0 + 0-8-2 Garratt of Class U1, which was introduced in 1926, was also destined to remain a solitary locomotive. Originally allocated LMS numbers 4967-4999, the entire class was renumbered in 1938 into the 7967-7999 block, thereby allowing their old numbers to be reused on Stanier Black Five locos then under construction. At Nationalisation, each number was increased by 40000. Kitmaster

(Models in detail continued in next chapter)

Above. **The four kits that made up the Series 2 Rolling Stock were introduced from 1960. The Railbus was first, followed rapidly by the Lowmac and Booth Crane. The last one to arrive was the Interfrigo, the only Airfix HO scale model.**

Below. **The Airfix Series 1 wagons represented incredible value for money at just two shillings each. The set of spare couplings is now considered scarce.**

3. RISE and FALL

AIRFIX PRODUCTS LTD.
'Products in Plastics'

Airfix Rolling Stock Kits

The advent of the plastic construction kit after the War has been well documented elsewhere. However, despite their involvement in assembly kits as early as 1949 and the large market for model railways, it was only in 1956 that Airfix Products Ltd. began their now-famous association with railway modelling.

Even then, the first series to see the light of day was the Trackside Series. A further four years were to elapse before Airfix contemplated a full-blown rolling stock kit. A press release in March 1960 at the Toy Fair, declared that Airfix would enter the 4 mm rolling stock market with a series of kits. Unusually, it was not a Series One 'pocket money' model, but a larger Series Two kit that was intended to launch the range. This was to be the Park Royal Railbus. However, it was beaten into production by the first of the Series One wagons and was not finally released until November 1960. The first of the amazing Series One wagons had been given to the press for review in July 1960. Not one, but two models were issued together. These were the Class B Tank Wagon and the *Presflo* cement hopper. The choice of a tank wagon, whilst on the face of it not very interesting, was an inspired one. All the ready-to-run models lacked detail and did not represent actual prototypes at this point. Consequently, a good and above all accurate model of a modern Class B Tank wagon was an immediate success. These wagons were well distributed around the country, in fact anywhere that a refinery was sited and could be seen in the hands of various locomotives. Your author regularly stood in awe on the west end of Basingstoke station watching the impressive Class 33 diesels hauling 30 or more such tankers up from the Exxon refinery at Fawley. I longed to model the whole train, but alas space restricted me to just six or seven tankers! Although Airfix provided markings for three different Esso tankers, they never considered the obvious attraction of issuing the kit in other petrochemical company liveries. That step was left to Dapol, who have recently issued it with BP markings.

The *Presflo* cement hopper, whilst similar to a pre-existing Hornby-Dublo model, provided a really superb little kit of a distinctive prototype. The *Railway Modeller* looked forward to seeing all that angle iron portrayed in plastic, noting that it was the sort of vehicle exactly suited to injection moulding techniques. The bright yellow plastic and excellent well-reproduced decal sheet made it very easy to depict an example in the Blue Circle cement fleet with minimal effort.

However, it was to be the third issue in the series that really caught the imagination of the modelling fraternity. This was the ubiquitous 16 ton steel mineral wagon. Built in their tens of thousands by British Railways and used for carrying all manner of traffic, this kit proved immensely popular. Whole block trains could now be constructed quickly and cheaply, as all these early Series One kits cost just two shillings each. Coming towards the end of 1961, about the time that Kitmaster released their excellent kit for the 9F, this was a modern image modeller's Mecca. All that was needed to complete the train was a standard 20 ton brake van and Airfix duly obliged in late 1961 with a well-received model of the same. Beautifully detailed and moulded in a dark brown plastic ready for painting, this kit set the standard for Brake Vans that others would have to follow. Not until late 1979, when Mainline introduced their RTR model, was it bettered.

Some of these early kits had extremely long production lives. Indeed, the Tank Wagon appeared in every Airfix catalogue except the final (17th) edition, and has been in production with Dapol for a further 10 years now. Similarly the Mineral Wagon enjoyed favour with Airfix, appearing in 14 of the 17 catalogues. Not so fortunate was the 10 ton Ventilated Meat Van, which had a lamentably short run of just three years in the early 1960s and was then mothballed until the penultimate catalogue in 1979 when it made a welcome return. This model portrayed the louvred ventilators to perfection and even had opening doors.

		April	1st	Sum.	2nd	Sum.	3rd	4th	5th	6th	7th	8th	9th	10th	11th	12th	13th-15th	16th	17th
No.	**Name**	**1961**	**1962**	**1962**	**1963**	**1963**	**1964**	**1965**	**67-68**	**1969**	**1970**	**1971**	**1972**	**1973**	**1974**	**1975**	**1976-78**	**1979**	**1980**
R1	12t Oil Tank Wagon	R1	R1	R1	R1	R1	R1	R1	R1	R1	R1	R1	LP	02656-3	02656-3	02656-3	02656-3	02656-3	
R2	Cement Wagon	R2	R2	R2	R2	R2	R2	R2										02662-8	
R3	10t Mineral Wagon		R3	R3	R3	R3	R3	R3	R3	R3	R3	R3	LP	02657-6			02657-6		02657-6
R4	Brake Van		R4	R4	R4	R4	R4	R4				R4	LP	02658-9	02658-9	02658-9	02658-9	02658-9	
R5	Cattle Wagon		R5	R5	R5	R5	R5	R5				R5	LP	02659-2			02659-2		02659-2
R6	24 couplings		R6	R6	R6	R6													
R7	Drewry Shunter		R7	R7	R7	R7	R7	R7	R7										
R8	10t Meat Van			R8	R8	R8	R8	R8										02661-5	
R9	Saddle Tank Pug						R9	R9	R9	R9	R9	R9	LP	02660-2	02660-2	02660-2	02660-2		02660-2
R10	Prestwin" silo wagon						R10	R10	R10										
R11	Stephenson`s Rocket						R11	R11	R11	R11	R11	R11	R11	01661-2	01661-2	01661-2	01661-2	01661-2	
R201	Park Royal Railbus	R201	R201	R201	R201	R201	R201	R201											
R202	Diesel Loco. Crane	R202	R202	R202	R202	R202	R202	R202											03622-3
R203	Interfrigo" Refrigerator			R203	R203	R203	R203	R203											
R204	Lowmac with JCB					R204	R204	R204	R204										
R205	J94 Saddle Tank						R205	R205	R205										
R301	Prairie Tank						R301	R301	R301	R301			LP	04655-6	04655-6	04655-6	04655-6	04655-6	
R302	City of Truro							R302	R302				LP	04654-3	04654-3	04654-3	04654-3		04654-3
R401	Evening Star							R401	R401	R401	R401	R401							
R402	Schools Class								R402	R402	R402	R402	R402	04652-7	04652-7	LP	04652-7		04652-7
R403	BR Mogul											R403	R403	04653-0	04653-0	LP	04653-0	04653-0	
R501	Battle of Britain								R501	R501	R501	R501	R501	05651-7	05651-7	05651-7	05651-7	05651-7	
R502	Evening Star											07/71	LP	05652-0	05652-0	05652-0	05652-0		05652-0

Note: LP denotes a kit shown in the catalogue or price list as Limited Production.
Note: Some kits were not illustrated in the catalogue although they were listed on the accompanying price lists.
Note: From Summer 1971, Evening Star moved up from Series Four (R401) to Series Five (R502).

Airfix rolling stock came and went in their catalogues. Some items had very short lives indeed, such as the Scammell Scarab, whilst the Mineral Wagon and Tank Wagon appeared to be in near continuous production for 20 years.

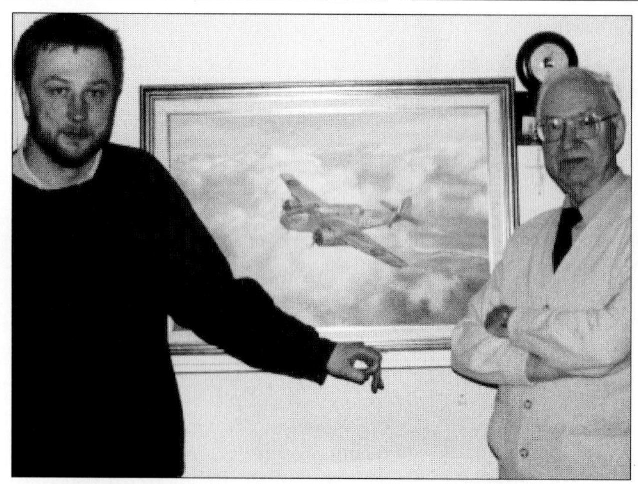

John Wells (left) of the Airfix Collectors Club together with Airfix artist Roy Cross admiring a Bristol Beaufort which Roy had recently completed.

Another popular model was the Cattle Wagon. Although based on an earlier GWR diagram, like all the other kits in this series, it was in fact a BR built vehicle. Representing a traffic flow which has long since disappeared from the railways, this was nonetheless a big seller in the 60s. Accuracy and attention to detail meant that

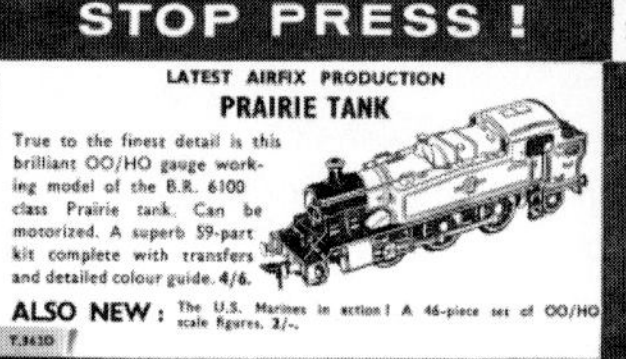

Airfix designers incorporated a removable partition inside which could be positioned to give a variety of sizes of stall. Naturally, all six doors could be made to open and the chassis had all the correct running gear.

Next in line for release was an unusual and now hard-to-find kit. Not so much a kit, in fact, as an accessory pack. This was R6, '24 Buckeye Couplings'. This pack provided enough extra couplings to convert a dozen wagons to the bizarre Airfix coupling system. According to the 2nd Edition catalogue 'Airfix have standardised on the NMRA buckeye coupling of type X2F. It allows automatic uncoupling with a simple ramp.' Fine, as long as it works, but as any one who has tried will know, it doesn't! Understandably deleted after just 18 months in the programme, these couplers must surely rate as one of the most ill-considered ideas of any toy manufacturer. Why NMRA instead of BRMSA or Simplex? Nobody seems to know. Like Kitmaster and their hook and eye arrangement, this vitally important part of the model seems to have been left to chance. The only easily fitted satisfactory coupling for these models is the Peco Simplex buckeye. It is close to impossible to fit the Airfix models with the Tri-ang tension lock coupling, which was establishing itself rapidly as the new standard at the time. Today, Dapol supply a useful little adaptor plate that will allow a Dapol or Airfix GMR coupling to be fitted, but frankly it is thirty years too late.

TABLE J - ENGINEERING TOOL CHANGES

Kit		Kitmaster	Part No. Airfix
1	Rocket	Metal stays 17	28/29 Plastic stays 31/32 crew added and footplate extended Pistons redesigned Rear coupling added All parts renumbered!
5	Schools	Moulded name Hook coupler KM steam pipe	19 Transfer name + nos. 33 NMRA buckeye replaced 31 Steam pipes added 34 Vacuum pipes added 32 3-link coupling added 33 Injector pipes added 22 Hole in buffer beam
6	Pug	Front beam plain Hook coupler	10A lamp irons added 17 NMRA buckeye replaced 17a 3-link coupling added Whistle added to roof Reversing rod added Guard irons and brake gear added
7	Prairie	KM pony truck	24/27 NMRA pony truck 24a/27a Steam/vacuum pipes added
11	BoB	Hook coupler	10 NMRA Buckeye replaced 27/31 Steam pipes added 25 Vacuum pipes added 26/32 Scale coupler added 27-30 Brake gear added 33/34 Front Steps Added
22	9F	Front pony KM Rear coupler KM	Front pony NMRA Rear coupler NMRA Steam/vacuum pipes added
24	Truro	Hook coupler	NMRA buckeye replaced Steam/vacuum pipes added Brake rods added Wheel balance weights 3-link coupling added
26	J94	Hook coupler	18 NMRA buckeye replaced 18a 3-link coupling added
30	Mogul	Front pony KM Hook coupler KM steam pipe	38 Front Pony NMRA 64 buckeye replaced 77/81 Steam pipes added 78/79 Scale couplings 80 Vacuum pipe rear
60	Arrow	Centre hub clear	Centre hub opaque

The seventh issue in this series was a milestone in kit history. Whilst the Railbus was technically the first Airfix vehicle to move under its own power, it was not a locomotive as such. That honour fell to the delightful Drewry Shunter, pattern number R7. Classified under the 1970 TOPS system as Class 04, these 204 hp diesel-mechanical shunters were a popular and widespread design. An early introduction under the Modernisation Plan and construction in large numbers put them at the head of the queue for a model. However, in reality these shunters were to have relatively short service lives with British Railways, being surpassed by the BR-built Class 03 shunter, with which they share certain similarities. Withdrawals began in the mid-60s and by 1972 very few survived in capital stock. Many of them did, however, go on to useful lives in industry. Numerous kits were built and motorised, notably with the E.A.M.E.S. of Reading chassis kit and latterly with the Mainline and Bachmann 03 chassis. Now, of course, one can simply buy the excellent Bachmann RTR model off the shelf. The Drewry disappeared from the range after the 5th Edition and only resurfaced under Dapol's aegis. The next issue in the Series One range was the reissued Kitmaster Pug, No. R9. Priced at just two shillings, this represented great value. Formerly, it retailed for 4s 6d as a Kitmaster kit. The final Series One wagon issue was an interesting prototype. The Prestwin Pressure Discharge Silo Wagon is a good model with a wealth of detail. Although Hornby-Dublo had already produced a similar wagon in the Fisons livery, once more the Airfix issue was considerably cheaper and managed to encompass more detail in the walkways and valves on top of the tanks. The late issue date for the Prestwin ensured that it appeared in a rather good Type 3 box. All the previous wagons first appeared in classical Type 2 boxes.

The larger Second Series kits covered some remarkable vehicles. Starting, as noted above, with the Park Royal Railbus, the range was used to introduce three other very interesting models. The first was the Booth Diesel Locomotive Crane. This unit was a self-propelled diesel-hydraulic crane capable of lifting 15 tons on the jib arm. Unfortunately, no model of the riding truck with the jib runner was forthcoming from Airfix and this remained a 'half-model'. It was rather good in operation, with a winding handle for the winch and a lifting, rotating jib. Mysteriously, this model was listed in the 17th Edition catalogue as a Series 3 kit, but was never issued as such.

Next out was Airfix' one and only HO scale model, pattern number R203, the 'Interfrigo' Refrigerator Van. This vehicle, although widely used throughout Europe, had little appeal to the British modeller. A rather insipid pink, white and blue box combined with the chosen HO scaling to make this a distinctly poor seller and it was quickly deleted. Today, it is sought after in certain European circles and etched detailing kits are available from two manufacturers, in Denmark and France, to complete it to modern standards. With the opening of the Channel Tunnel and renewed interest in trans-European freight operations, perhaps the Interfrigo will yet come into its own?

The JCB and Lowmac was last to be introduced and was a truly superb kit. The JCB 3 is an excellent piece of modelling and set the trend for a long line of outstanding OO scale civilian and military vehicles from Airfix. The Lowmac depicted was of the EU type, which nicely complemented Hornby-Dublo's EB version. Strangely, when Airfix introduced a ready-to-run version in the GMR range, it was of the Lowmac EK, thereby completing the trio.

These wagon kits represent a selection of prototypes from the early 1960s. Some were unexciting, everyday types like the mineral wagon or brake van. Others represented the cutting edge of rail transport design. Together, they provide a fascinating snapshot of British Railways freight transport at the height of the modernisation plan.

Airfix Acquire the Kitmaster Tools

The acquisition of all Kitmaster moulds and stock was formally announced in the *Railway Modeller* of December 1962, but it was several months before anything happened. Throughout 1963, Airfix continued to sell the stock and to supply orders for the promotional Nabisco models. Postmarks of 21.1.64 and 1.1.64 on Airfix postage labels are known to exist on Nabisco Deltic and 9F kit boxes.

After carefully test firing all the tools, Airfix began an evaluation to sort out those kits that could be easily reintroduced, those that would need some modification and those that should be scrapped altogether. The decision was taken to scrap the Class 08, the coaches and all the TT and Continental prototypes at this point. Due to the unique nature of the Kitmaster Hook and Eye coupling, and the earlier adoption of the NMRA Buckeye coupling for Airfix trackside rolling stock, there was a considerable delay while the tools were changed to accommodate new couplings. For some inexplicable reason, the Rocket kit had all the parts completely renumbered.

At the same time, Airfix engineers reduced the diameter and shape of the sprue runs and made some additions to the tools, usually by lengthening a main sprue, to incorporate more detail in the model. This enabled Airfix to save on the quantity of material used and to run the injectors at much higher pressure.

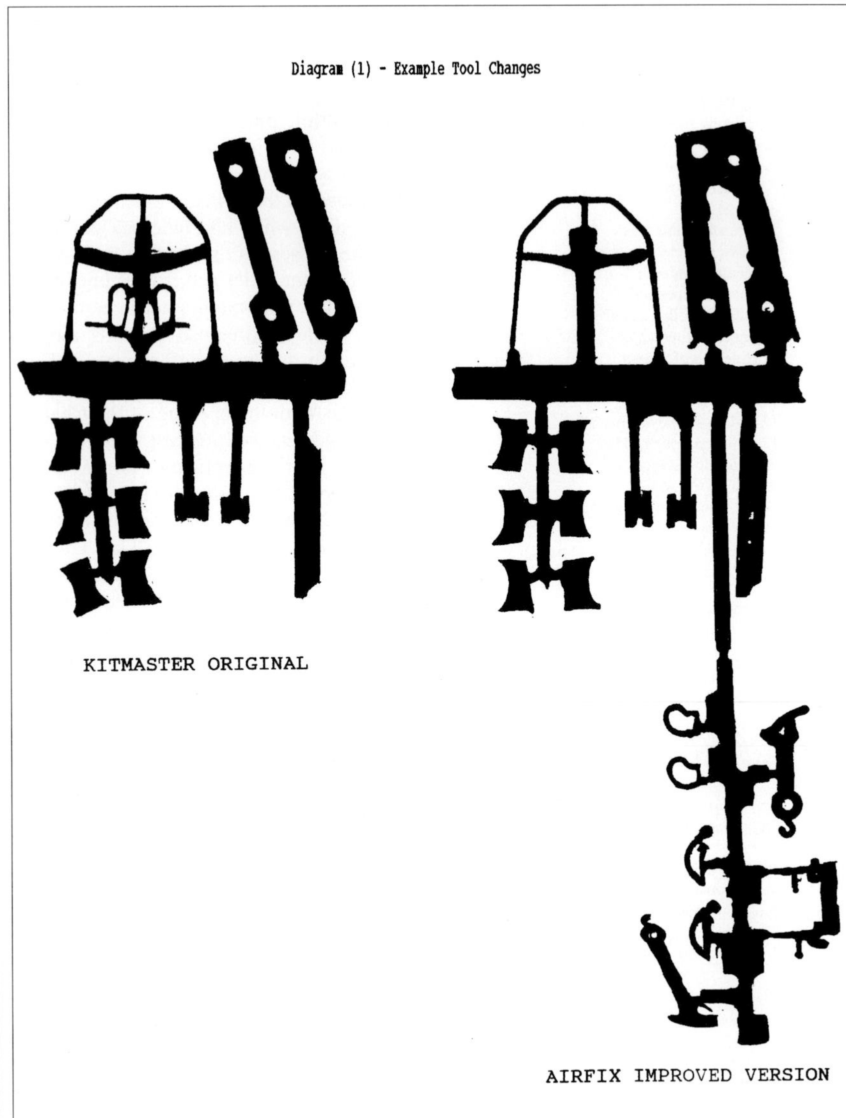

Airfix modified the Schools Class tool by adding an extra long sprue to take the new parts. These included NMRA type couplers, dummy screw couplings and new vacuum pipes. In addition the old Kitmaster vac pipes were shut off and a hole was added to the front buffer beam.

Consequently, the first reintroduction turned out to be none other than the Ariel Arrow motorcycle, ironically the last kit to be produced by Kitmaster. Even this early reintroduction did not escape the watchful eye of the Airfix engineers, who introduced a solid opaque moulding for the spokes instead of clear spokes. They also redrew the artwork to show the correct Birmingham registration number, 697 AOH, which had always appeared on the decal sheet, even in Kitmaster days. It was advertised in all the railway modelling magazines in July 1963, just six months after the takeover. Initially issued as Series 1 in a bag with an Airfix Type 2 header in blue and yellow, it soon received an excellent Type 3 header with a Roy Cross painting of the bike in a suitably muddy off-road location for a sports bike of this nature. For the Type 4 issue, it was boxed and moved up into Series 2, but retained the Cross artwork. It was last produced in 1980.

The first railway kit to reappear was the famous GWR 2-6-2T Large Prairie Tank, reissued in October of the same year. Only one change was apparent on the Prairie, the addition of optional scale three-link couplings as well as the NMRA replacement couplers on the pony trucks. This was actually the very first Airfix kit of any subject to appear in the new Type 3 'Ribbon Logo' box style. Conversely, the 'Limited Production' issue was one of the very last reissues in the Type 3 box and actually has Type 4 logos on the end panels, a fate which also befell the City of Truro. These last two kit issues are believed to date from 1972-3.

It took several years for all the other kits to re-emerge. Subsequently, they were in and out of the Airfix catalogue rather haphazardly, so that in the 16th edition catalogue the reintroduced 'Pug' locomotive was described rather mysteriously as 'Ohio Saddle Tank'. One can only assume that they confused 0-4-0 and Ohio phonetically and then failed to spot the mistake. The Airfix decal sheet for the Pug always described it as a 'Saddle 1 Tank' for some reason. Alternatively, perhaps the L&Y had shipped 'Pugs' to America without telling anyone! Considering that Airfix had the tools for the entire range, their choice of kits for reissue was surprisingly limited. Three of the best locomotives were honoured with Roy Cross paintings - the Schools Class *Harrow*, the BR Mogul and *Biggin Hill.* The Cross artwork is dramatically better than that used for the other models, showing far more attention to detail. When compared with Ken Rush's paintings for the original Kitmaster issues, the Cross artwork is in a different league. Indeed, the Cross box paintings show many details which are actually absent on the models, for example cylinder drain cocks on *Harrow*, various extra fittings on *Biggin Hill* and much of the ejector piping on the Mogul. However, Roy did make one big mistake, in the painting of the B.R. Mogul - the omission of the coupling rod, as described on page 35. This artwork survived the period of Type 4 boxes, but was largely superseded for Type 5, 6 and 7 issues. *Harrow* had a new and very different painting commissioned for the Type 6 issue, showing the locomotive leaving Charing Cross Station on a Kent Coast service. Why this was done is an enigma: the Pug, *City of Truro* and *Evening Star* all had modified original artwork in their Type 6 issues.

When Airfix was sold to Palitoy in 1982, all the surviving moulds were tested again and any that were considered life-expired were earmarked for scrapping. This is the point at which the name of each tool was chalked onto the casing. The Beyer-Garratt and Duchess were scrapped at this point.

The main Airfix engineering changes are summarised in Table J. In all cases, new instruction leaflets, retaining the original Kitmaster text, were prepared, new transfers were printed which included the name of the kit and new boxes were designed, primarily to appease the American market.

During the period of 'Limited Production', the Prairie and *City of Truro* were issued as Series 4 kits. These later reverted to Series 3. Likewise, the 9F was issued as Series 5 and reverted to Series 4, while the Pug started as Series 1 and went to Series 2. The Rocket was heavily retooled to include plastic stays for the chimney and a Victorian crew on an extended footplate. Although it was always a Series 1 kit, it appeared first in a small box, then in a plastic bag with paper header and finally in a blister-pack!

THE MODELS IN DETAIL - FOURTEEN

R201 - The Park Royal Railbus

Hailed as the future of rural rail transport, the plethora of rigid four-wheel Railbuses introduced by British Railways under the 1955 Modernisation Plan proved to be a great disappointment. However, this did not prevent Airfix from modelling a version of the Railbus built by Park Royal, but it did lead to the early deletion of the model from their catalogue. In November 1960, the *Stop Press* column of the then popular 'Believe it or not' series of Airfix advertisements carried details of the latest Airfix production, which was heralded as: 'A superbly detailed OO/HO scale model of the B.R. 50-seat Railbus. Seven inches long, it has sliding doors, free-running wheels and can be motorised easily. This 67-piece kit plus nine marking transfers costs three shillings.'

The kit was enthusiastically reviewed by the railway modelling press of the day and

This Airfix Railbus was easily motorised with a Hornby Pacer chassis. The power sledge from the Pacer snits snugly between the plastic side frames, whilst the rear pick-up axle can also be similarly transplanted.

as British Railways were in the midst of their modernisation programme, which would lead, ultimately, to the demise of the steam locomotive in daily use, the Railbus fitted in very well with anyone who was seeking to portray the railways at that period.

The prototype for the Airfix model was the 50-seat Park Royal Vehicles Ltd. Railbus, stock number M79971, which was put into service in 1958 on the Bedford - Hitchin branch of the London Midland Region. A total of five vehicles to this design were delivered. Four other manufacturers supplied B.R. with similar vehicles: A. C. Cars of Thames Ditton, D. Wickham and Co. of Ware, Wagen und Maschinenbau, GmbH of Donauwõrth, Germany and finally, Bristol Commercial Vehicles, Bristol. The Park Royal cars were powered by an underfloor 150 b.h.p. diesel engine, manufactured by British United Traction (B.U.T.), which was the trading name given to the joint company formed by Leyland Vehicles and A.E.C Ltd. Arguably, the Park Royal design was the most handsome and the Bristol the ugliest.

The main reason for building these vehicles was to cut operating costs on remote branch lines. The idea of lightweight railcars was not a new one, being quite common in some European countries, but unfortunately in the UK they were a commercial disaster, coming too late to save many unprofitable lines. The Park Royal vehicles also had an unnerving tendency to derail on facing points if taken at more than walking pace. All were withdrawn from service by 1968.

As far as can be established, the Airfix Railbus only ever appeared in a Series 2 box of the second Airfix design (Type 2) carrying pattern number R201. True to form for contemporary Airfix kits, there are two minor box-art variants:

a) Light malachite green railbus carrying the coach number 1179973. (the 11 should of course, be the letter 'M' to signify allocation to the L. M. Region of BR).

b) Dark multiple unit green version with the coach number almost obliterated.

The only indicators that Type 3 artwork may have been completed are the small illustrations on the side panels of the Airfix

The Railbus as produced by Airfix and Dapol. The M series numbering quickly changed to SC as these vehicles were sent to remote Scottish branches for most of their short lives.

ix

Just like the real thing!

Believe it or not, the nearer one is the Airfix model of the Railbus, 00 gauge (Kit 3/-). Behind it is a picture of the real thing.

That's how wonderfully realistic Airfix models are. Close attention to every detail gives them their faithful-to-the-original look—makes them true collector's pieces. And every Airfix series is to a constant scale. This means Airfix models look proportionally right, one against another, because they *are* right! You can't beat Airfix for realism—or value.

Constant Scale Construction Kits

From Model & Hobby Shops, Toy Shops and F. W. Woolworth

There are over 100 Airfix models from 2/- to 10/6.

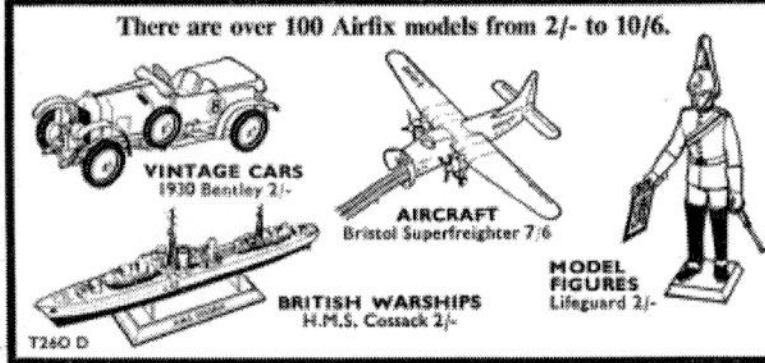

STOP PRESS!

Latest Airfix Production

B.R.
CATTLE WAGON

A realistic OO/HO gauge model of the B.R. 8-ton standard cattle wagon. Finely detailed, even to the wood grain. Hinged doors and loading ramps, choice of four coupling systems. Forty-part kit plus seven transfers, 2/-.
Also new: OO/HO GAUGE B.R. BRAKE VAN (20-ton). A beautifully detailed 45-part kit, 2/-.

PLEASE TELL YOUR FRIENDS ABOUT THE **RAILWAY MODELLER**

MAY 1961

J94 Saddle Tank kit, early issues of the L&Y Pug (small box) and the Series 4 *Evening Star* kit.

The kit comprised 47 parts moulded in green plastic, of which a number of shades exist. The remaining 20 were in clear plastic for the glazing. The darker green mouldings tend to appear, somewhat ironically, in the boxes with the lighter Malachite green artwork. A transfer sheet with nine subjects was provided, which included coach numbers (M79971), coach crests, front 'Speed Whiskers' (the forerunner of the yellow warning panels introduced in the mid 60s) and technical data markings. The two-character headcode (B1) was not supplied as a transfer, but was instead printed on the instruction sheet, which was presented in the usual Type 2 format. The style and feel of the kit is very similar to that of the superb Rosebud 'Kitmaster' range of B.R. Mk. 1 coaches.

R201 appeared in the first (1962), second, third and fourth edition Airfix catalogues and the seasonal leaflets which preceded them. The advent of the fifth edition (3/67) brought with it a general tidying up of pattern numbers, eliminating for the most part the remaining early four-digit pattern numbers and introducing fully computerised stock numbers. The other more drastic change was the deletion of the complete range of Series 2 railway rolling stock kits, some of which were destined never again to see the light of day under the Airfix marque. Kit No. 201 was now the Footbridge, in the Trackside Series.

That was to be the end of the only model of passenger carrying rolling stock made by Airfix, perhaps echoing the failure of the prototypes, which probably had rather limited appeal. This, of course, did not prevent several well known names producing motorising kits. Three that we know of are:

a) Arby Perfecta - better known for their motorising packs for Kitmaster locomotives. b) The Southgate Hobbyshop, nowadays known as Beatties. c) E.A.M.E.S. of Reading.

The Southgate Hobbyshop and E.A.M.E.S. conversions both provided replacement metal chassis, while the Perfecta kit (No. la) was a modification of that designed for the Kitmaster 'Pug' loco. All three based their designs around the slightly superior Tri-ang XT60 12v DC motor.

The Dapol issues come in a poly-bag complete with header card (similar to the early

First No.	Second No.	Name	Circa 1956	May 1957	Autumn 1958	Spring 1959	Summer 1959	February 1960	April 1961	Summer 1962	Autumn 1962
Series One											
4001	1	Country Inn	x	x	x	x	x	x	x	x	x
4002	2	Detached House	x	x	x	x	x	x	x	x	x
4003	3	Service Station	x	x	x	x	x	x	x	x	x
4004	4	General Store	x	x	x	x	x	x	x	x	x
4005	5	Signal Box	x	x	x	x	x	x	x	x	x
4006	6	Bungalow	x	x	x	x	x	x	x	x	x
4007	7	Station Platform		x	x	x	x	x	x	x	x
4008	8	Shop & flat		x	x	x	x	x	x	x	x
4009	9	Booking Hall			x	x	x	x	x	x	x
4010	10	Thatched Cottage			x	x	x	x	x	x	x
4018	11	Kiosks & steps			x	x	x	x	x	x	x
4012	12	Platform Fittings			x	x	x	x	x	x	x
4013	13	Station Accessories			x	x	x	x	x	x	x
4021	14	Trackside Accessories				x	x	x	x	x	x
4022	15	Level Crossing				x	x	x	x	x	x
4023	16	Signal Gantry					x	x	x	x	x
	17	Fencing and Gates						x	x	x	x
	18	Telegraph Poles						x	x	x	x
	19	Platform Canopy						x	x	x	x
	20	Scammel Scarab									x
Series 2											
4017	202?	Control Tower				x	x	x	x	x	x
4019	203?	Windmill				x	x	x	x	x	x
4014	201	Footbridge			x	x	x	x	x	x	x
4015	204	Village Church				x	x	x	x	x	x
	205	Travelling Crane						x	x	x	x
	206	Water Tower							x	x	x
	207	Girder Bridge							x	x	x
	208	Engine Shed							x	x	x
Series 3											
	302	Turntable								x	x
	03625-2	Platform Figures									1979
	03628-1	Railway Workmen									1980

This table shows how the full range of Trackside kits were introduced over the period 1956-62, with the two later figure sets for completeness.

Airfix Series 2 kits) and are mainly moulded in a medium shade of grey complete with the bonus of ready - to - run wheelsets using pinpoint metal axles. The transfers are exactly the same as the original Airfix sheet. Artwork for the header card is taken directly from the Airfix launch advert printed in maroon, as is done with most Dapol instructions and headers, making the preprinted two-character headcode appear rather unauthentic when used on the model. As with the original kit, motorising conversions have been manufactured for the Dapol model, by Branchlines of Exeter, who also produce an interior detailing kit.

An interesting twist in the tale concerns the doyen of the class, M79971, which ended its revenue-earning days operating on obscure lines in Scotland. Following withdrawal from service in 1968, it did not follow the fate of its stablemates by being reduced to scrap metal, but instead the body was separated from the chassis, grounded and used as a messroom in Millerhill marshalling yard until 1981. Because of the levels of asbestos present in the body, it could not be broken up in the normal manner, so it was taken to Pattersons Tip at Bishopbriggs in Glasgow, where it was unceremoniously buried!

THE MODELS IN DETAIL – FIFTEEN

Airfix Trackside Kits

The Airfix Trackside Range

Airfix first launched their enormously popular trackside range in 1956. It eventually comprised thirty-two different models, including two road vehicles (a Scammell Scarab and a Lambretta motor-scooter), three sets of figures and several 'Manyways' extendable kits which could be combined, such as the Girder Bridge, Footbridge, Engine Shed and Level Crossing. Thirty years later, they are nearly all still in production at Dapol, a tribute to the original toolmakers. These kits enabled modellers to construct entire towns and villages at modest cost, rapidly and with minimum skill. Indeed, your author well remembers constructing the Booking Hall in an afternoon and being well pleased with the results at the tender age of seven! It is precisely this aspect of the design, the ease of assembly and clear instructions that has made these kits so endearing over the years. Add to that the unquestionable utility of the various 'Manyways' extendable/adaptable kits and you can begin to see why they were so popular. Many famous layouts, from Charford to Acton Mainline, are to be seen sporting suitably cut-up and adapted bits of Signal Gantry and Girder Bridge, and one may while away many a happy hour at most Exhibitions playing 'Spot the Airfix Kits' with the 4 mm scale layouts!

The series was launched with an initial selection of six buildings, commencing with the Country Inn and retailing at a modest 1s 9d (7.5p). By 1958, a second series of larger kits had been introduced, starting with a very useful Footbridge, retailing at 3s (15p). These were all initially in bags, but later issues of Series 2 kits were issued in boxes.

Whilst some models, such as the Scammell Scarab 'Mechanical Horse' had lamentably short lives of under three years, several models were in virtually continuous production from 1956 to the present day. These include the Level Crossing and the famous Signal Box, modelled on the Midland Railway prototype at Oakham Level Crossing. Due to the celebrity status of the kit, the Heritage Department saw fit to grant the 'box Grade 1 Listed Building status. In fact, the Village Church is also based on a Grade 2 listed building, in this case the beautiful Norman church in the village of Godshill, Isle of Wight. However, apart from these two kits, no other specific buildings have been identified. There seems to be no direct link between the 'White Horse' or 'The Chequers' Country Inns and any real life pubs, although a number of the kits represent typical structures of their time, some of which have gone on to listed status.

For example, the classic oval W. H. Smith bookstall in the Kiosks and Steps kit is representative of the type now in preservation at the North Norfolk Railway, whilst at nearby Parham, one can see an excellently preserved WWII Airfield Control Tower of the type covered by the kit. Sadly, Braintree and Bocking station, whilst still in use, is no longer graced by the type of station name boards featured in the Platform Fittings kit, although plenty of enamel running-in boards of this type are to be seen at preservation centres around the country.

Most of the kits are reminiscent of the 1950s, especially the so-called 'Modern' buildings such as the Detached House, Gen-

4932

This interesting advertisement for the Trackside range dates from 1959 and shows that within just three years Airfix had tooled at least eighteen new kits in this range.

eral Store, Shop and Flat and, of course, the Bungalow, complete with VHF TV aerial on the roof!

The wide variety of lineside installations, such as Telegraph Poles, Engine Shed and the contents of Trackside Accessories, have provided endless numbers of parts and additional features to improve the detail of many a layout. When introduced in 1956, the earliest packaging for these kits used a common header design carrying line drawings in black on yellow of the first six kits. These distinguish each kit by a central title panel. They are unofficially referred to as Type 0 headers by Airfix Collectors Club members. As the series began to expand, a new design of header was required. The Type 1 header prominently features the 'Products in Plastic' logo on the left hand side and is printed in three bright colours - blue and red on a yellow field. Lettering is usually white reversed out on blue, an exception being the Windmill, which is predominantly green and red on white. Used for Series 1 kits Nos. 1-19 and the first four Series 2 kits, Nos. 201, 204, 4017 and 4019 (believed to have been allocated Pattern Nos. 202 and 203, but not taken up).

The first Series 1 in a classic Type 2 header was the Scammell Scarab transporter, No. 20. Type 2 is a full colour drawing on a white ground with coloured lettering and a distinctive vertical stripe down the

Table K The Airfix Trackside Range

First No.	Later No.	Description of Kit	Box or Bag Type 0	1	2	3	4	6	7
Series 1									
4001	1	Country Inn	x	x	x			x	
4002	2	Detached House	x	x	x			x	
4003	3	Service Station	x	x	x			x	
4004	4	General Store	x	x	x			x	
4005	5	Signal Box	x	x	x	x	x	x	x
4006	6	Bungalow	x	x	x			x	
4007	7	Station Platform		x	x	x	x	x	x
4008	8	Shop and Flat		x	x			x	
4009	9	Booking Hall		x	x			x	x
4010	10	Thatched Cottage		x	x			x	
4018	11	Kiosks and steps		x	x			x	x
4012	12	Platform Fittings		x	x			x	x
4013	13	Station Accessories		x	x	x (as S46)		x	x
4021	14	Trackside Accessories		x	x			x	x
4022	15	Level Crossing		x	x		x	x	x
4023	16	Signal Gantry		x	x			x	x
4024	17	Fencing and Gates		x	x		x	x	
	18	Telegraph Poles		x	x		x	x	x
	19	Platform Canopy		x	x			x	
	20	Scammell Scarab			x				

Note: Nos. 17,19 4017 and 4019 were all current in the same (2nd Edition) catalogue. Kit 4013 was later issued as S46 in OO/HO Figures range.

First No.	Later No.	Description of Kit	0	1	2	3	4	6	7
Series 2									
4017		Control Tower	202?	x	x		x		
4019		Windmill	203?	x	x			x	
4014	201	Footbridge		x	x	x	x	x	
4015	204	Village Church		x	x			x	
	205	Travelling Crane			x	x		x	
	206	Water Tower			x			x	
	207	Girder Bridge			x	x	x	x	
	208	Engine Shed			x	x	x	x	
Series 3									
	302	Turntable			x				
	03625-2	Platform Figures						x	
	03628-1	Railway Workmen							x
n/a		London Bus and Taxi	Not Released						
Series 1 OO/HO Scale Figures Series									
	S9	Farm Stock			x	x			
	S17	Civilians			x	x			
	S46	Station Accessories (reissue of 4013)				x			

middle of the illustration in a contrasting colour. The Type 2 Girder Bridge kit features a rather good representation of a green liveried Class 40 1-Co-Co-1 Diesel, by an unknown artist, possibly Harold Oates. Type 2 was used for all the trackside kits as they were reissued and all the rolling stock kits as they were introduced until the Prestwin Silo wagon was issued in 1963. The Prestwin is the only one of the original Series 1 wagons in a Type 3 box. All the reissued Kitmaster locos appeared in Type 3 boxes at first. Type 3 is the classic 1963-72 design with the so-called 'Ribbon' logo for Airfix or 'Red Flash' logo. The original Roy Cross paintings were commissioned by Airfix for Type 3 boxes. Although Roy did paint three of the reissued Kitmaster locomotives, he did not do the rest of the locos: that artist is as yet unknown. Roy was also commissioned for some reissued Trackside Series 1 kits with Type 3 or 4 header cards. These are all rather scarce and consist of the Signal Box, Platform Section, Level Crossing, Telegraph Poles, and Fencing and gates. He also completed artwork for certain Series 2 kits in boxes: Girder Bridge (Roy's favourite, featuring a BR liveried Class 47 diesel locomotive), Travelling Crane, Footbridge and Engine Shed. The latter carries a very decent representation of a BR(W) 57XX Pannier Tank and is one of the better subjects in this series.

Trackside kits were produced in their vintage 1960 Type 2 headers well into the 70s. After a period of withdrawal from the catalogues, they were reissued en masse in Series 3 during 1980. The Type 6 box is a standard design for all kits and is, frankly, hideous. Coloured in bright yellow with a blue "scene" featuring all the kits, it does little to justify the exorbitant list price of a Series 3 kit, some with as few as 16 parts! Only one new kit was added to the range in this style box, Platform Figures. An excellent representation of people in various poses, luggage trolleys and station staff, it is moulded in polystyrene.

The final Trackside issue is also rather scarce and came in a Type 7 Oval logo box showing a Midland Railway Compound locomotive, possibly at Bromsgrove, in a blue/black half-tone. A picture of the completed kit is superimposed on top. Again, this was a new model and once more it was another excellent set of figures, this time Railway Workmen. As with Platform Figures, it was moulded in polystyrene and there were three identical sprues of figures in each kit. It was never catalogued, Airfix Ltd. being sold before this could happen. Both tools are with Dapol. The last two were very late additions to the range, Platform Figures being introduced in 1978 in a Type 6 box and the uncatalogued Railway Workmen appearing in a Type 7 box in 1979. Both are extremely scarce in original Airfix packaging, but were reissued by Dapol. They differ from the two sets of figures in the OO/HO Figures series in being real polystyrene mouldings, not polyethylene as normally used for figures. The first of the series was the sought-after Civilians set. This featured an excellent Vespa motor scooter and lots of useful people, including public service figures such as policemen and a nurse. The second kit is Platform Accessories, which started life as a Trackside kit, but by 1968 had moved into the OO/HO Figures series in a proper blue Type 3 Figures box. This later kit is now available from Dapol moulded in polystyrene. In addition, Airfix also produced a very nice set of Farm Stock in the same range.

The Airfield Control Tower kit has been the subject of some controversy over the years. Palitoy maintained that it was not a 'Trackside' kit, although the 1962 advertisements and the Airfix complaint slip clearly show it in the "Trackside" range! When released in 1959 as Pattern No. 4017, it was clearly a Trackside kit, but upon reintroduction in the 12th Airfix catalogue it had become 03305-1 numbered in the AFV/Diorama range. Subsequently, it became 03380-2 in the 13th Catalogue, but was listed with Series 3 Aircraft Kits! It was reissued again by Airfix in 1991 in the Airfield series. It is the only Trackside tool not owned by Dapol.

The Un-released Trackside Kit

Airfix had completed a set of drawings for a 'compendium kit', similar to the R.A.F. Emergency, Refuelling and Recovery Sets, which was to have been added to the range of Trackside OO/HO scale models. The kit would have depicted two 4 mm scale civilian vehicles: a London Transport RT bus plus an FX3 London taxi cab. As far as is known, no artwork was prepared and no tooling made. Patterns may exist, however. This kit would probably have been a Series 3 issue along with the R.A.F. Recovery Set. It was abandoned during 1980. *See page 98 -99.*

Just what would those three unreleased kits have looked like? As far as is known, no artwork was produced for them, but here we present a selection of modern interpretations. The Class USA tank and the A3 Pacific are by John Rimmer, lecturer in Fine Art at de Montfort University, whilst the CN U-4-A is by freelance designer Trevor Tremethick

The Class USA tank engines were obtained by the Southern Railway from ex-War Department locomotives which were surplus following the outbreak of peace. Extensive modifications were made at Eastleigh, after which all of the class were put to work in the Southampton area. Notably, these engines replaced ageing B4 Class locos in Southampton Docks itself.

The A3 portrayed here is 60100 *Spearmint*, whereas the Kitmaster model would have been *Flying Scotsman*. The locomotive is shown somewhere on the Waverley route from Edinburgh to Carlisle, a favourite location for photographs of this class in the 1950s.

Trevor has decided to picture the mighty U-4-A in a typical Canadian scene, which may, or may not, be Toronto. What is sure is that these smart streamliners provided the backbone of the Toronto-Montreal service for many years.

4. RUMOURS AND POSTULATIONS

Perhaps the most recurrent theme in the Kitmaster collecting world is the continuous stream of rumours and speculation surrounding the company. Whilst 90% of this is apocryphal, there is a certain element of truth in some of the rumours. Also included here are some of the better substantiated theories about what would have happened next. These are summarised as:

Rumours

1. The A3 was produced.
2. The USA Tank was produced.
3. The TT motor bogie was produced.
4. The Motor Bogies were made by Tri-ang Railways.
5. The Coach kit tooling was lost at sea.
6. The CN U-4-A 4-8-4 was produced.

Postulations

1 The next design would be a WD 2-8-0 Austerity.
2 The next boxed set would be the Midland Pullman set.

RUMOURS

1. *The A3 was produced.*

This is the most common rumour and may just have some truth in it. Firstly, the record should be put straight. No artwork was ever produced for the packaging and the kit was never put on retail sale to the public. However, three different sources claim to have seen a clear plastic 'test firing' of the mould for the A3. They claim that it was in a clear plastic bag with no markings, decals or instructions., just as one might expect for a factory test run. Nick Gilman mentions that the proprietor of a Bedford model shop had one around 1974. These kits, if they exist, would be limited to perhaps half a dozen at most. There is a very strong possibility that they are incomplete. Since more than one tool was required for some kits, Kitmaster may have been in the middle of tooling up when the sale was agreed. This attractive little hypothesis is supported in two ways: it accounts for the existence of one or more (incomplete) test shots and it also explains why this brand new model was never put into production by Airfix. As yet, nobody has been able to show the author one first hand, but if they really do exist in some form they would be highly prized collectors' items. Jack Gain is said to have worked on the pattern for this model and also for the USA tank, but this does not mean that tools were necessarily produced. British Transfer Printing Co. Ltd. did print the transfers and it is possible that boxes were also completed. The transfer sheet was definitely for a *Flying Scotsman* in LNER livery, including the black and white lining and the number 4472. The LNER insignia were printed inside the tender lining in a similar manner to that for the Class 9F decal sheet. Nameplates were NOT included: presumably, these would have been in raised letters as on earlier kits, a retrograde step in comparison to the *Evening Star* and *City of Truro* with their neatly reproduced nameplates.

2. *The USA Tank was produced.*

This theory has the same currency as the first, except that nobody claims to have seen a test firing. Instead, a source believed to have worked at Raunds told Kitmaster Newsletter that 'Six units were made (up) and given to the sales force to show to distributors'. Other sources have been told of 9 or 12 kits. This does not, of course, mean that it was tooled up. It just means that several models were mocked up from the pattern or drawings, a normal part of the modelmaker's procedure in any case. Mock-ups should exist for all the kits, although nobody is looking for them very seriously, apart from the USA tank!

3. *The TT motor bogie was produced.*

This is 99% untrue... Kitmaster certainly produced a couple of prototypes for promotion and press reviews, but they abandoned production of the bogie in July 1961 and even issued a press release to this effect, repeated in the *Railway Modeller* of that month.

4. *The Motor Bogies were made by Tri-ang Railways.*

This story is easy to lay to rest. The author has written confirmation from Richard Lines, proprietor of Tri-ang Railways at the time, who says that at no time did they ever supply parts or bogies to Kitmaster. Indeed, he says that they were not very pleased by the striking similarity of the Kitmaster bogie to their own successful design for the SR EMU and Blue Pullman sets. The design was shamelessly copied by Messrs. Rosebud and all the bogies were assembled 'in-house' from parts bought in around the country. Armatures were wound on site at Raunds and carbon brushes were also assembled by the doll workers.

5. *The tooling for the coaches was lost at sea.*

Though false in itself, this rumour is connected directly with a true story. The Kitmaster tooling was never sent anywhere by ship. However, *Frog* did send a batch of tools out to Tri-ang in New Zealand on a ship which sank in a tropical storm. The (now somewhat rusty) steel tools continue to lie in 300ft of water on the floor of the Pacific, should you be thinking of a rescue bid...

6. *The CN U-4-A 4-8-4 was produced.*

At a recent Colchester MRC Exhibition, an exhibitor claimed, vociferously, that he had seen a complete box for the CN U-4-A in a shop called 'Angels' in the Mile End Road in London during 1962. The box was in the window with a label saying 'Coming Soon'. He was quite specific about the artwork, claiming that it was a night scene with the loco travelling right-to-left instead of the Rosebud standard left-to-right. It has not been possible to confirm this story, neither did he see the contents of the box. It may well be that packaging samples for the three new kits were despatched to key dealers, but this does not explain why only one person can remember them.

POSTULATIONS

1 *The next design would be a WD 2-8-0 Austerity.*

This interesting theory was a frequent topic of discussion after the 1962 range had been announced. Certainly, the type would have been a popular choice. Large numbers of these engines were still in service at the time, both at home and, perhaps more importantly for Kitmaster, overseas. The type had not been covered at all by the British manufacturers of ready-to-run equipment and a suitable chassis for motorising, the Hornby-Dublo Stanier 8F, was freely available from Meccano. Perhaps it was the similar duties and geographical distribution of the self-same 'Eight Freights' that precluded the early choice of an Austerity 2-8-0 for inclusion in the range? We shall never know of course, but a good model of the type would certainly not have gone amiss with the British outline modelling fraternity. However, a correspondent in Wiltshire wrote to Rosebud in 1962 and was told that 'next year's range may include something of interest to GWR modellers'. What this means is unclear, it could be another GWR locomotive such as a Pannier, Manor or Grange to follow the huge success of the Truro and Prairie, or it could have heralded a series of pre-Nationalisation coaches. Dennis Franklin, who left Rosebud in 1960, would have liked a King in the range, but it is not known if the idea was ever pursued.

2. *The next boxed set would be the Midland Pullman set.*

This theory is certainly logical. Bringing together a 'Complete Train' kit of the six Midland Pullman cars would have been impressive if nothing else. One can speculate as to whether a KM1 (or two) would have been included. This would have taken the approximate cost up to 72 shillings, nearly double the cost of the previous P2 and P3 sets. Even without a power bogie, it would cost in the region of 62 shillings, but what a sight it would have made! Compare this with the rather poor Tri-ang Train Set of the Blue Pullman with just three cars in it and you begin to appreciate what could have been done.

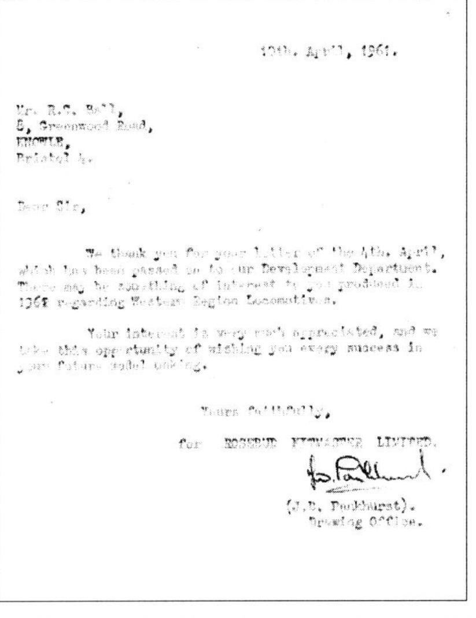

19th. April, 1961.

Mr. R.C. Bell,
8, Greenwood Road,
KNOWLE,
Bristol 4.

Dear Sir,

We thank you for your letter of the 4th. April, which has been passed on to our Development Department. There may be something of interest to you produced in 1962 regarding Western Region Locomotives.

Your interest is very much appreciated, and we take this opportunity of wishing you every success in your future model making.

Yours faithfully,

for ROSEBUD KITMASTER LIMITED.

(J.D. Parkhurst).
Drawing Office.

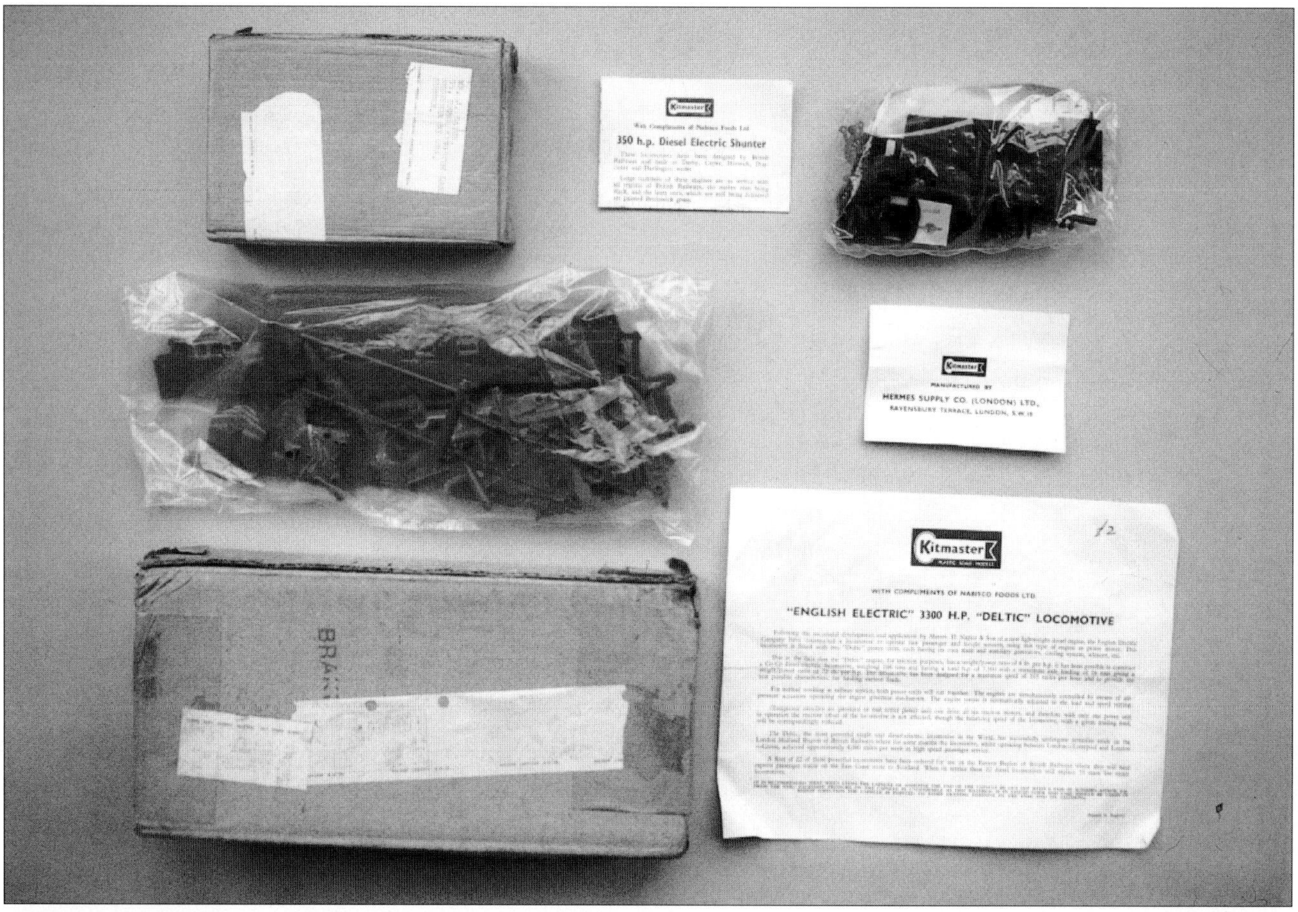

The Nabisco kits were issued in plain brown mailing boxes. Each kit was in a polythene bag with an instruction sheet drawn by the Airfix drawing office. The kits were despatched by Airfix and each carried an Airfix postage meter label.

Weirdest object in the Kitmaster range must surely be the Fireball XL5 spaceship. These kits were given away with Zoom ice loollies during 1963 and are, strictly speaking, an Airfix product. However the application form does state 'your Kitmaster model..'.

5. COLLABORATIONS

Nabisco and the Hermes Supply Company

The Hermes Supply Company first appears in the Kitmaster story when it used some of the surplus stock from Airfix to fulfil a supply contract with Nabisco Foods. It would appear that HSC was a fully owned subsidiary of the Airfix Holdings Group and is listed as such in the 1973 Airfix Report and Accounts. All the Nabisco kits were actually despatched by Airfix and the two companies had postal addresses in the same area of Southwest London. The mailing boxes carry Airfix franking machine labels.

The Nabisco kits were obtained by collecting tokens from packets of Shredded Wheat, which together with a postal order, could be redeemed for a 'Train Kit' from a fairly limited selection. There were two types of token on each box. Blue 'X' tokens could be exchanged for an entirely free 'Shunting Locomotive' - actually Kit No. 2, the 350 hp Diesel Electric Shunter. For the larger kits, yellow 'Z' tokens had to be redeemed with a part-payment of the cost of the loco. The details are shown in the table below.

Kit Number	Kit Colour	Nabisco Description	Token colour	Number Required	Normal Price	Offer Price	Postage Charge	Postage Cost
2	Black	Free Shunting Engine	Blue	4	4s 6d	Free	10d	6d
10	Blue	Deltic Diesel	Yellow	2	10s 6d	5s 11d	nil	10½d
22	Black	Evening Star	Yellow	2	10s 6d	5s 11d	nil	10½d
28	Maroon	Dining car and						
15	Green	Corridor/brake coach	Yellow	2	16s 0d	8s 9d	nil	1s 4½d

As can be readily seen from the table, the so-called 'Free' shunter actually cost 4d and the others were roughly half-price when the postage is taken into account! Supply of these kits to customers began in January 1963. The Nabisco promotional kits were limited to what was in stock in large enough quantities to fulfil the expected orders from the happy Shredded Wheat-eating modellers of the day! Consequently, although you could select the RFO and BSK coaches, you had no choice about the colour. Invariably, it seems, all RFOs were red and all BSKs were green, both in the same box!

Hermes issued their own instruction sheets for these kits, based on the latest revisions of the Kitmaster instructionals. These were almost certainly produced by the Airfix drawing office, being stylistically identical to contemporary Airfix Type 2 kits. An example of a blue Rosebud Format 1 instruction sheet overprinted with the legend 'With the Compliments of Nabisco Foods' is known to exist for the *Deltic* kit. They also produced their own complaint slip, which bore a striking resemblance to the Airfix complaint slip. The word 'Rosebud' was carefully removed from the logo on both items. The kits were actually despatched by Airfix, providing strong evidence of the link between the two companies. The stock was finally exhausted in January 1964, almost two years after the sale of Rosebud Kitmaster Ltd.

Hermes subsequently moved to Sunbury-on-Thames and, in June 1963, issued the unique Fireball XL 5 rocket kit. The 1:100 model of the Fireball XL5 was a promotion carried by Lyons Maid on 'Zoom' Ice Lolly products, in which a plastic kit of Steve Zodiac's Fireball XL5 was sent in exchange for tokens. The kit was packed in a clear plastic bag inside a plain Hermes/Nabisco type box only, and does not carry any reference to Kitmaster. However, the advertisements in *Airfix Magazine* and *Boys Own Paper* all refer to it in the small print of the coupon as '...your Kitmaster Fireball model...'. It was issued in June 1963 by the Hermes Supply Co. and is, strictly speaking, not a Kitmaster product. There is a complaint slip from the Hermes Supply Co. as in Nabisco kits. Although the tool is no longer known, the kit made a recent reappearance as a resin model with whitemetal fittings thanks to Tony James at Comet Miniatures who even persuaded Gerry Anderson to help improve some design flaws in the original model!

So successful was the XL5 promotional kit, that in 1964 Hermes obtained a contract to produce a similar model of the Stingray. Neither of these kits is a true Kitmaster model, although the XL5 is often cited as such. In a July 1963 advert in *The Victor* comic, the Lyons Maid XL5 is described (in the small print) as Kitmaster, but the kit carries no indication of this. Interestingly, it also indicates that whilst Lyons Maid customers can obtain the kit for

Original advertisement from Airfix Magazine for the Fireball XL5 promotion.

4s 6d, the 'normal' price is 9s. There is, however, no evidence of this kit ever having been supplied to trade customers.

Both the Stingray and XL5 are extremely rare items now, often commanding in excess of £500 when sold.

The Humber Oil Company Ltd. 'Humbrol'

Kitmaster always recommended Humbrol Railway Colours for completing the models to best effect. Humbrol colours were becoming well established in the late 1950s and early 1960s, so this relationship blossomed.

As early as 1960, Humbrol advertisements carried the wording 'Ideal for Kitmaster locomotives'. The joint marketing programme started mid-way through 1960. First, a special chart showing the available colours was produced with both the Rosebud Kitmaster and Humbrol logos, and one was packed with every kit from mid-1960 onwards.

Second, Humbrol produced a convenient card pack which contained eight capsules of enamel paints for lining and finishing the

Table H Kitmaster/Humbrol Joint Promotional Campaign

Item		Date
Humbrol/Kitmaster Colour Chart	Type A	1959 -1960
Humbrol/Kitmaster Colour Chart	Type B	1960-1962
Humbrol Railway Colours Card		1960-63
Humbrol / Kitmaster general ad	RM	4.61
Half page J94 / Humbrol ad	McM	5.61
Half page J94 / Humbrol ad	BOP	5.61
Full page J94 / Humbrol ad	BOP	8.61
Half page J94 / Humbrol ad	MRN	9.61
Half page 4MT / Humbrol ad	MoM	9.61
Half page 4MT / Humbrol ad	RM	10.61
Half page 4MT / Humbrol ad	MRC	11.61
Half page 4MT / Humbrol ad	RM	11.61
Half page Pullman/Humbrol ad	MRC	12.61
Quarter page Pullman/Humbrol ad	MRC	1.62
Quarter page Pullman/Humbrol ad	AM	1.62
Full page Pullman/HMS York ad	AM	2.62

AM=Airfix Magazine RM=Railway Modeller MRC=Model Railway Constructor MRN=Model Railway News BOP=Boys' Own Paper MoM=Model Maker McM=Meccano Magazine

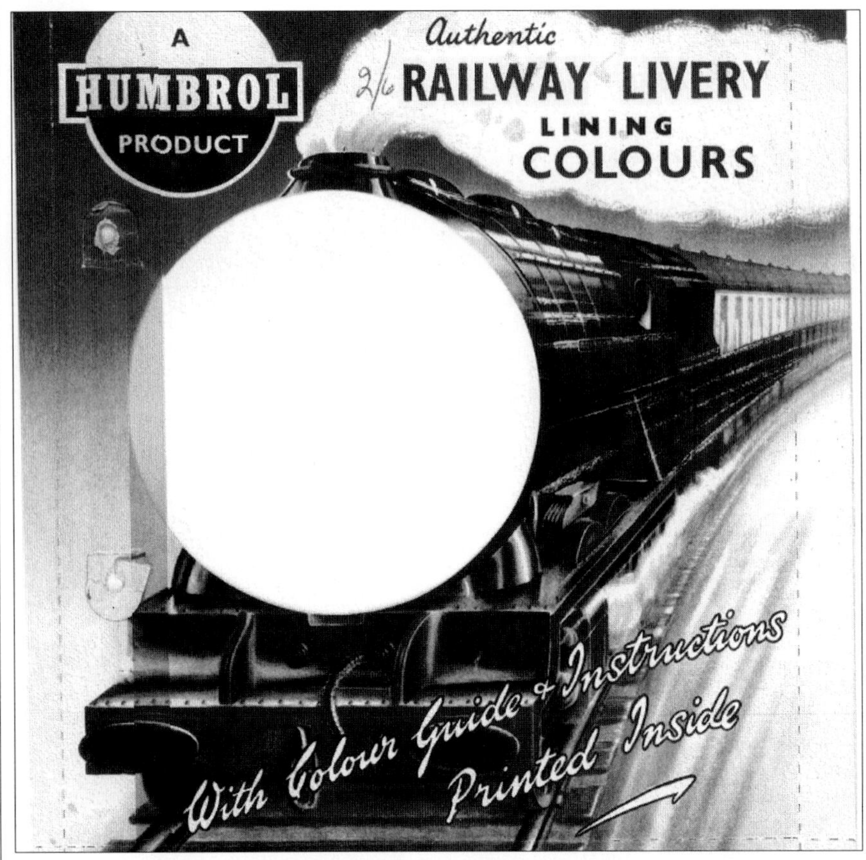

***Top.* The front of the Humbrol Railway Lining Colours card. The circular hole was filled with a clear plastic tray which acted as a mixing pallette. *Below.* On the rear, the first twelve Kitmaster locomotives are prominently featured. The inside gives detailed mixing instructions for given colours used by British railway companies.**

locomotives together with a brush. The reverse side of the card showed nine of the current Kitmaster kits. Both company logos are shown in full colour and the locomotives are reproduced from the original 1959 catalogue artwork. The gelatine capsules contained only basic colours, whilst the details printed inside the sealed card explained how to mix them and the best techniques for applying them. These cards are extremely scarce today. Finally, joint advertising campaigns promoting Humbrol colours for Kitmaster kits started with a non-specific advertisement in the April 1961 edition of *Railway Modeller*. This was followed by a series of 'specific' advertisements featuring a photograph of a recent Kitmaster release, a stylised Kitmaster logo and text about the suitability of Humbrol paint.

These advertisements are important because they were the only published examples for the J94 tank and the BR Mogul, coming at a time when cash flow was becoming difficult at Rosebud and the advertising budget had been slashed. They are also important because they were the only advertisements for a Kitmaster product ever to appear in Boys' Own Paper.

The Colour Charts were published by Humbrol and included in the kits from 1960 onwards. They show the full range of colours available for railway modellers, including some Canadian liveries. Each colour is numbered and Kitmaster refer to these numbers in their later instruction sheets. There were two editions of this 'Kitmaster Colour Chart'.

The advent of the French Mountain locomotive eventually led to Humbrol producing SNCF Loco Green to enable this interesting model to be correctly painted. This in itself necessitated a reprint of the colour chart to include the new colour, No. 134 in the series. This reprint can be dated to July or August 1961 using contemporary advertisements.

The two advertisements for the J94 which appear in *Boys' Own Paper*, May 61 and Aug 61, mark the period during which SNCF Green was introduced. The first advertisement states that there are 33 colours in the range; three months later this had risen to 34 colours.

Surprisingly, the paint in the presentation sets is not branded Humbrol, although that in the P2 set resembles the capsules on the Railway Colours card and the glue in the P2 and P3 sets is Humbrol Britfix 77 packed in specially branded "Kitmaster" ½ oz tubes. These lead tubes are printed in full colour on one side with the Kitmaster logo and on the other side with the Humbrol logo.

The Humbrol/Kitmaster relationship appears to have outlasted the Rosebud company by some years. A copy of *Model Railway News* from June 1972 clearly shows a Kitmaster produced 9F, complete with hook and eye coupling, in an advert for Railway Colours!

Unfortunately, Humbrol themselves have no record of any of this, as their entire archive was destroyed by a catastrophic fire in 1988.

The Pritchard Patent Product Co. Ltd. 'Peco'

The involvement of Peco in the Kitmaster story is twofold: firstly, they were the sole agents for the range of Arby Perfecta Kits introduced from 1960 onwards and secondly, they introduced their own interior kits for the Kitmaster Coaches.

The Arby "Perfecta" motorising kits are dealt with in the section covering all chassis and motorising kits.

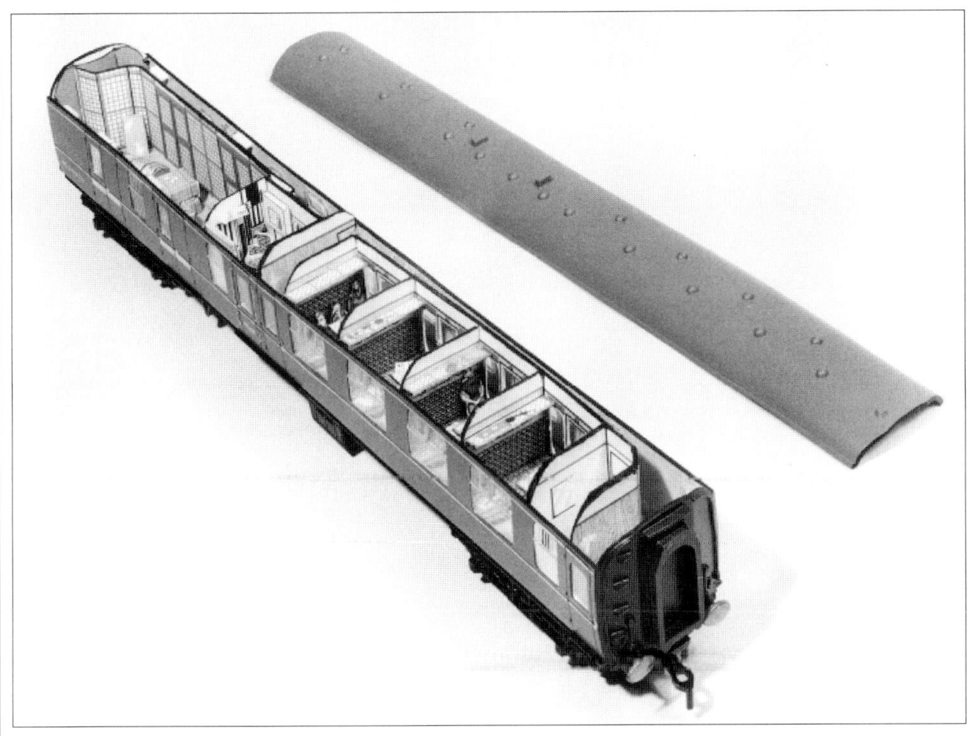

to provide interior fittings. Even so, only the Pullman cars were treated in this way, the two HO coaches (Nos. 27 and 29) never having interiors supplied.

Peco also had a marketing alliance with Kitmaster. Many of the early kits included a small black and blue leaflet produced by Peco which promotes the *Railway Modeller* and shows pictures borrowed from an article on motorising the Pug. Similar leaflets, which were longer and printed in black and red, were also produced by Peco and included in certain Tri-ang Railways TT Train Sets. The text makes it clear that now the purchaser had acquired a Kitmaster model, he needed to read *Railway Modeller* in order to make it go! In exchange, Peco took the 1960 Kitmaster catalogue as a loose insert in the July issue of that year.

***Above top.* As can be seen, the Peco card kits for the Kitmaster coaches really do add a finishing touch. Not only are they full colour, but additional items such as passengers, luggage and even newspapers, were included.**

***Left.* There were four different interior kits available, one each for the Corridor Brake 2nd and Corridor Composite and two for the Corridor Second. This enabled it to be built in Open or Compartment configuration.**

PECO COACH INTERIORS

The successful introduction of scale-length Mk 1 BR coaches in the 1960 Kitmaster range was a great step forward. Enthusiasts everywhere could at last build proper scale models of the modern rolling stock being introduced at that time. However, the kits, whilst offering many innovative features, lacked any sort of interior detail. This led Peco to develop a range of interior kits for the three Kitmaster 'OO' scale coaches.

These card kits came as flat packs wrapped in acetate film. Each kit built one complete interior for either a BSK, SK, SO or CK interior. Both the SK and SO interiors were fitted to the same Kitmaster coach shell, No. 14, the Corridor Second. The kits, despite their simple material, were exceptionally well designed and proved very popular. In addition to the major structural components of the coach, they provided interior fittings such as toilets, hand basins, guard's periscopes and mirrors. Also included were people and baggage, all folded up from card! When carefully constructed, these full colour interiors look far better than the plain plastic moulding of the Tri-ang coaches.

In addition, the kits lent themselves to adaptations. The CK kit can easily be made to fit the Tri-ang Railways Thompson LNER CK, which never had an interior. They can also be used for a range of other conversions. In fact, they were so successful that they are still in print even today, albeit in limited numbers. Peco advertised them extensively at the time and many different Peco advertisements exist which refer to the coach kits, often in connection with the 'Perfecta' kits mentioned above.

Kitmaster themselves recognised the importance of interiors and with the introduction of the Mk 1 Restaurant First Open coach (No. 28) in late 1961 they began

Perhaps the Arby Perfecta Kits are the best known after-market motorisation kits. The series ran to five different kits, with a re-issue of No.1 to cover both the Pug and the Railbus.

Arby Perfecta kits gave you everything you needed to motorise a Kitmaster loco bar the motor itself. Most used the XT.60 or X.04 motors from Tri-ang, but Kit No.1 for the Pug used a Romford Terrier motor.

6. CHASSIS and MOTORISING KITS

The advent of a range of inexpensive static locomotive construction kits inevitably led to the introduction of many different products to enable them to run under their own power. We have already considered the Kitmaster solution to the problem: the Motor Bogie and the Motorised Box Van. Now we shall consider some of the numerous products which emerged throughout the 60s to enable Kitmaster locos to be motorised.

This section is divided into two parts: those kits which provided only a chassis and those which attempted to provide all the necessary parts.

Motorising Kits

[A] ARBY 'PERFECTA' KITS

Perhaps the most famous, and sought-after, of all the kits introduced are the original Arby 'Perfecta' kits.

Table I Arby Perfecta Kits

Perfecta kit for Kitmaster	Issued	Priced	Motor
No. 1 L and Y Pug	Oct 59	8s 9d	Terrier
No. 1a Pug and Railbus	Mar 61	8s 9d	XT60 or Terrier
No .2 Italian Tank	Apr 60	8s 9d	XT60
No. 3 Prairie Tank	May 60	11s 8d	XT60
No. 4 BoB Pacific	Jun 60	11s 8d	XT60 or X04
(No. 5 Duchess	Jul 60	11s 8d	X04)
No. 5 City of Truro	Mar 61	11s 8d	X04

Professionally designed and packaged, each Perfecta contained enough parts to modify a Kitmaster locomotive for 12 volt operation. All that was needed in addition was a motor. The sole concessionaires for Perfecta were Peco Products.

The Perfecta kits, of which five were produced, but six advertised, came in professionally produced packs featuring a two-colour header card, either red, blue or green on black, containing full instructions and diagrams as well as templates for the parts that needed cutting. The kits contained sleeves for axles, metal tyres for the wheels, pickup assemblies, phosphor bronze strip pickups, a cog and worm, and even replacement plastic mouldings for certain body parts. These last parts were contained on a single injection moulded sprue in black polystyrene. Although the first kit to be launched was designed for the 'Pug', it was later redesigned to enable use with the Airfix Railbus. The Railbus was issued in 1961 and the necessary changes to Perfecta kit No.1 were put in place quite rapidly. The redesign resulted in a switch to the optional Tri-ang XT60 motor, used in the other Perfecta kits. The original kit No. 1 had used a Romford 'Terrier' motor.

There is some uncertainty as to whether Perfecta Kit No. 5 for the Duchess Pacific was actually issued. It was never advertised by Peco after the initial introductory range advertisement. Anyone who has one of these kits is asked to contact the Collectors Club. Certainly, the fifth kit to be released was for *City of Truro* and this has been confirmed by the Club.

[B] N and KC KEYSER (K's)

Although K's never actually produced a 'motorising kit' as such, they did produce a range of motor bogies for Kitmaster locos. These were as follows *(overleaf)*

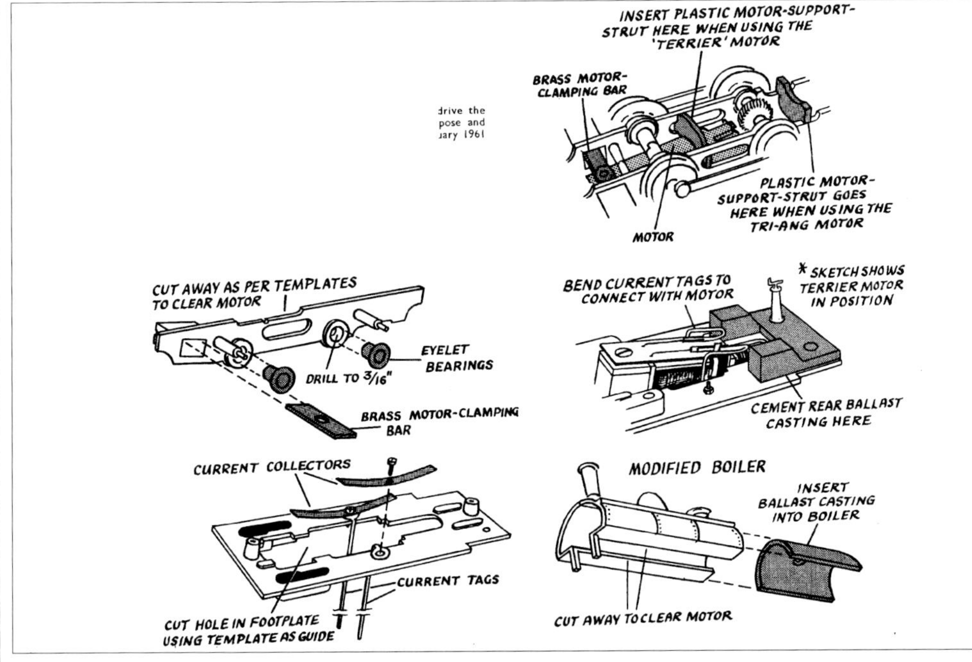

Top left. **The ingenuity of the Arby Perfecta system has to be admired. The Pug kit even included cast chassis and body weights for better adhesion.**

Left. **Perfecta kits came with well drawn and detailed instructions.**

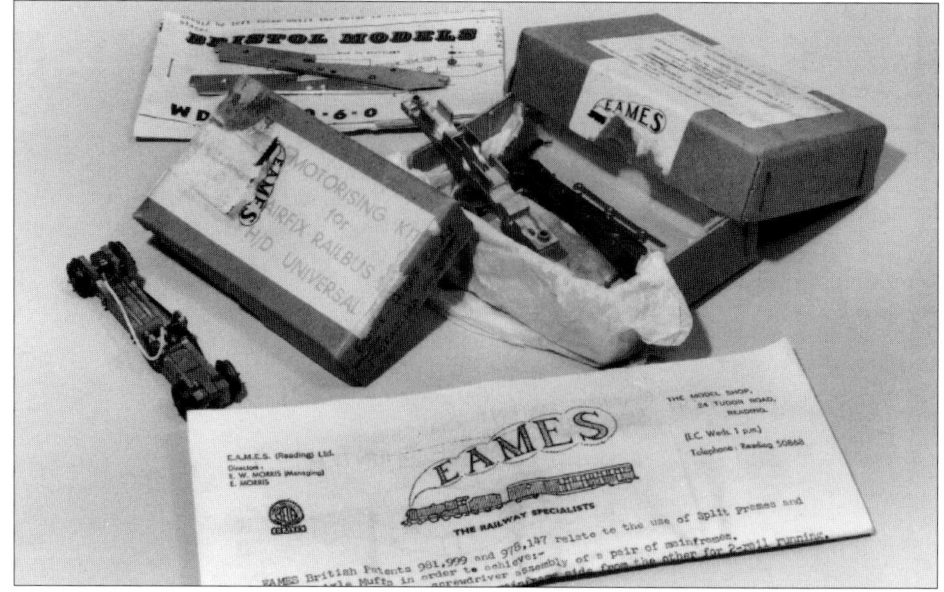

The Airfix re-issues produced a second flurry of motorisation kits. Amongst the most advanced were those from Bristol Models and Eames. The latter employed split axle pick-up for their Drewry shunter chassis.

1] General long wheelbase power bogie for large steam locomotive tenders, such as *Evening Star* and *Duchess of Gloucester*, introduced in July 1960.

2] Medium wheelbase bogie for the prototype Deltic plus special cast sideframes, introduced in May 1962, priced £2.3.6d + 3s 6d for the sideframes.

3] Short wheelbase bogie for the driving motor brake first of the Midland Pullman plus special sideframes, introduced in February 1962 Price £2.2.9d + 1s 6d for the sideframes.

Of these, the tender units are most common today. The Collectors Club has recently handled both a 9F and a Stirling 8ft Single locomotive motorised in this way. The others are extremely elusive. The favourite Deltic motorising method seems to have been a Tri-ang Class 31 or 37 chassis or, occasionally, a Hornby-Dublo Deltic chassis. Most Midland Pullmans were motorised with either the KM1 Kitmaster motor bogie or the Tri-ang DMU motor bogie, from which the former was shamelessly copied!

[C] SURREY MODEL CENTRE - SMRS
Surrey Model Centre (SMRS) was actually the first in this market with its motorising pack for the Schools Class loco. A straightforward 0-4-0 chassis was provided in brass, largely replacing the existing plastic one and having an X.04 motor mount (but no motor). Current collection and power transmission were all housed in the brass chassis unit, making this an easy conversion. The existing front bogie and valve gear were retained, but a metal coupling rod was provided. Correct scale metal wheels were also included. In general, this was a quick and neat conversion, but few survive today.

Chassis Kits

Many different chassis kits were produced, in whitemetal, brass and more recently, in etched nickel silver. The best of these are

Many Airfix issues were motorised with these Wilro Models 'Simplas' chassis packs and matching Romford wheel packs. They covered the entire range of Airfix locomotives.

The famous K's motorised tender chassis was available in two lengths, 7ft 6ins or 6ft 6ins wheelbase and was also produced as a motor bogie for the *Deltic* with cast sideframes.

undoubtedly the superb second edition Kemilway chassis for the Mogul and the Bulleid Pacific. Unfortunately, neither is currently in production. However, Comet and Crownline do make excellent chassis for the Battle of Britain, whilst Branchlines of Exeter make excellent chassis kits for the Mogul, Class 08, Class 04 and Railbus.

Others in this field included the 'Simplas' chassis range produced in 1967 by Wilro Models Ltd. of 20 Clarence Road, Clapton, London E5. Messrs Williams and Roland (hence Wil-Ro) designed, manufactured and marketed these Simplas chassis kits from their Model Shop. The centricast machine was in the back of the shop and these two affable gentlemen persuaded local model builders to donate any unwanted whitemetal scrap parts to their melting pot! They produced at least seven chassis, for the Pug, *Evening Star, City of Truro*, *Biggin Hill*, J94, Prairie Tank and Schools, each using the appropriate Romford wheel pack. They were attempting a kit for the Railbus when they split up their partnership and closed the business. It is therefore unlikely that this kit was marketed. E.A.M.E.S. of Reading already had a Railbus chassis kit on the market, so one wonders why they bothered in the first place. Also worth noting is the current production 'Simple Chassis' for *City of Truro* and *Biggin Hill* by West Coast Kit Centre.

Both Romford and Westward produced packs of wheels and bearings for the Class 9F, although no separate chassis existed.

A complete "motorised"
TENDER CHASSIS

***ready to run—only* 42/-—inclu**

Ideal for motorising your KITMASTER tender locos 7 ft. 6
L.M.S. City; 6 ft. 6 in. x 6 ft. 6 in. for Stirling, M. N

Now that we have redesigned all the loco kits to include f
we are able to offer the chassis as a separate unit. Set inc
Brass frames, frame spacers, coupling rods (correctly shaped), ca
keeper plate, seating block for K's motor, and all screws and washers.

Price only 10/6 including P.T.

Do you know? Humbrol now produce
31 different colours for model railways

LNER Loco, Green	101	LMS Maroon. BR Loco-Hauled Stock, Maroon	108	BR Loco-Hauled Stock, Lining	115	CPR Tuscan Red	123
GWR Coach Stock, Chocolate	102	BR Roof Paint, Lead	109	BR Coach Stock, Crimson. LMS Crimson Lake	116	CPR Grey	124
GWR Coach Stock, Cream	103	BR Freight Stock, Red Bauxite	110	GE Blue	117	CNR Yellow	125
GWR Standard Loco, Green	104	BR Freight Stock, Grey	111	LNER Garter Blue	118	CNR Green	126
GWR Freight Stock, Grey	105	BR Interior Paint, Stone	112	Track Colour (Matt)	119	Also available:— Black	127
SR Green, Malachite	106	BR Multi-Unit Stock, Green	113	Signal Yellow	120	White	128
LMS Wagon, Grey	107	BR Coach Stock, Cream	114	Signal Red	121	Silver	129
				CPR Yellow	122	Gold	130
						Copper	131

All 1/- per tin Full range always in stock together with K's special track colour at 1/9 per tin.

PRECISION MODEL ENGINEERS
Hanover Court · 197 Uxbridge Road · Shepherds Bush W.12
Proprietors: N. & K. C. Keyser Telephone: SHEpherds Bush 5254

★ K's—GOOD VALUE · FINE QUALITY AND DETAILS SECOND-TO-NONE

Get **MORE** and more pleasure **OUT OF YOUR HOBBY**

just keep an eye on us!

FOR EXAMPLE YOU CAN
motorize your Kitmaster "Schools" model with our **POWER UNIT**
TRI-ANG motor with full scale wheels complete with full instructions for fitting ... £2/12/6
ALSO AVAILABLE FOR TRI-ANG TRACK ... £2/8/-

BASEBOARDS
2in. x 1in. machined framing faced with ⅛in. Sundela semi-hardboard.

SIZE	PLAIN	MATT GREEN PAINTED
6ft. x 4ft.	£3/0/0	£3/10/0
5ft. x 3ft.	£2/10/0	£3/0/0

Carriage 7/6 in England.
4 legs 2in. x 2in. with fixing bolts: 15/-

SETS FOR CHRISTMAS
We can supply sets in Tri-ang or Trix complete with mains transformer unit and either 6ft. x 4ft. or 5ft. x 3ft. baseboard.
Prices from £7 or from 20/- deposit and 8 monthly payments of 16/6.

REMEMBER
We supply all model railway goods on
10 WEEKS' or 9 MONTHS' CREDIT

Send for **DETAILED LISTS**

ALL MODEL RAILWAY EQUIPMENT STOCKED
TRI-ANG, TRIX, WRENN, MASTERMODELS, FALLER, HORNBY-DUBLO, VOLLMER, MODELCRAFT. AIRFIX, PECO, H & M CONTROLLERS, LILIPUT. Mail orders welcomed. POST FREE

Surrey Model Railway Supermarket S. FRENCH & SONS LTD.
Dept. RMT. 450 EWELL ROAD, TOLWORTH, SURREY Telephone ELMbridge 1325
PLEASE TELL YOUR FRIENDS ABOUT THE RAILWAY MODELLER

G and G Scale Models produced a chassis pack, which included a turned brass chimney and dome, in etched brass for the Stirling Single, whilst H and N produced a rudimentary kit for the Pug.

Current production is limited to the aforementioned Crownline chassis and West Coast Kit Centre's 'Simple Chassis' range which includes the BR Mogul, Pug, *City of Truro* and Battle of Britain.

ASSEMBLY INSTRUCTIONS
FOR YOUR
"SCHOOLS" CLASS LOCOMOTIVE
KIT No. 5

"SCHOOLS" CLASS LOCOMOTIVES

The "Schools" Class 3 cylinder 4-4-0 type locomotives, with names chosen from those of famous schools were designed and built by the former Southern Railway to haul express trains on lines where larger and heavier locomotives were not permitted to run, particularly on the route from London to Hastings via Tonbridge, which had tunnels of restricted width.
The Driving Wheels are 6'7" in diameter and the total weight of the Engine and Tender in working order is 109 tons 10 cwts and many of the detail parts are standard with other classes of locomotives.
The "Schools" were the most powerful locomotives of their wheel arrangement (4-4-0) in Europe and their pleasing appearance and reliability made them immediate favourites with the travelling public as well as the railway staff.
As more were built their use extended from Hastings route to those from London to Dover, Portsmouth and Bournemouth, where they not only replaced older locomotives but worked on similar duties to those undertaken by the larger and heavier "King Arthur" Class.
No major alterations to the design have been found necessary, but the addition of wind plates alongside the smokebox to prevent down draught of smoke and steam from obscuring the view from the cab have modified the general appearance, together with the larger diameter chimney fitted to engines with a multiple jet blast pipe. At one time, when the speeding up of trains to Bournemouth was being considered, a temporary streamlined (or air smoothed) casing was fitted to one engine for experimental purposes in order to reduce wind resistance, but the idea was eventually abandoned.
During the 1939-45 war, following enemy air attacks on trains, one engine was fitted with an armoured cab as protection for the engine, but it was found unnecessary to fit further engines, the R.A.F. and other defences having taken action to prevent such attacks. Another engine while standing on the Cannon Street railway bridge over the Thames received a direct bomb hit on the cab, but damage to the bridge was prevented and the engine was eventually repaired. The enginemen escaped injury, having left the cab shortly before the bomb fell.

YOUR KITMASTER MODEL

This "Schools" Class Locomotive model embodies virtually all the detail and moveable features of the actual Locomotive, and has been designed to fit on standard OO and HO track (16.5 mm.).

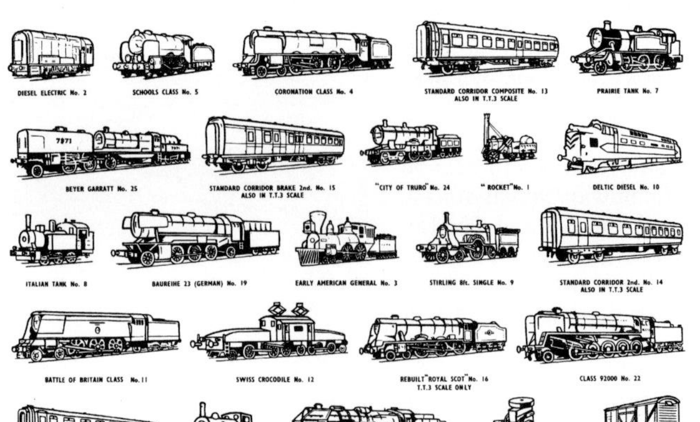

This is the rare Format 2 instruction sheet for the Schools , complete with a mini-catalogue of Kitmaster products.

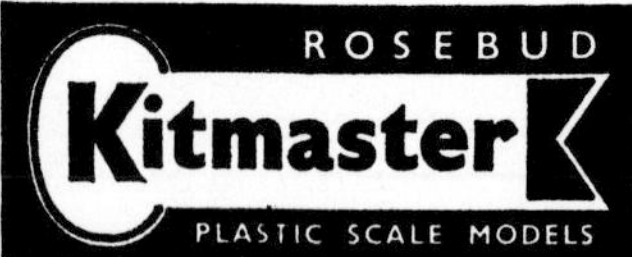

BRITISH RAILWAYS O-6-O SADDLE TANK
J94 CLASS. KIT No. 26.

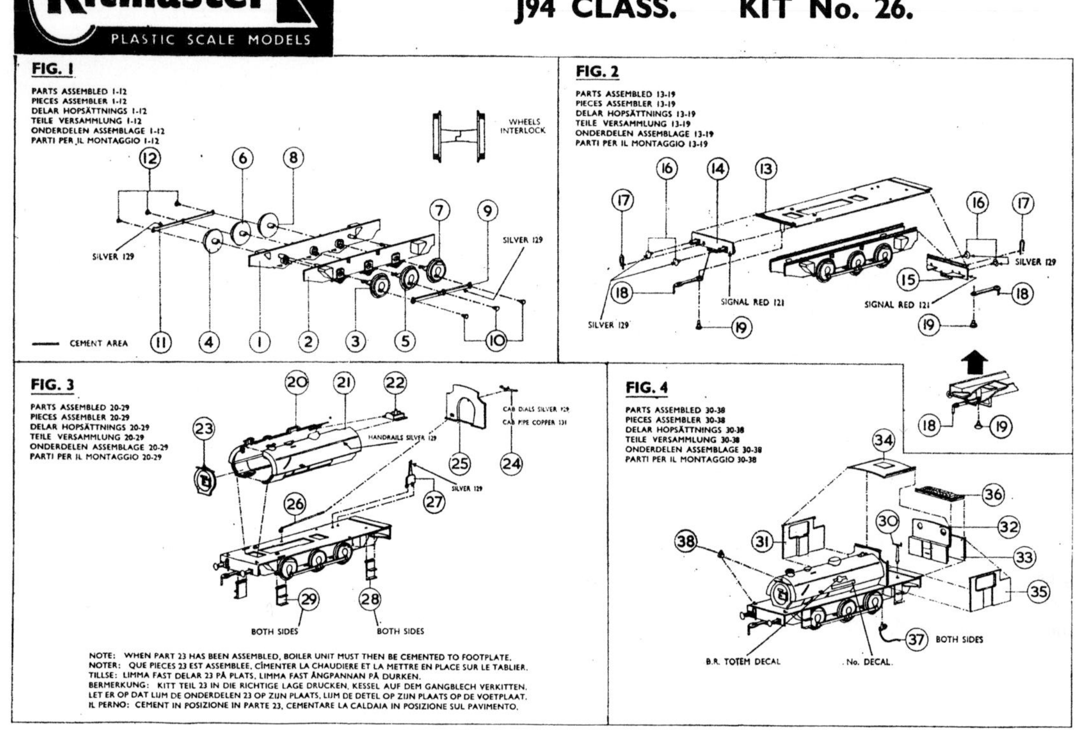

HISTORY

These Locomotives were designed by Mr. R. A. Riddles, C.B.E. Introduced during the Second World War and purchased from The Ministry of Supply in 1946. Built by Hudswell-Clarke, Bagnall, Stephenson and Hawthorns, Hunslet Engineering Co., Barclay, and Vulcan Foundry, from 1944 to 1947. Several of the same class purchased by industrial concerns and the Port of London Authority ; several also still owned by the W.D.

The weight of these Locomotives in working order is 48 tons. 5 cwts., the diameter of the coupled wheels is 4 ft. 3 ins. and have a tractive effort of 23,870 lbs. 2 inside cylinders of 18 ins. dia. x 26 ins. stroke, and boiler pressure of 170 lbs./sq in.

75 of these Locomotives were built, numbered 68006—68080. The Eastern Region has 25, 3 are at Bidston on the L.M. Region, and 4 others allocated to Rowsley for working on the Cromford and High Peak Railway from Middelton Top. The rest are on the N.E. Region. Chief purpose of these Locomotives is heavy shunting duties.

PAINTING YOUR MODEL

To ensure the correct authenticity of colour we recommend the use of "HUMBROL" Railway Enamel for this model. The numbers of which are given on Assembly drawing.

We wish to take this opportunity to express our gratitude to British Railways in furnishing drawings and photographs without which we could not have developed this model.

SHOULD ANY PARTS BE MISSING WRITE TO ROSEBUD KITMASTER LTD., RAUNDS, NORTHAMPTONSHIRE, ENGLAND.

Your Name ....

Street Address ....

Town ....

County ....

The box cover design of this Kit is the subject of Registered Design Application.

Printed in England

The words "ROSEBUD KITMASTER" are a Registered Trade Mark.

The last style of instruction sheet is in two colours and a big improvement on the earlier offering.

7. The KITMASTER and AIRFIX COMPENDIUM

This part of the book attempts to list all known production kits and planned kits identified in promotional material. A key to the abbreviations used in the text is given here. For an explanation of the symbols in the Notes column, please see 'Notes to Tables' which follow.

Kit Colour:
This is the colour of the plastic used to mould the kit, as shown in Table [a].

Table [a] : Colours of plastics used by Kitmaster

A = Apple Green	B = Black
Br = Brown	C = Clear Glazing
D = Dark Brunswick Green	G = Light Emerald Green
I = Pink (Pale Red)	K = Dark Grey
L = Light Grey	M = Metal parts
N = Nanking Blue	O = Dark Olive Green
P = Beige (Pale Yellow)	R = Red
S = Silver	U = Ultramarine Blue
W = White	Y = Yellow

Packaging and Box Type:
Box type refers to the dimensions of the boxes. Two materials were used. Earlier models were contained in strong cardboard boxes with the design printed on a paper surface covering the cardboard, but with kit No. 26 (J94 Saddle Tank), a change to card boxes (which were generally larger and floppier) was made. These have the design printed directly on the surface. A change was also made to the colour specification for the box designs. TT Scale models are printed with yellow logos on a pale blue background, whilst OO Scale models are Royal Blue on pale greenish-yellow backgrounds. From kit No. 26 onwards, the Kitmaster logo was redesigned to take up slightly less room on a Type 1 box. The new condensed logo was also printed in deep violet blue instead of royal blue and the background colour changed from greenish-yellow to yellowish-green (i.e. greener). The Motor Bogie and Box Van always had a smaller condensed logo due to lack of space on the box. These boxes were clearly printed by a different firm to the others as the colours are paler and have a dull matt finish. Most boxes were supplied by H. W. Chapman of Wellingborough, who also supplied cartons which would hold up to twenty-four finished kits each for onward shipment.

From 1960 onwards, all the boxes were sealed in an acetate wrapper similar to cellophane. It is still possible to find kits in the original wrapper. Additionally, some kits had the parts enclosed in a plastic bag. This tended to be the case with the Presentation sets, where the lack of box lids would otherwise have caused a problem. Examples of kits packed in plastic bags bearing the original Rosebud logo (used for the Dolls range) are known to exist, with two separate examples of Pullman Kitchen cars treated in this way having been discovered so far.

All Nabisco kits were despatched in plastic bags inside a plain brown box stamped with the name of the kit. Several sizes were used, depending on the number of kits ordered.

Dimensions of the principal box types were as shown in Table [b].

Design Patents:
Rosebud always sought to protect their famous box designs from competitors and cheaper imitations. To this end, each instruction sheet carried the legend 'The box illustration on the front of this kit is the subject of a Registered Design Application.' Early kits in the series also had the appropriate Application Number included. Interestingly, The General and the Pug were the first two to be registered, as shown in the table overleaf. The applications were lodged by Rosebud's Patent Agent, Messrs. Haseltine, Lake and Co., of 28 Southampton Buildings, Chancery Lane, London, W.C.2.

Unfortunately, the 'Statements of Novelty' relating to these designs have now been destroyed and are no longer in the Designs Registry. After this point, no Application Numbers were shown, even on the later redrawn sheets for the Battle of Britain and Deltic. According to the Patent Office, there are no more applications in the name of Rosebud Kitmaster Ltd.

Instruction Format:
Several different instruction formats were used for Kitmaster kits. The first eleven kits had Format 1 sheets. These are an early version of the instruction sheet with a large Kitmaster logo in the top left corner, surmounting a black and white half-tone of the finished locomotive. Step-by-step instructions in English are shown, together with a brief description of the Class. The reverse side has an exploded assembly diagram, except some examples of the Italian tank which were erroneously packed with single sided sheets. These Format 1 sheets were used for the first twelve models throughout 1959 and 1960, but commencing in December 1960, certain popular kits, including the Schools and Battle of Britain, had their sheets reprinted in the multilingual Format 2. The necessity of reprinting the Battle of Britain sheet in Format 2 arose through the issue of the P2 Presentation Set. On the outside of that set, the instructions are quoted as being in six languages. Whilst this was not a problem with the coaches, it was for the locomotive, which had first been issued with a Format 1 sheet. The Deltic, Schools, Stirling, Italian Tank, Pug, Duchess and Battle of Britain are all known with Format 1 sheets printed in blue ink. We can deduce, by dating these examples from catalogues and decals, that they were first printed in Format 1 in black, then Format 1 in blue and finally in Format 2.

The second style has only the exploded diagram on the reverse side, but features a 'mini-catalogue' of drawings showing other available kits on the front side, normally in the top right corner. These multilingual sheets are very large and have detailed assembly instructions, with the Class description printed in English, French, German, Dutch, Swedish and Italian. This type of sheet was used exclusively for kits 12-25, released in 1960, as well as the reprints mentioned above. Starting with the 1961 programme of introductions, new reduced sheets were introduced. The J94 Saddle Tank [26]

Table [c] : Printing Colours of Kitmaster Boxes

Scale	Kit Nos.	Logo Colour	Background Colour
OO	1-15,19,22-25, P1	Royal Blue	Greenish-Yellow
TT	16-18,20-21, P3	Deep Yellow	Pale Duck Egg Blue
OO	26,28,30-33, P2	Violet-Blue	Yellowish-Green
HO	27,29,34	Violet Blue	Yellowish Green
OO	KM1 and KM2	Matt Royal Blue	Pale Greenish-Yellow

Table [b] : Principle Box Types - Dimensions

Type	L mm W H	L ins W H	Used for kits:
1	144 x 93 x 39	5.75 x 3.75 x 1.5	1/2/6/8/26
2	208 x 93 x 39	8.25 x 3.75 x 1.5	3/7
3	370 x 126 x 39	14.50 x 5.00 x 1.5	4/10/11/12/19/22/28/31/32/33
4	297 x 92 x 39	11.75 x 3.75 x 1.5	5/9/13/14/15/24/30/27/29
5	240 x 92 x 39	9.50 x 3.75 x 1.5	16
6	255 x 80 x 39	10.00 x 3.25 x 1.5	17/18/20/21
7	420 x 126 x 39	16.50 x 5.00 x 1.5	23/25
8	424 x 126 x 39	16.75 x 5.00 x 1.5	34
9	152 x 102 x 36	6.00 x 4.00 x 1.0	60
10	442 x 216 x 39	16.50 x 8.50 x 1.5	P1
11	660 x 225 x 39	25.50 x 8.75 x 1.5	P2
12	750 x 216 x 39	30.00 x 8.50 x 1.5	P3
13	116 x 93 x 39	4.25 x 3.75 x 1.5	KM1/KM2
N1	152 x 102 x 45	6.00 x 4.00 x 1.7	Nabisco 2
N2	342 x 137 x 56	13.50 x 5.33 x 2.3	Nabisco 22/11
N3	275 x 140 x 88	11.00 x 5.50 x 3.5	Nabisco 28/15

KITMASTER— BRITAIN'S FIRST TRUE SCALE PLASTIC LOCO KITS

Exhibited at the Corn Exchange

WHILE the name Rosebud is new in railway modelling circles, the firm is an old-established one with considerable experience in plastics. Its Kitmaster range of OO gauge plastic locomotive kits will, we feel sure, prove highly popular among all modellers, as first and foremost they are scale models moulded in polystyrene, and provided with revolving wheels and working motion in the same material. The four locomotives immediately available are:

Rocket, 4/6.
Diesel electric shunter, 4/6.
General, 6/6.
Schools, 7/6.

It is intended to introduce a model a month from May onwards in the following order:

May	L. & Y. "Pug" 0-4-0 saddle tank, 4/6
June	Stirling single, 7/6
July	G.W. Big Prairie, 6/6
August	"Princess" Coronation Pacific, 10/6
September	Italian State Railways 0-6-0T, 4/6
October	"Deltic" diesel electric Co-Co, 10/6
November	"Battle of Britain," 10/6
December	Swiss 1C-C1 "Crocodile" electric loco, 10/6

The first Kitmaster to be produced, the diesel shunter, together with the parts supplied.

It will be seen that the initial range has a reasonable balance between old-time and modern locomotives and that Southern fans are once again well served. These models are essentially display items, and while the plastic parts do revolve freely, we doubt if they would be suitable for normal use on a layout. The models could, however, be fitted to a chassis, and even when the cost of this is added the price of the completed locomotive will still be reasonable. The kits also provide an inexpensive way of adding interest to a locomotive depot. Alternatively, how about staging a "Transport through the ages" exhibition at your station? Then, of course, there remains the primary intention of collecting a display of models of historic interest.

The prices are such that anyone can afford to acquire a wide range of these attractive kits and will doubtless do so, and we feel it will not be long before we see versions on many layouts.

Table [d] : Registered Design Applications

Kit No.	Application No.	Date of Application	Date Registered	Certificate Issued
1	891075	13 Nov 1958	13 Nov 1958	27 April 1959
2	891076	13 Nov 1958	13 Nov 1958	27 April 1959
3	891073	13 Nov 1958	13 Nov 1958	27 April 1959
4	891077	13 Nov 1958	13 Nov 1958	27 April 1959
5	891078	13 Nov 1958	13 Nov 1958	27 April 1959
6	891074	13 Nov 1958	13 Nov 1958	27 April 1959

"Article in respect of which design is registered: A box primarily for a toy construction kit."

appeared with one of these later sheets, which were two colour (normally red and black) to indicate glue lines and moved away from the primitive single exploded diagram to a more user-friendly series of assembly diagrams. This is designated Format 3.

However, this format dispensed with the long multi-lingual instructions as well, and shortened the description, so that the entire sheet fits on a single side of Foolscap paper. Previously, the Format 2 instructions covered both sides of an Imperial Folio sheet. Quite a drastic revision!

The final retail kit to be produced, the Ariel Arrow, has a double-sided two-colour instruction sheet with multiple diagrams, akin to later Airfix offerings. This is designated Format 4.

Table [e]: Sheet Formats

Type	Style
1	Large picture and one exploded diagram
2	One exploded diagram and mini-catalogue
3	Two colour exploded multiple diagrams, single side
4	Two colour exploded multiple diagrams, double side
5	Fireball XL5 - Hand drawn single exploded diagram
6	Motor Bogie fitting sheet
7	Motor maintenance sheet
N	Nabisco instruction sheet

The Nabisco versions of the kits had their own entirely different instruction sheets, designated Format N. These have only a small Kitmaster logo, minus the Rosebud name, positioned centrally. In addition, they have the wording 'With Compliments of Nabisco Foods Limited'. They comprise full assembly instructions and an exploded diagram only, and are very similar to Airfix Type 2 kit instruction sheets. It is interesting to note that the Nabisco version of the OO gauge Restaurant Car is a single diagram, whereas the actual Kitmaster sheet was a multidiagram offering. In fact, all the Nabisco sheets included entirely new drawings, often superior to the original sheet. Thus the Deltic kit has an extra diagram showing how to assemble the bogies, not available in the Format 1 kit instructional. It is probable that these sheets were drawn by the Airfix drawing office, as they bear a strong resemblance to Airfix Type 2 kit instructionals. There is also material evidence of a blue Format 1 Deltic sheet overprinted in black with the wording 'With the compliments of Nabisco Foods Ltd.' in the top right-hand corner.

Not fitting in with any of this is the Fireball XL5 sheet. This Format 5 sheet is a crude hand-drawn single exploded diagram with no descriptive text, just the bare essentials for assembly. It carries no reference to Kitmaster and was despatched by the Hermes Supply Co. Motor Bogie and Motor Box Van instruction sheets fall into two categories. Both products share a common sheet which details care and maintenance of the motor. Glued to the inside of the box lid is a sheet showing how to fit the alternative Peco or Tri-ang couplings. Finally, the Motor Bogie has separate monochrome instructions on how to fit the Motor Bogie to the coach shell.

Transfer Sheets

As far as can be ascertained, all the transfer sheets were printed in Coventry by British Transfer Printing Co. Ltd. of Harefield Road, now part of the Eyelith group. They also printed decals for the unreleased A3 kit. There are several variations in the transfer sheets (decals) included with some kits. The first production of British locomotives in British Railways livery contained the 1957 "totem" emblem of the lion-on-wheel heraldic device facing both left and right. However, the British Transport Commission had only been granted the use of the left-facing emblem as a heraldic device for use as a corporate mark by the College of Arms. Shortly afterwards, therefore, all locomotives had the right-facing emblem replaced by a second left-facing one. After this was pointed out to Kitmaster by the BR Publicity office at Euston, Kitmaster reprinted the transfer sheets for kits 2, 4, 5, 6, 7, 11 and 16 accordingly. There is no indication on the sheet that the decals have been reprinted and the kits were otherwise identical. Later kits such as 22, 25 , 26 and 30 were only produced with left-facing lions.

Type LR Left and Right-facing emblems used up until mid 1960
Type LL Both Left-facing emblems used after this time.

NOTES TO TABLES

Tables One and Two

Afx indicates that this kit was released by Airfix.
Dap indicates that this kit was released by Dapol.
Nab indicates a confirmed issue of a Nabisco branded kit by Hermes Supply Co.
Com indicates that a resin model made from the original Hermes model has been issued by Comet miniatures.

[6] The Stirling Single was moulded in two different colours of green, which are quite distinct. The early models were in Apple Green, but this was changed to Light Emerald Green, probably around 1960. There are no other detail differences. Both colours were used for kits in the P1 Presentation Set. During 1962, G and G Scale Products produced an etched brass chassis kit for the Stirling at a price of 25s, which included a brass boiler dome and safety valve unit.

[7] Although Airfix had the Deltic mould, it was never put into production.

9 Pullman Cars. These kits had three alternative colours for the seat mouldings: pink, white and beige.

11 There is an unsubstantiated report, in Kitmaster Newsletter Vol. 1 No. 1, from an ex-employee who worked at Grove Street to the effect that six SR Class USA tank engines were produced and given to the salesmen to show to dealers. There is yet another rumour that some test firings in clear plastic of a

Flying Scotsman mould were made. Several third hand reports of people with a clear kit in a plastic bag with no header or instructions, are known, but as yet no one has been able to show one to the author. The existence of tools for these locos seems

Text continues on page 70

Glossary of Terms

Instructional	=	Instruction Sheet, Instructions
Decals	=	Transfer Sheet
Sprue	=	Runner, plastic feeder holding parts together
Kitmaster	=	Rosebud Kitmaster Ltd.
Rosebud	=	Rosebud Dolls Ltd.

TABLE ONE: Kitmaster Production details

Number	Scale	Livery	1959*/**1960** Catalogue Description	Notes	Kit Col	Box Typ	Ins Fmt	Nab	Afx	Dap	Com
1 *	OO		'Rocket'		YM	1	1		x	x	
2 *	OO		Diesel Electric - 2-lights		B	1	1				
2 *	OO		Diesel Electric - 4 lights		B	1	1	x			
3 *	HO		Early American General		BM	2	1				
4 *	OO		Coronation Class		B	3	1				
5 *	OO		Schools Class		B	4	1/2		x	x	
6 *	OO		Saddle Tank		B	1	1		x	x	
7 *	OO		Prairie Tank		B	2	1		x	x	
8 *	OO		Italian Tank		B	1	1				
9 *	OO		Stirling 8ft Single	6	A/G	4	1				
10*	OO		Deltic Diesel	7	CU/L	3	1	x		x	
11*	OO		Battle of Britain Class		B	3	1/2		x	x	
12*	OO		Swiss Crocodile		CB	3	2				
13	OO	Maroon	Standard Corridor Composite		BCRK	4	2				
13	OO	Green	Standard Corridor Composite		BCDK	4	2				
14	OO	Maroon	Standard Corridor 2nd		BCRK	4	2				
14	OO	Green	Standard Corridor 2nd		BCDK	4	2				
15	OO	Maroon	Standard Corridor Brake 2nd		BCRK	4	2				
15	OO	Green	Standard Corridor Brake 2nd		BCDK	4	2	x			
16	TT		Rebuilt "Royal Scot"		M B	5	2				
17	TT	Maroon	Standard Corridor Brake 2nd		BCRK	6	2				
17	TT	Green	Standard Corridor Brake 2nd		BCDK	6	2				
18	TT	Maroon	Standard Corridor Composite		BCRK	6	2				
18	TT	Green	Standard Corridor Composite		BCDK	6	2				
19	OO		Baureihe 23 (German)		B	3	2				
20	TT	Maroon	Standard Corridor 2nd		BCRK	6	2				
20	TT	Green	Standard Corridor 2nd		BCDK	6	2				
21	TT	Maroon	Standard Restaurant 1st		WBCRK	6	2				
21	TT	Green	Standard Restaurant 1st		WBCDK	6	2				
22	OO		Class 92000		B	3	2	x	x	x	
23	OO		241P Mountain (French)		B	7	2				
24	OO		"City of Truro"		B	4	2		x	x	
25	OO		Beyer-Garratt		B	7	2				
26	OO		J94 0-6-0ST		B	1	3		x		
27	HO		DB B4yge Coach		CBO	6	3				
28	OO	Maroon	Standard Restaurant 1st	14	IWBCRKU	3	3	x			
28	OO	Green	Standard Restaurant 1st	14	IWBCDKU	3	3				
29	HO		SNCF A9 myfi Coach		CS	6	3				
30	OO		BR 4MT Mogul Class 76000		B	4	3		x	x	
31	OO		Midland Pullman Power	9	IWPCBKN	3	3				
32	OO		Midland Pullman Ktchn	9	IWPCBKN	3	3				
33	OO		Midland Pullman Parlr	9	IWPCBKN	3	3				
34	HO		New York Central Hudson		B	8	3				
35	OO		SR Class USA Tank		Not Released						
36	OO		A3 Flying Scotsman		Not Released						
37	HO		CN U-4-A		Not Released						
60	1:16		Ariel Arrow Motorcycle		PC	9	4		x		
—	1:100		Fireball XL5	12	SC	N3	5				x

Presentation Sets *including Set No. and Contents*

P1	1/4/9	100 Years of British Steam	MYGB	10	1
P2	11/13/14/15	Battle of Britain Set	KCBD	11	1/2
P3	16/17/18/20/21	TT3 Royal Scot Set	MKIWCBR	12	2

Ready-to-Run Motor Bogie *'Kits'*

KM1	OO	Motor Bogie	-	13	6
KM2	OO	Motor Box Van	Br	13	7
KM3	TT	Motor Bogie	Not Released		

Notes see page 70

TABLE TWO: Release Dates and Prices

No.	1961 Catalogue Description	Release Dates *In Cat.*	*Actual*	Original Price	1961 Price	1960 Trade	Peco Kit
1	Rocket	02.59	04.59	4s 6d	3s 6d	2s 7d	
2	Diesel Electric Shunter	01.59	04.59	4s 6d	3s 6d	2s 7d	
3	Early American 'General'	01.59	04.59	6s 6d	5s 0d	1s 11d	
4	Coronation Class	08.59	11.59	10s 6d	10s 6d	5s 0d	11s 8d
5	Schools Class Harrow	03.59	04.59	7s 6d	10s 6d	4s 3d	
6	Saddle Tank	05.59	05.59	4s 6d	3s 6d	2s 7d	8s 9d
7	Prairie Tank	07.59	10.59	6s 6d	5s 0d	1s 11	11s 8d
8	Italian Tank	09.59	12.59	4s 6d	3s 6d	2s 7d	8s 9d
9	Stirling	06.59	09.59	7s 6d	4s 4d		
10	Deltic Diesel	10.59	01.60	10s 6d	5s		
11	Battle of Britain Class	11.59	02.60	10s 6d	5s	11s 8d	
12	Giant Swiss Crocodile	12.59	03.60	10s 6d	5s		
13	BR Standard Corridor Composite	02.60	04.60	6s 6d	2s		
14	BR Standard Corridor Second	02.60	04.60	6s 6d	2s	2s 9d [1]	
15	BR Standard Corridor Brake 2nd	02.60	04.60	6s 6d	2s	2s 9d	
16	Rebuilt Royal Scot	04.60	05.60	6s 11d	4s		
17	BR Standard Corridor Brake 2nd	05.60	06.60	5s 11d	1s 5d		
18	BR Standard Corridor Composite	05.60	06.60	5s 11d	1s 5d		
19	German Baureihe 23	06.60	07.60	10s 6d	5s		
20	BR Standard Corridor Second	07.60	08.60	5s 11d	1s 5d		
21	BR Standard Restaurant 1st	07.60	08.60	6s 6d	2s		
22	BR Class 92000	08.60	09.60	10s 6d	5s		
23	French 241P Mountain	09.60	10.60	12s 6d	7s 2d		
24	City of Truro	10.60	11.60	7s 6d	4s 4d		
25	Beyer-Garratt	11.60/Sp 61		12s 6d	7s 2d		
26	ER Saddle Tank Class J94	Sp 61		3s 6d			
27	German Coach Type B4yge	Sp 61		7s 6d			
28	BR Standard Restaurant 1st	Sp 61		9s 6d			
29	French Coach Type A9 myfi/1958	Sum 61		8s 6d			
30	BR Mogul Class 76000	Sum 61		7s 6d			
31	Midland Pullman Power Car	Sum 61		10s 6d			
32	Midland Pullman Kitchen Car	Sum 61		10s 6d			
33	Midland Pullman Parlour Car	Sum 61		10s 6d			
34	New York Central Hudson Type J3a	Win 61		3s 6d			
35	SR Tank Class USA	Win 61	No kit	13s 6d			
36	ER Gresley A3 'Flying Scotsman'	Win 61	No kit	10s 6d			
37	Canadian National Railways Type U-4A	Win 61	No kit	13s 6d			
60	Ariel Arrow Super Sports Model	N/A	Mar 62	5s 11d	See Note 13, page 70		
—	Steve Zodiac's Fireball XL5	N/A	July 62	4s 6d			
	Presentation Sets						
P1	100 Years of British Steam	10.59	11.59	27s 6d	15s 9d		
P2	Battle of Britain Set	4.60	10.60	37s 6d	21s 5d		
P3	TT3 Royal Scot Set	8.60	12.60	37s 6d	21s 5d		
	Ready-to-Run Motor Bogie *Kits*				Actual	Advance	
KM1	OO Motor Bogie	7.60		32s 6d	27s 6d	15s 9d	
KM2	OO Motor Box Van	7.60		39s 6d	35s 0d	20s	
KM3	TT Motor Bogie See Note 10	7.60		(32s 6d)	27s 6d	15s 9d	

Note that the 'Actual' price shown for the Motor Bogies is the price given in the Retail catalogue for 1960/61, whereas the 'Advance' prices are those shown as being the suggested retail prices for 1960 in the 1960 Trade Price List. This reflects the increased supply costs of the motorised items to Rosebud.

Notes see page 70

TABLE THREE: Press Coverage

No.	Short Description	First Advert	Reviews RM	MRN	MRC	Interior[2] Perfecta	Simplas Chassis	Airfix reintro
1	Rocket	04.59	04.59		04.59			10.64
2	08 Shunter	04.59			03.59			
3	General	04.59	04.59		04.59			
4	Coronation	11.59	12.59	11.59	11.59	07.60		
5	Schools	04.59		7.59	06.59		?1968	05.68
6	L&Y Pug	05.59	05.59	7.59	12.59	10.59	03.67	03.64
7	Prairie Tank	10.59	10.59	10.59	10.59	05.60	10.67	10.63
8	Italian Tank	12.59	12.59			04.60		
9	Stirling	09.59	10.59	10.59	08.59			
10	Deltic	01.60	03.60	03.60				
11	B o B	02.60	02.60	02.60	02.60	06.60	?1968/9	04.68
12	Crocodile	03.60	04.60					
13	Mk 1 CK	04.60	03.60					
14	Mk 1 SK	04.60	03.60			03.60	Date?	
14	Mk 1 SO	04.60	03.60			10.60		
15	Mk 1 BSK	04.60	05.60			07.60		
16	Royal Scot	05.60	07.60	08.60	08.60			
17	Mk 1 BSK	06.60	08.60	08.60	08.60			
18	Mk 1 CK	06.60	07.60					
19	Baureihe	07.60	09.60		10.60			
20	Mk 1 SK	08.60	08.60					
21	Mk 1 RFO	08.60	07.60					
22	9F 2-10-0	09.60	01.61	01.61	01.61		10.67	12.64
23	Mountain	10.60	02.61	04.61	04.61			
24	City of Truro	11.60	03.61	04.61		03.61	04.67	04.65
25	Beyer-Garratt	05.61	05.61	05.61	06.61			
26	J94 0-6-0ST	05.61[3]	05.61	05.61	05.61		10.67	01.64
27	DB Coach	07.61	07.61	07.61	07.61			
28	Mk 1 RFO			07.61	07.61			
29	A9 myfi			08.61	08.61			
30	BR Mogul	10.61[4]?	10.61	11.61	10.61			07.71
31	Power Car	02.62[8]	12.61	12.61	12.61			
32	Kitchen	12.61	12.61	12.61				
33	Parlour	12.61	01.62	12.61				
34	Hudson	02.62[5]		03.62				
KM1	Motor Bogie		07.61	07.61	12.61			
60	Ariel Arrow		07.63					07.63
P2	Battle of Britain			01.62				

RM = Railway Modeller
MRN = Model Railway News
MRC = Model Railway Constructor

Notes see page 70

TABLE FOUR : Names and Numbers

No	*Instruction sheet name*	*Alternatives*
1	George Stephenson's Locomotive 'Rocket'	
2	BR Standard 350 hp Diesel Electric Shunting Locomotive D3421	
3	Early American 'General' Locomotive	
4	British Railways (London Midland Region) 4-6-2 'Coronation' Class Locomotives	46225 Duchess of Gloucester
5	'Schools' Class Locomotive	30919 Harrow
6	0-4-0 Saddle Tank	51212
7	British Railways (Western Region) 6100 Class Prairie Tank Locomotive	6167
8	Italian State Railways Class 835 Tank Locomotive	162
9	Stirling 8ft 'Single' Locomotive No 1	
10	English Electric 3,300 hp Deltic Locomotive	
11	British Railways (Southern Region) 'Battle of Britain' Class Locomotive	34057 Biggin Hill
12	Swiss Federal Railways 'Crocodile' Series Be6/8	13305
13	BR Standard Corridor Composite M16001	M15627/019/243 W15111/598/430 E15307/144/16017
13	SR Green version only M16001	S15042/573/888/903/580/873
14	BR Standard Corridor Second M25589	M24133/405/861 W24165/341/719 E24222/531/25027
14	SR Green version only M25589	S24320/305/169/326/318/311
15	BR Standard Corridor Brake 2nd M35114	M34090/105/671 W34152/297/763 E34422/590/35157
15	SR Green version only M35114	S34256/621/158/945/279/35020
16	Rebuilt Royal Scot Locomotive (ex LMSR) 46100 Royal Scot	46110 Grenadier Guardsman 46169 Boy Scout
17	BR Standard Corridor Brake 2nd M35114	M34090/105/671 W34152/297/763 E34422/590/35157
17	SR Green version only M35114	S34256/621/158/945/279/35020
18	BR Standard Corridor Composite M16001	M15627/019/243 W15111/598/430 E15307/144/16017
18	SR Green version only M16001	S15042/573/888/903/580/873
19	German Federal Railways Class 23 Locomotive 23014	23001 23008 23014
20	BR Standard Corridor Second M25589	M24133/405/861 W24165/341/719 E24222/531/25027
20	SR Green version only M25589	S24320/305/169/326/318/311
21	BR Standard Restaurant 1st M5	M4/5/6/S9/W7/8/E1/2/3/10/11
21	SR Green version M5	M4/5/6/S9/W7/8/E1/2/3/10/11
22	BR Standard Class 92000 Locomotive 92220	92203, 92134
23	French 241P Mountain	241P.026 241P.027 241P.029
24	GWR 'City' Class Locomotive 3440 City of Truro	
25	Beyer-Garratt 2-6-6-2 Freight Locomotive (Ex-L.M.S.) 7971	7987, 47994
26	ER Saddle Tank Class J94 68022	68028 68051 68076
27	German Coach Type B4yge	
28	BR Standard Restaurant 1st M5	M4/5/6/S9/W7/8/E1/2/3/10/11
28	SR Green version M5	M4/5/6/S9/W7/8/E1/2/3/10/1
29	French Coach Type A9 myfi/1958	
30	BR Mogul Class 76000	76093, 76114
31	Midland Pullman Power Car Type 1 First Class M60090	- A F
32	Midland Pullman Kitchen Car Type 4 First Class	- B E
33	Midland Pullman Parlour Car Type 6 First Class	- C D
34	New York Central Hudson J3a Locomotive (4-6-4) 5405	
60	Ariel Arrow Super Sports Model ONV 989	697 AOH

TABLE FIVE: Airfix Re-Releases Reissued Kitmaster Rolling Stock:

KM No.	Airfix No.	Dapol No.	Airfix Description	Series	Type	Colour	Reissue
1	R11	C46	Stephenson's Rocket	1	3 Box	Y	12.64
1	R11	C46	Stephenson's Rocket	1	3 Bag	Y	1966
1	016612	C46	Stephenson's Rocket	1	4 Blis	Y	1973
5	R402	C35	Schools Class Harrow	4	3	D	05.68
5	046527	C35	Schools Class Harrow	4	4	D	1973
5	046527	C35	Schools Class Harrow	4	6	D	1978
6	R9	C26	Saddle Tank Pug	1	3	B	03.64
6	R9	C26	Saddle Tank Pug	1	3LP	B	1972
6	026602	C26	Saddle Tank Pug	2	5	B	1980
6	026602	C26	Saddle Tank Pug	2	6	B	1982
7	R301	C62	Prairie Tank	3	3	D	10.63
7	036561	C62	Prairie Tank	3	3LP	D	1972
7	046556	C62	Prairie Tank	4	4	D	1973
10	N/A	C09	Deltic	N/A	N/A	U	1984
11	R501	C48	Battle of Britain Class	5	3	D	04.68
11	056517	C48	Battle of Britain Class	5	4	D	1973
22	R401	C49	Evening Star	4	3	B	12.64
22	R502	C49	Evening Star	5	3	B	07.71
22	056520	C49	Evening Star	5	4	B	1973
24	R302	C61	City of Truro	3	3	B	04.65
24	036524	C61	City of Truro	4	3LP	B	1972
24	046543	C61	City of Truro	4	6	B	1976
26	R205	C34	Class J94 Saddle Tank	2	3	B	01.64
30	R403	C59	BR Mogul	4	3	B	07.71
30	046530	C59	BR Mogul	4	4	B	1973
60	1635	—	Ariel Arrow Motorcycle	1	2	P	07.63
60	014805		Ariel Arrow Motorcycle	1	3	P	1965
60	024811		Ariel Arrow Motorcycle	2	4	P	1971

NOTES TO TABLE FIVE

The above table gives information about the Airfix production of Kitmaster locomotives as well as their own tooled-up kits for the Drewry Shunter, the Railbus and wagons of various descriptions. Airfix originally catalogued all their kits by a 'Pattern No.', which was engraved on the tool. As office automation began to have an impact on Haldane Place in the early 1970s, the Type 4 boxes started to show the Pattern No. together with a computerised number. This eventually became the standard number for cataloguing the kits. Since the first digit after the leading zero is the Series number, if a kit changed Series, it was given a new number. This was also true of the old Pattern No. system as applied to the larger kits.

Hence Pattern No. **R4**01 is a **R**ailway Series **4** kit, whilst R502 is the same kit, but in a Series **5** box.

Airfix periodically withdrew their rolling stock kits, only to reintroduce them again later, and many box variations exist. Some of the 1972 reintroductions are marked 'Limited Production' on the box cover, although all subsequently went into mass production. Limited Production kits are not as rare as those without this marking! Various colours of plastic were used for wagons in addition to those shown, for example the Brake Van in bright red and the Cattle Wagon in tan or very dark brown.

Airfix Box types -
1958-1963 Type 2 Has a solid wide stripe down the middle.
1963-1973 Type 3 Has a red flashed rectangular Airfix logo at bottom right.
1967-1973 Type 3LP Has Limited Production wording next to logo.
1973-1977 Type 4 Has a circular Airfix logo, the colour of the box art.
1977-1978 Type 5 Red/white/black logo English/French wording White border to box.
1979-1982 Type 6 Has red/white/black oval logo on full colour box. with no border.

It should be noted that the Ariel Arrow, City of Truro and Evening Star, together with all the Series 1 wagons and some of the others, changed series during their lifetime. When first reintroduced, the Arrow was packed as a Series 1 kit in a clear plastic bag with a paper header/ instructional. When last produced, in 1981, it was packaged as a Series 2 kit in a conventional box with a separate instruction sheet. Many Airfix Series 1 kits reverted to Series 2 during their production lives. The Evening Star kit was designated as a Series Five model with Pattern No. R502 for the 1972 limited production run, having moved up from a short spell in Series 4, upon which it was allocated Pattern No. R401 (both are tabulated left). In 1979, it was issued in a Type 6 box in Series 5, this is a scarce kit. Only the Rocket ever appeared in a Series 1 'Blister-Pack'. The Lowmac with JCB was issued with two different instruction sheets due to a numbering error on diagram 2 of the sheet, which resulted in all numbers being increased by 1. This was quickly reprinted with the correct numbering.

Original Airfix production rolling stock:

Airfix No.	Dapol No.	Airfix Description	Series	Type	Colour	Reissue
R1	C36	12t Oil Tank Wagon	1	2	B	07.60
02656-3	C36	12t Oil Tank Wagon	2	3	B	1973
R2	C40	'Presflo' Cement Wagon	1	2	Y	07.60
02662-8	C40	'Presflo' Cement Wagon	2	3	Y	1978
R3	C37	10t Mineral Wagon	1	2	L	03.61
02657-6	C37	10t Mineral Wagon	2	3	L	1973
R4	C38	Brake Van	1	2	Br	05.61
02658-9	C38	Brake Van	2	3	Br	1973
R5	C39	Cattle Wagon	1	2	Br	05.61
02659-2	C39	Cattle Wagon	2	3	Br	1973
R6		24 Buckeye couplings	1	2	B	01.64
R7	C60	Drewry Shunter Class 04	1	2	B	10.61
R8	C41	10t Meat Van	1	2	R	08.62
02661-5	C41	10t Meat Van	2	3	R	1978
R10	C43	"Prestwin" Silo Wagon	1	3	Br	04.64
R201	C47	Park Royal Railbus	2	2	D	12.60
R202	C28	15 ton Diesel Loco. Crane	2	2	R	03.61
03622-3	C28	15 ton Diesel Loco. Crane	3	6	R	1980*
R203	C42	'Interfrigo' Refrigerator	2	2	W	07.62
R204	C45	14t Lowmac with JCB Load	2	2	Br/Y	07.63

*The Diesel Crane in a Series 3 box was clearly shown in the first few Airfix GMR ready-to-run catalogues, in the kit section. It even appeared in the text of the Railways section of the 17th Edition (1980) kit catalogue, but is thought not to have been issued.

None of the Series 2 Airfix rolling stock ever appeared in the Roy Cross style Type 3 packaging, although the Railbus was certainly redrawn for a Type 3 issue - it can be seen as such on the side panels of the larger locomotive kits. Consequently, these Type 2 Series 2 boxes remained in production for much of the 1960s, long after all the other kits had progressed to Type 3 artwork. Interestingly, the Prairie Tank locomotive was the first Airfix kit to appear in Type 3 boxes. It was also one of the last. When reissued as a Limited Production, the end panels were already drawn as Type 4 (with a circular Airfix logo) but the front panel remained Type 3, one of the very last to do so.

unlikely, however, since it would mean that at the time of the Airfix takeover, the tooling for a USA class tank and an A3 was in existence. Airfix would surely have wanted to release these models straight away as they would have been very popular. Any clarification of this story would be gratefully received. *See Rumours and Postulations section.*

12 The 1:100 model of Fireball XL5 was a promotion carried by Lyons Maid on 'Zoom' Ice Lolly products, through which a plastic kit of Steve Zodiac's Fireball XL5 was sent in exchange for tokens plus a charge of 4s 6d - as detailed on page 55.

TABLE TWO ONLY

[1] Peco introduced two interior kits for the Corridor 2nd. The first was introduced in March 1960, for the SK interior, priced at 2s 9d. This was followed in October 1960 by the SO interior, also at a price of 2s 9d.

TABLE THREE

[2] Simplas Chassis were produced and marketed by Wilro Models Ltd., 20 Clarence Road, London E5.

[3] Humbrol advertised the J94 with a picture to promote Humbrol Railway Colours in MRN 9/61.

[4] Humbrol advertised the Mogul with a picture to promote Humbrol Railway Colours in RM 10/61 and 11/61.

[5] Referred to in an article in *Railway Modeller* 10.62, p. 242, as the introduction date.

[8] Humbrol advertised the Pullman Power Car with a picture to promote Humbrol Railway Colours in Airfix Magazine 2/62.

TABLES FOUR AND ONE

14 Other numbers for vehicles with this body shell (First Class Open) with Mk 1 BR1 bogies) would be: 1953- build year: M3000/1/2. All regional prefixes were carried by these vehicles. Note: Build year 1953, FO's 3003-3007 were outshopped with a centre door added. This was the only change to the vehicle as supplied in the kit. All FO/RFO outshopped after this differ considerably in ventilator positions and internal arrangement. RFO kit No. 28 was produced with both white and pale pink interiors and, in several cases, Deltic's ultramarine blue plastic interior!

KITMASTER MEDIA CAMPAIGN

Rosebud Kitmaster launched their famous range of kits with a spectacular, not to say expensive, advertising campaign. During the spring and summer of 1959, it was impossible to miss this barrage of advertising. Each month, a different and highly original advert would appear in the major magazines of the period. In the second year of production, the campaign continued, but in a different selection of titles. Out went *Model Aircraft* magazine and in came *Model Maker*. This impressive launch campaign, covering twelve separate publications, ensured that Kitmaster was the name on everyone's lips by the end of 1960. At that point, all paid-for advertising ceased and Kitmaster relied heavily on editorials and reviews. There was no shortage of these either, as the kits afforded plenty of opportunities for conversions and motorising. After the initial wave of motorising, a second series of articles appeared from 1967 onwards as Airfix progressively reintroduced their range of modified kits. The last advertising to be done by Rosebud was a joint campaign with Humbrol, which ran throughout 1961 and into early 1962. The table opposite summarises the major part of the initial Kitmaster launch campaign. Each advertisement carried a code letter and number combination, usually in the bottom left-hand corner. These are shown in the table and a key is given below. KMC 5 was used for two entirely different advertisements for The Duchess. One is a full page portrait format and was used exclusively for Ian Allan ABC Spotter's Guides, while the other is landscape format and was in wider use. We are lacking any information on the issues left blank. The symbol ~ indicates that nothing appeared in that issue and the issue has been verified by the Collectors' Club. Persons with information on the vacant cells in the table are asked to contact the Secretary. An additional note: Due to a nationwide printing strike, no journals appeared in July 1959, except for 'Emergency Issues' of some Ian Allan titles.

Publications

Rosebud produced three catalogues, one for each year of the company's existence. All were printed on a single sheet of paper, double sided in four-colour photolithography.

Catalogue 1 1959-1960

This familiar little catalogue was included with most of the early kits. There are at least ten known versions, including four UK reprints, plus two Irish, two US export, several French and Italian versions and even an Austrian version! The reprints were necessitated by poor reproduction and the need to add the Raunds address block to the rear panel. Different typefaces were used for the second and third reprints.

Catalogue 2 1960-1961

This is the more elusive 1960 catalogue. It was packed together with the P2 and P3 Presentation sets and was also distributed free with the July 1960 *Railway Modeller*. It does not seem to have been included with any other kits. It is slightly larger than the

It's a great day for model enthusiasts when a new 'Kitmaster' appears. Here's this month's —an authentic scale model of the Italian Tank locomotive, used for shunting duties by the Italian State Railways. Like all 'Kitmaster' models it's for use on OO and HO gauge tracks.

Hurry to your nearest model or toy shop

LET'S STICK TOGETHER! - British Plastic Assembly Railway Kits 1955-1970

TABLE SIX - MEDIA CAMPAIGN for the KITMASTER LAUNCH

This table summarizes the advertisements appearing in support of the Kitmaster launch during 1959/60

Date of Issue	Railway Modeller	Model Railway News	Model Railway Constructor	Model Aircraft	Meccano Magazine	Model Maker	Ian Allan Publications	Trains Illustrated	Express Weekly	Issue Date	Hobbies Weekly	Issue Date	The Eagle	Aero Modeller
04/59	KMC1	KMC1	~			~	Range Ad	KMC1		8.4.59	KMC1	4.4.59	KMC1	
05/59	KMC2	KCM2				~	ABC Directories	KMC2		6.5.59	KCM2	2.5.59	KMC2	
06/59	KMC2	KM2	~	KCM2		~	~	KMC2		*10.6.59*	*KCM2?*	6.6.59	KMC2	
07/59	~	~	~	~	~	~	~	~	~		~	Printing	~	
08/50	-	-	-	-	-	-	-	-	-		-	Strike	-	
09/59	KMC3	KMC3	KMC3		KMC3	~	~	KMC3		9.9.59	(KMC3)	5.9.59	KMC3	
10/59	KMC4	KMC4	~		KMC4	~	~	KMC4		7.10.59	KMC4	3.10.59	KMC4	
11/59	KMC5	KMC5	~	KMC5	KMC5	~	KMC5	KMC5		11.11.59	KMC5	7.11.59	KMC5	
12/59	KMC6	KMC6	~	KMC6	KMC6	~	ABC Directories	KMC6		9.12.59	KMC6	12.12.59	KMC6	
01/60	KC10	KC10	KC10		KC10	KC10	~							
02/60	KC11	KC11	KC11		KC11	KC11	~							
03/60	KC12	KC12	KC12		KC12	KC12	~							
04/60	KC13	KC13	KC13		KC13	KC13	~							
05/60	KC14	KC14	KC14		KC14	KC14	~							
06/60	KC15	KC15	KC15		KC15	KC15	~							
07/60	KC16	KC16	KC16		KC16	~	~							
08/60	KC15	KC15	KC15		KC15	KC17	~							
09/60	KC17	KL17	KC17		KC17	~	~							
10/60	KC18	KC18	KC18		KC18	~	~							
11/60	KC19	KC19	~		KC19	~	Range Ad							
12/60	KC20	KC20	K20		KC18	~	Book of Model Railways							
After this point there were no more advertisements placed by Kitmaster until the joint campaign with Humbrol started.														

1959 catalogue and opens out to twice the size. It has all the TT kits and the power bogies included, and goes up to kit No. 25, the Beyer-Garratt. Note that, at this stage, the BR 9F is shown in BR black livery and is not *Evening Star*, that the OO coaches are shown as available in green and maroon, whilst the TT coaches are only shown in maroon. The bogies are wrongly described as being for 12.15 Volt operation instead of 12-15 Volt!. It was also produced in all the major languages and the Archive contains Dutch and Italian copies.

Dimensions: 145 x 75 mm closed, 285 x 145 mm opened flat.

Catalogue 3 1961-1962

The most impressive yet. Full colour *Evening Star* on the front, opens in a peculiar manner to a full A3 sheet. Shows all railway kits, including Nos. 35/36/37 (not produced), but not the motorcycle. Printed in all the languages used by Kitmaster. Confirmed

Continued on page 76

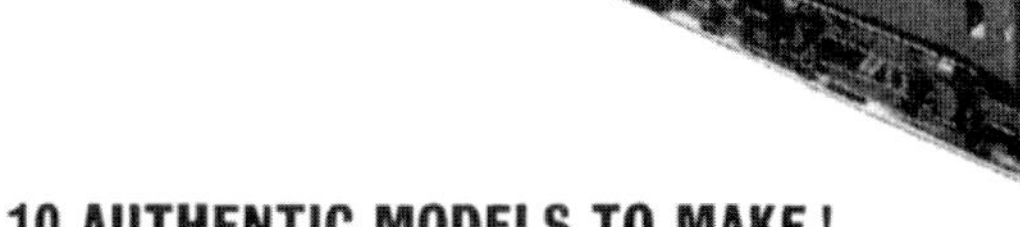

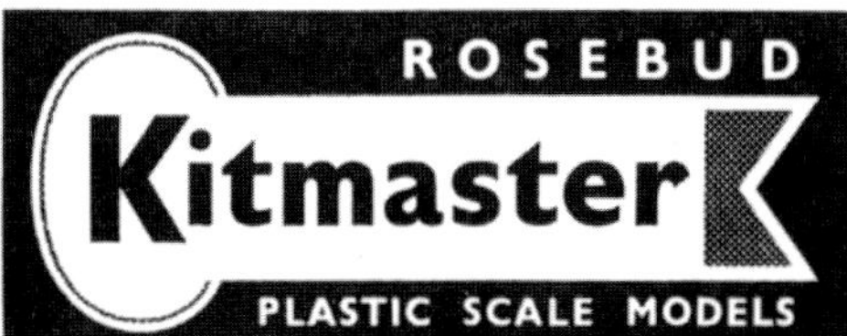

RUSH TO BUY

Kitmaster's latest

Battle of Britain Class

If you collect world-famous locomotives, here's one you must not miss: Battle of Britain Class 'Biggin Hill'. It's No. 11 in Kitmaster's authentic series of plastic scale model loco kits, actually made from British Railways blueprints. Build it to-day—to run on OO and HO gauge tracks. Price 10/6d.

ROSEBUD KITMASTER LIMITED

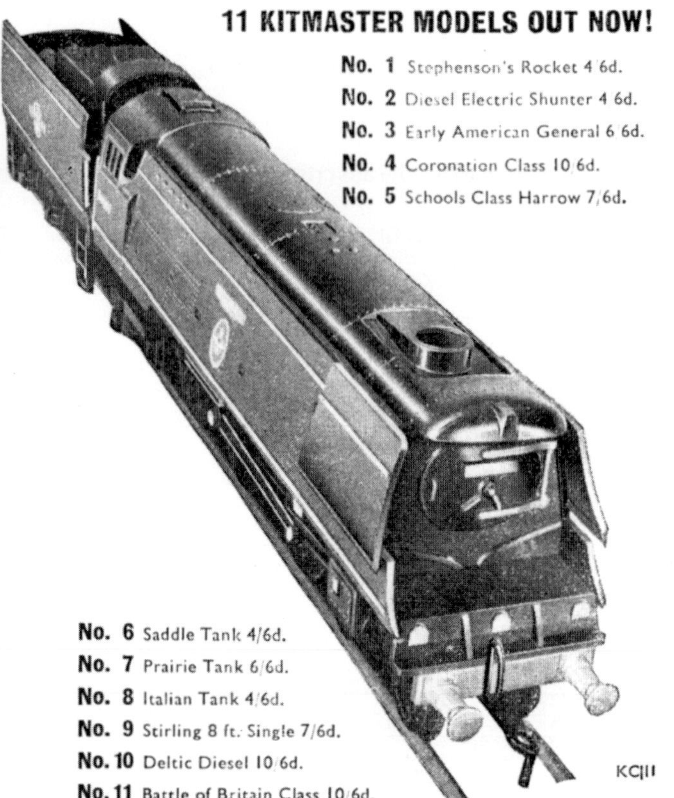

11 KITMASTER MODELS OUT NOW!

No. 1 Stephenson's Rocket 4/6d.
No. 2 Diesel Electric Shunter 4/6d.
No. 3 Early American General 6/6d.
No. 4 Coronation Class 10/6d.
No. 5 Schools Class Harrow 7/6d.
No. 6 Saddle Tank 4/6d.
No. 7 Prairie Tank 6/6d.
No. 8 Italian Tank 4/6d.
No. 9 Stirling 8 ft. Single 7/6d.
No. 10 Deltic Diesel 10/6d.
No. 11 Battle of Britain Class 10/6d.

KCl11

AT MODEL AND TOY SHOPS EVERYWHERE

a brilliant new Kitmaster to add to your collection!

GIANT SWISS 'CROCODILE' 10/6d.
This powerful engine hauls heavy loads in the Swiss Alps. You'll want to see it and make it right away! It's No. 12 in Kitmaster's famous series of *authentic* scale model locomotive kits with moving parts, for use on OO-HO gauge tracks. Ask for the new 1960 Kitmaster catalogue.

AT MODEL AND TOY SHOPS EVERYWHERE!

ROSEBUD KITMASTER LIMITED

12 AUTHENTIC MODELS NOW!

No. 1 Stephenson's Rocket	4/6d.	No. 7 Prairie Tank	6/6d.
No. 2 Diesel Electric Shunter	4/6d.	No. 8 Italian Tank	4/6d.
No. 3 Early American 'General'	6/6d.	No. 9 Stirling 8 feet Single	7/6d.
No. 4 Coronation Class	10/6d.	No. 10 Deltic Diesel	10/6d.
No. 5 Schools Class Harrow	7/6d.	No. 11 Battle of Britain Class	10/6d.
No. 6 Saddle Tank	4/6d.	No. 12 Giant Swiss 'Crocodile'	10/6d.

KC12

The first KITMASTER COACHES

From today, you can build *complete* Kitmaster train sets! This is because Kitmaster have just added British Railways COACHES to their famous series of plastic scale model locomotives. Like the other Kitmasters in your collection, these B.R. Coaches are built exactly to scale—with moving parts to work on OO-HO gauge tracks. See them at model and toy shops today!

... and here they are

No. 13	Corridor Composite Coach	6/6
No. 14	Corridor Second Coach	6/6
No. 15	Corridor Brake Second Coach	6/6

ALREADY ISSUED:

No. 1	Stephenson's Rocket	4/6d.
No. 2	Diesel Electric Shunter	4/6d.
No. 3	Early American 'General'	6/6d.
No. 4	Coronation Class	10/6d.
No. 5	Schools Class 'Harrow'	7/6d.
No. 6	Saddle Tank	4/6d.
No. 7	Prairie Tank	6/6d.
No. 8	Italian Tank	4/6d.
No. 9	Stirling 8 foot Single	7/6d.
No. 10	Deltic Diesel	10/6d.
No. 11	Battle of Britain Class	10/6d.
No. 12	Giant Swiss 'Crocodile'	10/6d.

ROSEBUD KITMASTER LIMITED

KC13

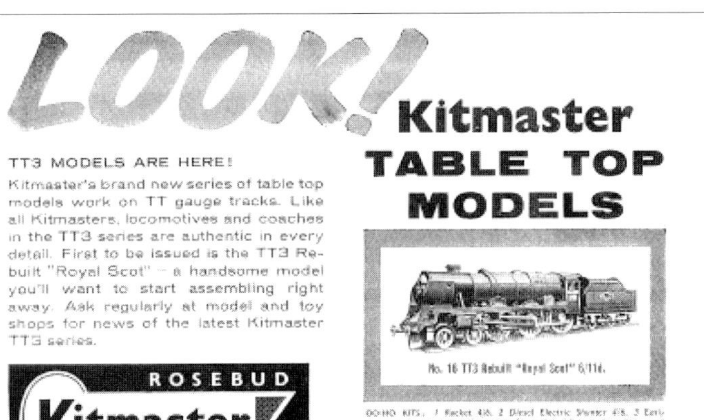

Kitmaster

NEW **TT3** SERIES

TT enthusiasts take note! The first three models in Kitmaster's exciting new TT3 series are in the shops now. Wonderful to build . . . to collect . . . to run on your TT tracks. Hurry! Be among the first to build them.

TT3 No. 16 Re-built 'Royal Scot' 6/11d.
TT3 No. 17 Corridor Brake Second Coach 5/11d.
TT3 No. 18 Corridor Composite Coach 5/11d.

Fifteen OO gauge models now available.
Ask at your usual MODEL or TOY SHOP.

ROSEBUD KITMASTER LIMITED

KC15

LOCOMOTIVE REALISM

No. 19 Baureihe 23

NEW: "BAUREIHE 23" 10/6d

Judge it for yourself when you make Kitmaster's latest — the famous "Baureihe 23" from Germany. You can build an **international** collection of locos and coaches with sixteen OO-models and three for TT gauge tracks. New Kitmasters are issued every month! If you appreciate realism—start collecting Kitmaster models today.

FROM ALL MODEL AND TOY SHOPS

. . . by Kitmaster

OO Kits: *1 Rocket 4/6, 2 Diesel Electric Shunter 4/6, 3 Early American 'General' 6/6, 4 Coronation Class 10/6, 5 Schools Class 'Harrow' 7/6, 6 Saddle Tank 4/6, 7 Prairie Tank 6/6, 8 Italian Tank 4/6, 9 Stirling 8 foot Single 7/6, 10 Deltic Diesel 10/6, 11 Battle of Britain 10/6, 12 Swiss Crocodile 10/6, 13, 14, 15 B.R. Coaches 6/6 each.* TT3 Kits: *16 Rebuilt 'Royal Scot' 6/11, 17, and 18 B.R. Coaches 5/11 each.*

ROSEBUD KITMASTER LIMITED

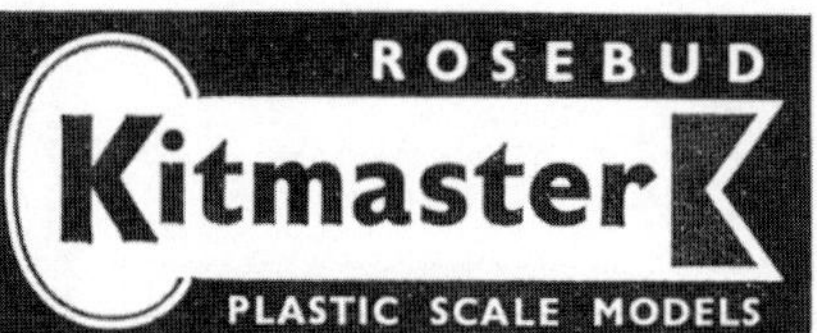

Kitmaster
NEW **TT3** SERIES

Here's big news for TT enthusiasts! The full range of Kitmaster's exciting new TT3 series is in the shops now. Four perfect scale models of B.R. Coaches to build yourself . . . plus the famous Re-built 'Royal Scot'. If you're a TT collector you must own all the models in the TT3 series. Hurry! See them at your favourite model shop today.

TT3 No. 16 Re-built 'Royal Scot' 6/11d.
TT3 No. 17 Corridor Brake Second Coach 5/11d.
TT3 No. 18 Corridor Composite Coach 5/11d.
TT3 No. 20 Corridor Second Coach 5/11d.
TT3 No. 21 Restaurant First Coach 6/6d.

Sixteen OO gauge models now available. Ask at your usual MODEL or TOY SHOP.

ROSEBUD
Kitmaster
PLASTIC SCALE MODELS

'OSEBUD KITMASTER LIMITED

add this new model to your

KITMASTER COLLECTION

Here's your chance to build a completely authentic model of Europe's most powerful express passenger locomotive. It's the French Railways 241P "Mountain" which hauls the famous "Mistral Express". It's the latest of Kitmaster's world famous list of locos and coach kits. The "Mountain" will bring your international collection of locomotives right up-to-date. Don't miss it! Ask to see it at your favourite model or toy shop today.
For OO gauge tracks.

KIT No. 23 FRENCH 241P "MOUNTAIN" 12/6

✳ LOOK OUT FOR NEXT MONTH'S NEW MODEL!

ROSEBUD KITMASTER LIMITED

Look! the latest

KITMASTER MODEL

KIT No. 24 'CITY of TRURO' 7/6

The 'City of Truro' was built in 1903 and was the first British locomotive to attain a speed of over 100 m.p.h. Now Kitmaster add this historic locomotive to their world famous list of loco and coach kits, and reproduce it in completely authentic detail. The 'City of Truro' is an actual scale model made from official blue prints and checked by British Railways designers. See it in your favourite model or toy shop, today. You can't afford to miss it! For 00 gauge tracks.

KC19

* LOOK OUT FOR NEXT MONTH'S NEW MODEL!

ROSEBUD KITMASTER LIMITED

British Railways' last steam locomotive

92000 CLASS "EVENING STAR" 10/6

–no Kitmaster collection is up-to-date without it

Western Region's "Evening Star" is the last of a long and glorious line of British-built steam locomotives. Named only in March this year, Kitmaster have added this history-making loco to their world-famous list of loco and coach kits.

Ask to see kit No. 22 for OO gauges *today!*

NOW AVAILABLE: *nineteen 00 gauge models, five TT3 models. At your usual model or toy shop.*

ROSEBUD KITMASTER LIMITED.

Add this new model to your

KITMASTER COLLECTION

Add the world-famous Stirling 8ft. Single to your Kitmaster collection. It was built in 1873 for the Great Northern Railway, had 8ft. diameter driving wheels, and was capable of 80 m.p.h. This authentic model is in all good model and toy shops *now*.

No. 9 Stirling 8ft. Single **7/6**

HAVE YOU MADE THESE EARLIER MODELS?

No. 1. Stephenson's "Rocket" **4/6**
No. 2. Diesel-electric shunter **4/6**
No. 3. Early American "General" **6/6**
No. 5. Schools class "Harrow" **7/6**
No. 6. Saddle tank **4/6**

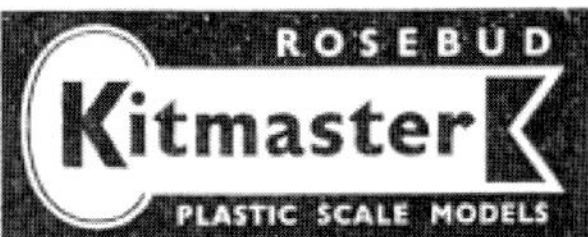

Authentic models with moving parts
Can be used on OO and HO gauge tracks

ROSEBUD KITMASTER LIMITED

Date	Code	Kit No(s)	Size on Page
04/59	KMC1	1,2,3,5	Full
05/59	KMC2	6	Full
06/59	KM2	6	Full
09/59	KMC3	9	Half
10/59	KMC4	7	Half
11/59	KMC5	4	Half
12/59	KMC6	8	Half
01/60	KC10	10	Half
02/60	KC11	11	Half
03/60	KC12	12	Half
04/60	KC13	13,14,15	Half
05/60	KC14	16	Half
06/60	KC15	16,17,18	Half
07/60	KC16	19	Half
08/60	KC15	16,17,18,20,21	Half
09/60	KC17	22	Half
10/60	KC18	23	Half
11/60	KC19	24	Half
12/60	KC20	22	Half

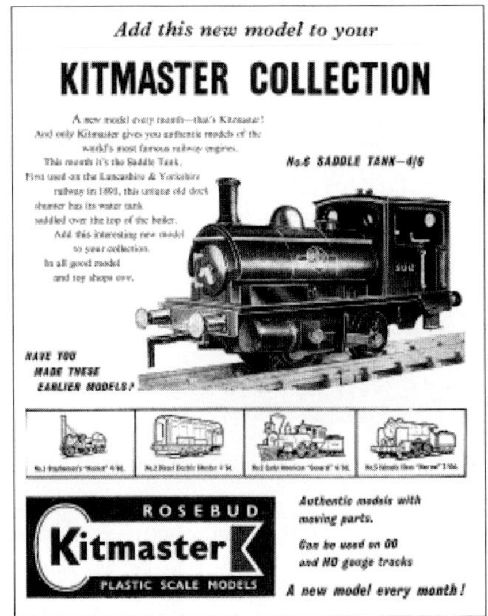

printings in KMCC archives include German, French, Italian and Swedish, also an interesting South African version with prices in Sterling and in Rand!
Dimensions: 140 x 190 mm closed, 280 x 380 mm opened flat.

Dealer Catalogues

These are certainly known to exist for 1959 and 1960, and were also presumably available for 1961. The 1959 catalogue resembles a larger version of the 1959 Retail leaflet, with the same artwork for the Pug and Duchess, but measuring 7 5/8" x 9 5/8" (194 x 244 mm) when closed. It is printed in full colour and is in the form of a simple four-page folder. The first twelve kits are illustrated. The catalogue details the advertising campaign for the initial launch and promotes special shop display units featuring an 0-6-0 diesel emerging from a tunnel mouth on a special plinth, which can also hold a kit box. It is extremely rare, far more so than the 1960 catalogue, but why this should be is not apparent.

The 1960 catalogue resembles a larger version of the 1960 Retail leaflet, with the same artwork for the Pug and Duchess with the date 1960 in the top right corner. However, this 12-page booklet is the same size as the 1959 trade catalogue. It is printed in full colour throughout and describes the range in some detail, including the Presentation Sets, with a mock up of the TT3 Set box. Special displays are promised and much is made of the new introductions planned for 1960. The catalogue comes with a separate smaller four-page Trade Price List, printed in black and red, featuring the Deltic artwork first used for advertisement KMC 12.

Colour Charts

These were published by Humbrol and included in the kits from 1960 onwards. They show the full range of colours available for Railway Modellers, including some Canadian liveries. Each colour is numbered and these numbers are referred to by Kitmaster in the instruction sheets. There were two editions of this 'Kitmaster Colour Chart'. Early editions, i.e. up to May 1961, do not show No. 134 SNCF Green, whilst those from August 1961 onwards include this colour. This meant reorganising the bottom half of the sheet. From this date, Humbrol advertised that '...one is included with every kit...'. We can speculate that this colour was introduced partly in response to the Kitmaster release of the SNCF Mountain Locomotive, as no other proprietary kits of

1959 KITMASTER CATALOGUES
Dimensions: 125 x 90 mm closed, 250 x 90 mm opened flat.

Type A Early 1959	Address block missing. Kit No. 2 is spaced with 2 dots only.
Type B Mid 1959	Address block added, upper and lower case letters. Kit No. 2 is spaced with 3 dots.
Type C Late 1959	Address block is 4 lines all capital letters. Kit No. 2 is spaced with 3 dots.
Type D Early 1960	Full address block, plus the name of the printer added to it. All in caps.
Type E USA 1 1959	Text includes OO scale, US address added, prices in US $
Type F USA 2 1960	Text reset to exclude OO scale, US address added, prices in US $
Type G Eire 1	Type A, but carries bold type inside "Prices only valid in Eire" with higher £ prices shown. Kit No. 10 spaced with two dots, Regd. TM is above Made in England.
Type H Eire 2	As above, except kit No. 10 has no dots, Made in England is above Regd. TM. This was included with some P1 sets.
Type AZ Australian	As Type A but with higher prices in shillings.
Type AI1 Italian	As Type A above, but text in Italian: Lire price of Prairie is LT575
Type AI2 Italian	As Type AI1, but price of Prairie corrected to read LT825
Type AI2b Italian	As Type AI2, but text now printed in blue ink throughout.
Type AU Universal	As Type A above, but no prices. English text. Used in Canada.
Type AUb Universal	As Type A above, but prices blocked out in black overprint.
Type AS Swedish	As Type A above, but text in Swedish, confirmed
Type AD German	As Type A above, but text in German
Type AA Austria	As Type A above, but text in German , prices in Austrian Schillings, confirmed.
Type AF French	As Type A above, but text in French, confirmed
Type AN Dutch	As Type A above, but text in Dutch

lining the models. Dimensions: 190 x 203 mm closed, 380 x 203 mm opened flat.

Gauges and Scales
Kitmaster models were modelled to four constant scales, 1:76 for the OO models, 1:87 for the HO kits, 1:100 for the TT3 models, and 1:16 for the Ariel Arrow. Only the Arrow shows the actual scale ratio on the box front. The railway kits show the gauge to which the axles are set. Consequently, the claim on the front of the boxes of 1:76 kits that they are 'Suitable for OO and HO gauge track' is misleading. The earlier Continental prototypes, [8] [12] [19] [23] as noted above, were designed to OO 4 mm Scale, whilst the French rolling stock existed. Dimensions: 90 x 96 mm closed, 90 x 192 mm open flat. Type A (Early type) Bottom right corner has no colour. Type B (Later type) Bottom right corner shows SNCF Green No. 134.

The 1960 Kitmaster Trade Catalogue carried this wonderful page on the forthcoming Motor Bogies. Unfortunately, the TT bogie never got beyond review samples.

Colour Card
The Humbrol/Kitmaster Lining Colours Colour Card is now a very scarce item indeed. The card is a set of Humbrol Enamel Colours in small gelatin capsules mounted on a plastic 'palette' of circular shape which is itself held between a sheet of folded and glued card. The card is printed in full colour on the outside and features both company logos. The front depicts a heavily stylised Duchess, with the palette forming the smokebox front. The reverse has nine of the 1959 catalogued locomotives printed in full colour, whilst the inside gives useful hints and tips on mixing the primary colours to obtain certain railway lining colours and on later ones, the DB and SNCF coaches, the General, the Hudson and ill-fated CN U-4-a, [27] [29] [34] and [37], were, or would have been, modelled in HO scale for export markets.

The OO kits were built to 4 mm/ft scale with 16mm gauge wheels. The HO scale 3.5 mm/ft kits have the same gauge of 16mm, but these kits were proportionally smaller. This is best seen when a Kitmaster Mountain is compared with a continental model of the

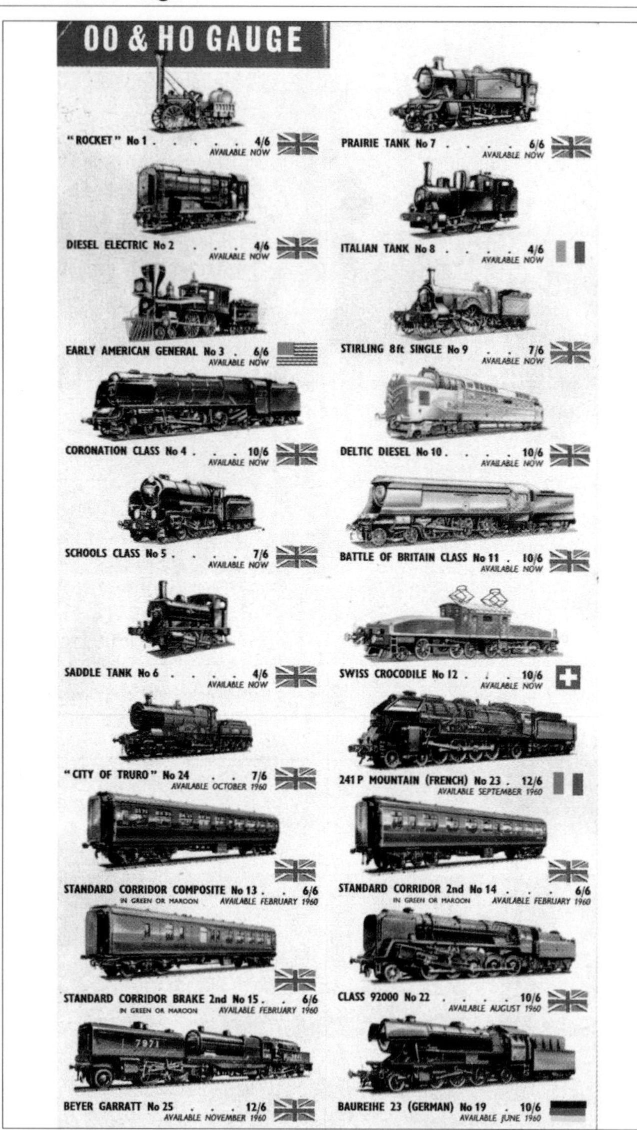

Inside of the fold-out 1960 catalogue leaflet.

***Evening Star* graced the front cover of Kitmaster's 1961 retail catalogue.**

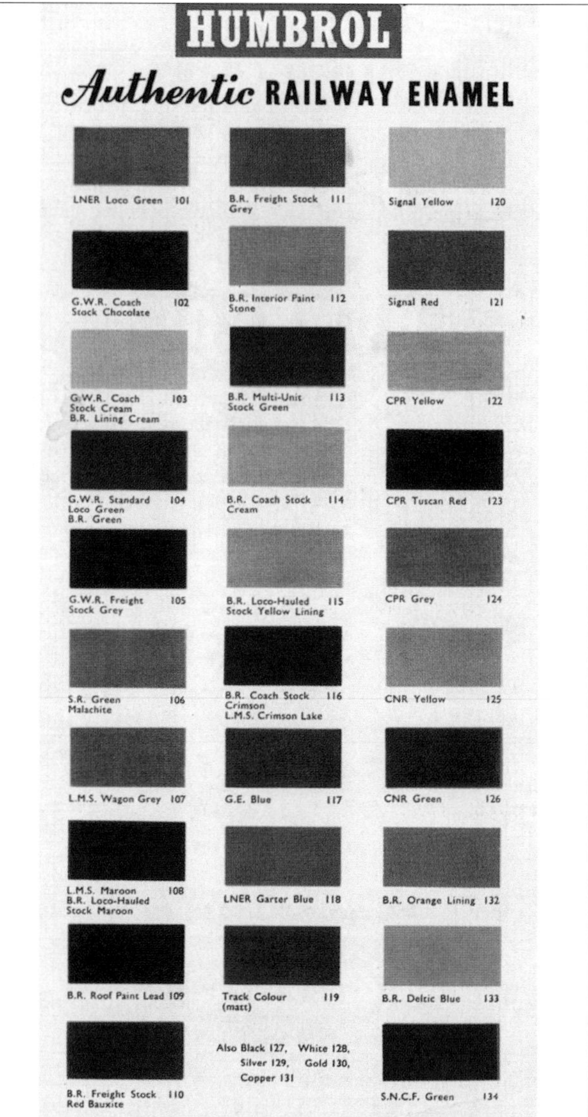

The Humbrol Colour Chart was packed with most kits. It exists in two versions, with and without SNCF green.

same locomotive, for example, from Jouef. The dimensions of the Kitmaster version show it to be completely over-scale.

This also applies to some of the other Continental models in the range, notably [3] [8] [12] and [19]. However, the German B4 [27] and SNCF Mistral [29] coaches are very well proportioned for Continental modelling. Perhaps this explains the disappointing European sales of some of the kits, since although they would indeed run on HO gauge track, the completed OO scale model would appear gargantuan when running with HO scale rolling stock.

TT3 Scale, at 3 mm/ft, also suffered from these problems of incompatible gauge/scale ratio. The gauge was set at 12 mm by Tri-ang Railways when they introduced TT (which stands for Table Top) Scale, which is incorrect for the 3 mm scale. Thus, the TT Rebuilt Royal Scot on TT track seems just as badly proportioned as the OO Coronation Pacific on OO track.

It is worth noting that the original Airfix rolling stock was also described as being for OO and HO gauge track. In fact, all the Airfix rolling stock kits were made to OO scale except the 'Interfrigo' Refrigerator wagon, which was HO scale because of the Continental prototype.

Front cover of the 1960 Trade Price List featuring the Deltic artwork from the 10th Kitmaster press advertisement.

Above and below right. **Two pages from the 1959 Kitmaster Trade Catalogue outlining their media plan and introducing the World's first fully plastic scale model railway kit.**

KITMASTER and AIRFIX in COLOUR

ROSEBUD
Kitmaster
PLASTIC SCALE MODELS
1960

Kitmaster models, when properly assembled, can make really attractive additions to any layout. Here we present them in all their glory. Built exactly as per the instruction sheets and finished according to the colour painting guide in each kit, behold Rosebud-Kitmaster in colour... The 1960 catalogue heralds the great things to come; below, the mighty Coronation Pacific.

Extreme contrast – the 'ice cream cart' (as its juvenile – and not so juvenile – admirers termed the DELTIC) and the WR 61XX suburban tank.

The possibilities of kit bashing – above, Kitmaster coaches transmuted into Southern Electric. Below – the renowned shunter, only likely to be bettered by Bachmann's new effort.

The Kitmaster models were customarily painted in fairly garish fashion – witness the Royal Scot – but the Blue Pullmans were often very effectively done.

One of the most celebrated of all – BIGGIN HILL.

The 2-2-4-0 that was... the BR 76000 Mogul. Below – the Airfix shunter and railbus.

100 years of steam – with the Stirling Single below.

From sublime to ridiculous – Kitmaster shop display and the various dolls.

Motorise your kit! These were effectively the beginnings of a vast expansion in 'kit bashing'. Below: Kitmaster's superb 'Ariel' motorbikes – boxed and packaged.

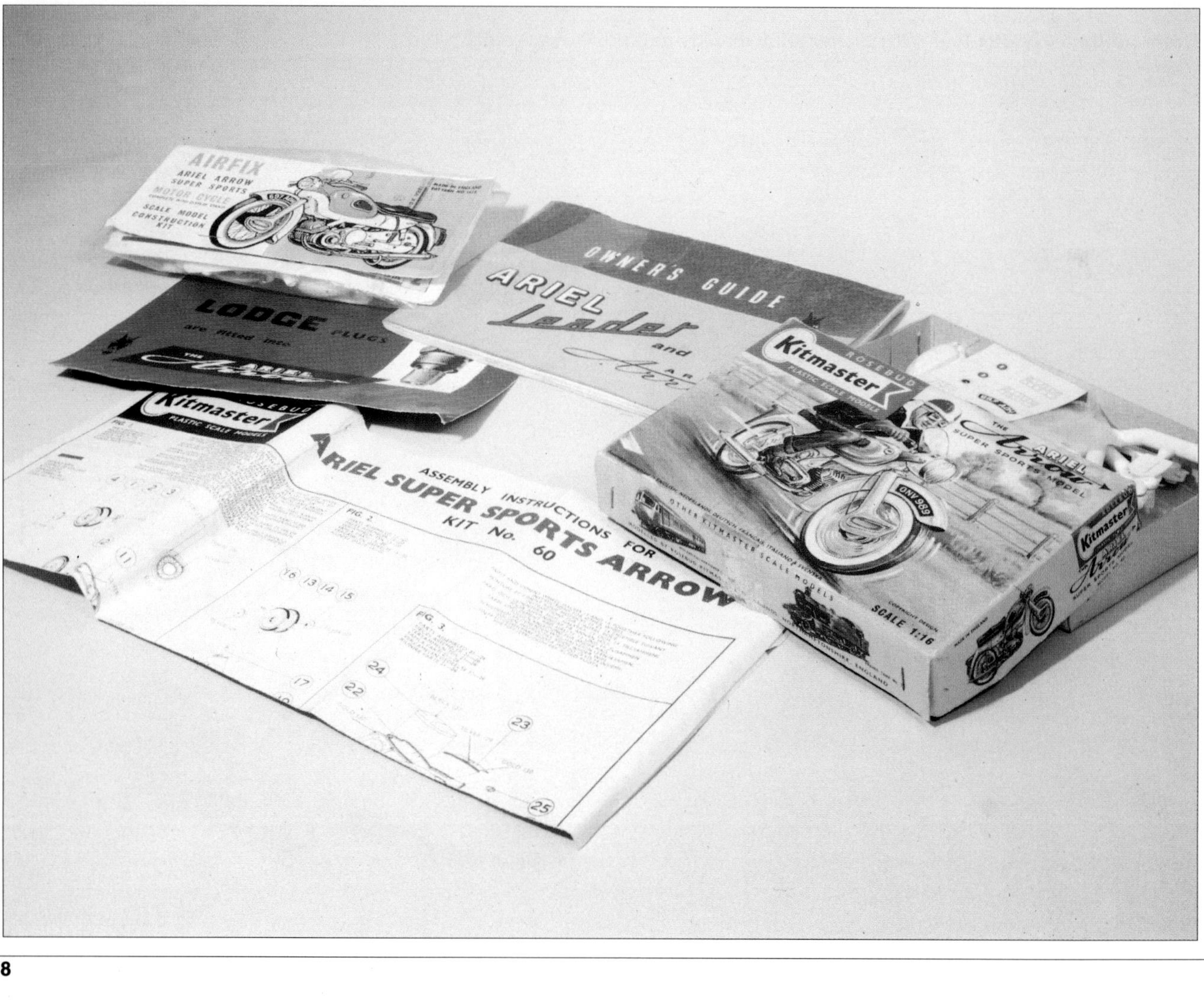

Box portrait of the L&Y Pug, deep in a stylised Lancashire industrial landscape – below, 'Rocket' variety.

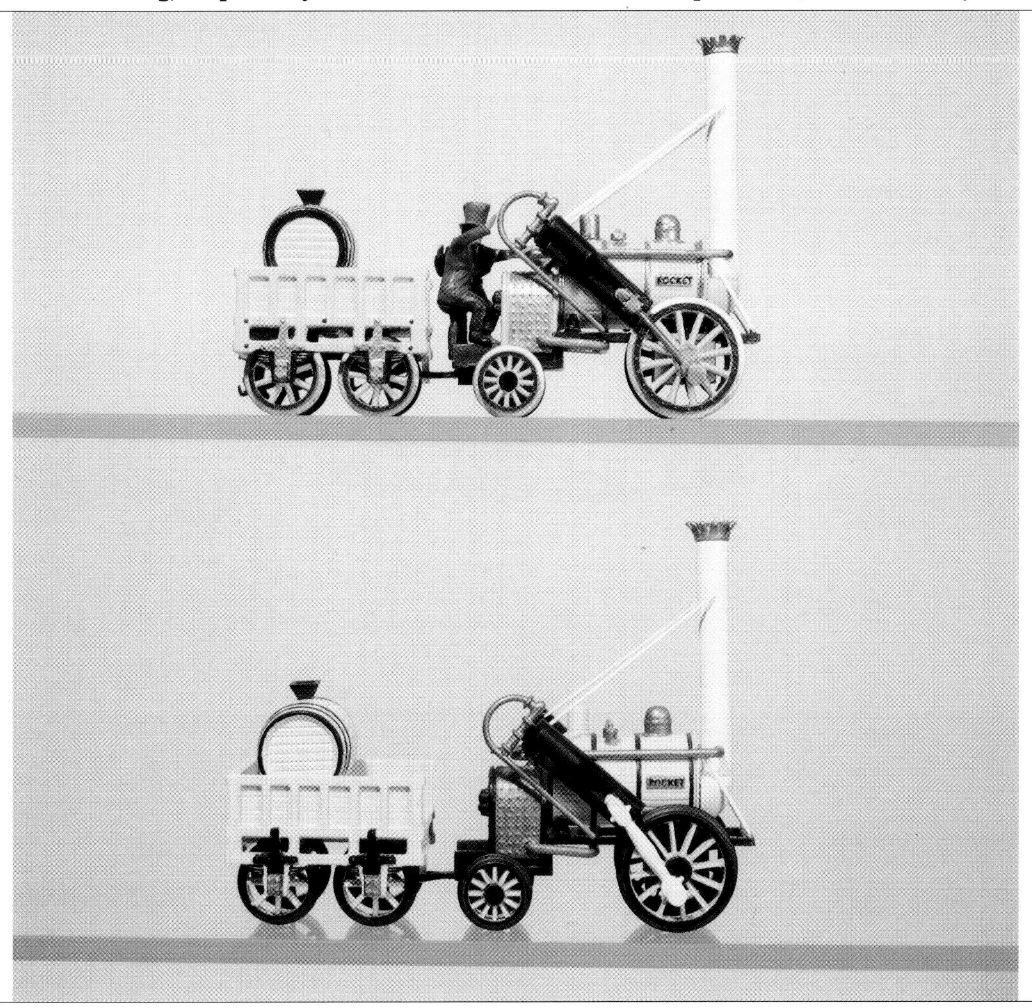

The scale-correctness and detail of the Kitmaster coaches ensured their popular success. The adaptations and variations that stretched away before the modeller were endless.

In a modellers' market now awash with every conceivable detail variation of coaching and wagon stock, it is hard to recall now just how much of an impact the Kitmaster models made.

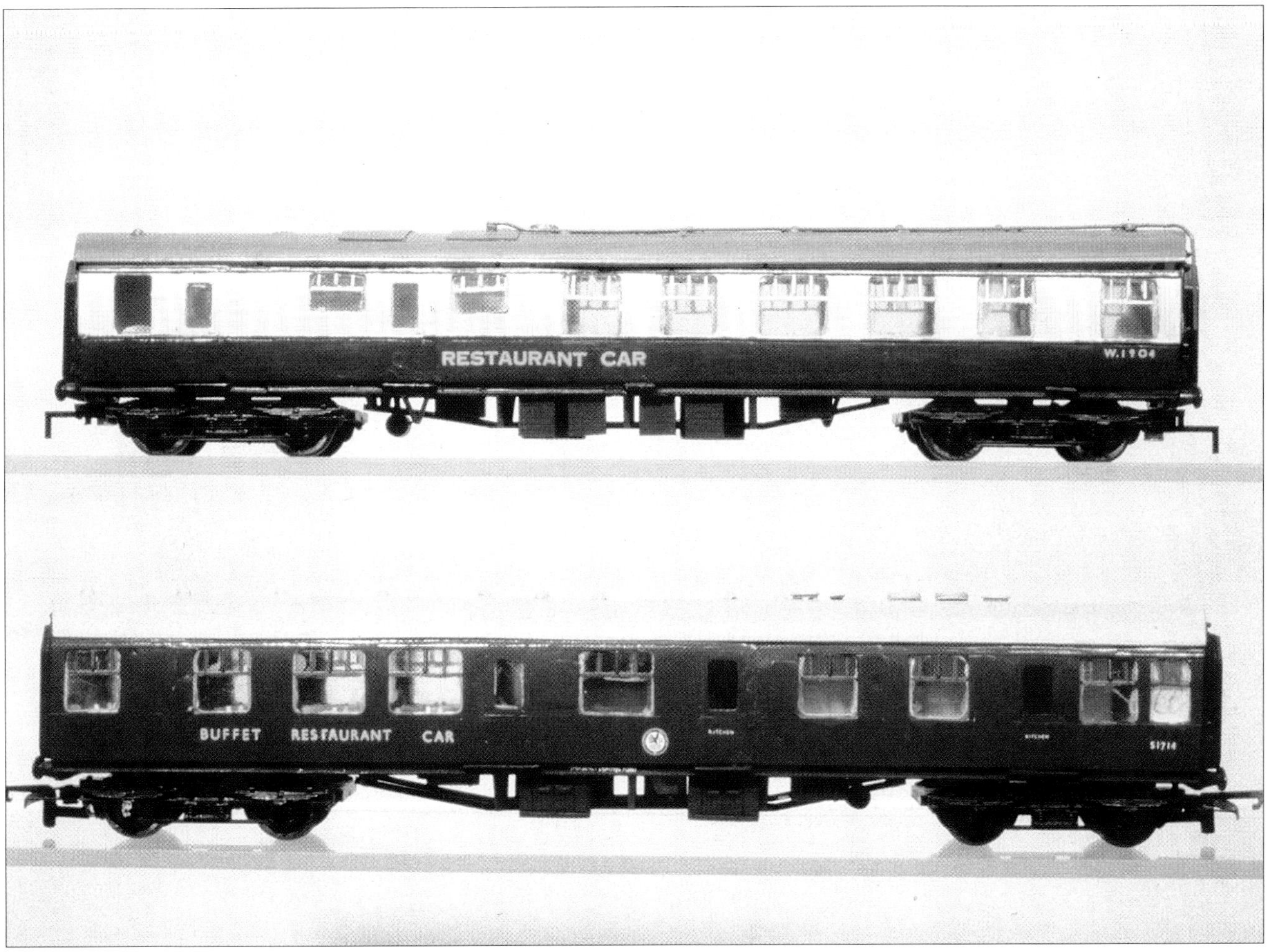

Wild West meets the French – the eclectic quality of the kits was one of their principal attractions.

Few would have thought to motorise the *Krokodil*, though one correspondent reported a motorised version from a layout on public display near Melbourne in Australia, along with various UK and American proprietary items. Below – *Peco's Perfect Partitions!*

APPENDIX ONE - INDEX TO RAILWAY JOURNAL ENTRIES

[A] Railway Modeller

Date	Page	Description
3.59	XV	Review of range and [2]
	VI	H A Blunt Retailer's announcement of [1] [2] [3] [5]
4.59	XIII	KMC1 Full page ad for [1] [2] [3] [5]
	100	Review of [1] [3]
5.59	VII	KMC2 Full page ad for [6]
	124	Review of [6]
6.59	IX	KMC2 Full page ad for [6]
	148	Article: Changes in P.T. - Kitmaster not affected
7.59	157	Feature: Motorising the Kitmaster Pug
9.59	X	KMC3 half page ad for [9]
10.59	V	Peco Perfecta (1) for [6]
	VIII	KMC4 half page ad for [7]
	XI	Ad for Surrey Models motorising kit for [5]
	224	Review of Perfecta kit (1)
	226	Review of [9].
	227	Review of [7].
11.59	XVII	KMC5 half page ad for [4]
	XII	Ad for Surrey Models motorising kit for [5]
	251	Mention of [4]
12.59	VIII	KMC6 half page ad for [8]
	276	Letter suggesting [6] is not a Pug
	251	Review of [4] [8]
1.60	xxiv	KC 10 Half page ad for [10]
	18	Article: Notes on Kitmaster Models [4]
2.60	VI	KC 11 half page ad for [11]
	42	Letters: Answers to Pug letter (qv 12.59)
	47	Review of [11]
3.60	X	KC 12 half page ad for [12]
	XXV	Gamages ad for [13/14/15]
	74	Review of OO and TT Coaches and [10]
	74	Peco announce Perfecta kits for :
		(2) Italian Tank Available — Apr
		(3) Prairie — May
		(4) BoB Pacific — Jun
		(5) Duchess — Jul
	74	Photograph of [10]
	75	Review of Peco Coach Interiors
4.60	VII	Peco ad for coach interiors + Perfecta (2) for [8]
	XVI	KC 13 half page ad [13] [14] [15]
	98	Review of [12]
5.60	VII	Full page ad for Perfecta (2) for [8]
	X	KC 14 half page ad for [16]
	121	Review of Perfecta (2) for [8]
	121	Review of [13] [15]
6.60	II	KC 15 half page ad for [16] [17] [18]
7.60	X	KC 16 half page ad for [19]
	171	Review of [16] [18] [21]
	169	Review of BSK interior kit and [16]
8.60	VI	KC15 half page ad [16] [17] [18] [20] [21]
	195	Review of [17] [20]
9.60	V	Full page ad Peco Perfecta var. and interiors
	218	Review of [19]
	XIII	KC17 half page ad for [22]
10.60	VIII	Peco ad for SO Interior
	XXXI	KC18 Ad for [23]
	232/3	Feature: Motorising Old Timers (The General)
11.60	VII	Full page ad for Perfecta (4)
	266	Article: The Kitmaster Lamp
	206	Motorising the Railbus with a Rivarossi motor
	271	Review of (4) for [11]
	XVII	KC19 half page ad for [24]
12.60	III	Peco ad for interiors and Perfectas
	XIV	KC20 half page ad for [22]
1.61	XXI	H A Blunt composite prices for KM/Perfecta
	14	Article : Kitmaster Variations
	23	Review of [22]
2.61	40/1	Motorising the Railbus with Perfecta kit No. 1
3.61	78	Review of [24] [23]
4.61	X	Kitmaster/Humbrol Ad
5.61	112/3	Feature: Motorising the City of Truro
	122	Article: Kitmaster Modifications
	122	Article: Replacing Kitmaster Coach Windows
	129	Review of [25] [26]
	129	Airfix introduce cattle wagon and Brake van
7.61	V	Retailer Ad for [27] [28]
	169	Article: EM-ing the Kitmaster Coaches
	175	Review of KM1 and [27]
	???	Situations Vacant - Modelmaker required, apply Rosebud Kitmaster!
8.61	V	Full page Peco interiors ad
	191	Article: Bringing the Deltic up to date
	191	Article: Lining KM Coaches
	192	Article: Flexible coach connections
	193	Article: Fitting KM coach windows
10.61	XXVI	Humbrol/Kitmaster ad featuring the Mogul
	235/6	Feature: Motorising the Mogul
	253	Review of [30]
11.61	XXVIII	Humbrol/Kitmaster ad featuring the Mogul
12.61	VI	Ad for Perfecta (1)
	302	Review of [31]
	305	Southgate chassis for Railbus intro
2.62	39	Kitmaster Prairie to 4-4-2 Atlantic!
	XIX	K's Pullman motor bogies and sideframes
3.62	FC	'A Corner Station'- pic shows four KM locos
	54	Charford - pic is 'denationalised' 21C157
	64	A Sludge Tender - conversion from Schools
	64/5	Corridor connections for KM Coaches
	65	Kitmaster Diesel Pullman
	67	Motorising the Prairie
4.62	91	Duchess to Jubilee
	98	Brass motorising kit for Stirling
5.62	115	'Painting Simplified' Stirling/9F etc..
	117	Motorising the J94
	118	Transformer wagon with KM parts
	118	Airfix couplings on KM coach bogies
7.62	170	W and H announce wheel kits for KM locos
8.62	175	Layout- Belindavon and Llanderek - many KM
10.62	240	A Kitmaster-Fleischmann conversion - Hudson
11.62	259	Various Pug conversions
	266	Extra weight for plastic kit locos
12.62	297	Announcement: Airfix purchase moulds and stock
3.63	57/58	Various KM in action
6.63	134	Kitmaster coach windows
	143	Tender conversion using [4] parts
7.63	VII	Ariel Arrow reintroduced by Airfix
		Airfix introduce Lowmac and JCB
8.63	IX	Tri-ang Blue Pullman introduced
9.63	FC/198	'The Long Thin Look' 6-car Pullman set pics
10.63	VII	Ad for Airfix Prairie Tank
	232	'A 4 Car EMU' Pic of KM1 in use
	252	News of the Airfix Prairie [7] reintroduction with new pic
11.63	XIX	H A Blunt Prairie Pack ad Kit/Romford wheels/Phantom motor
1.64		Airfix reintroduce [26]
3.64		Airfix reintroduce [6]
12.64		Airfix reintroduce [1]
5.65		Airfix reintroduce [24]
12.65	317	Midland Pullman in action
4.68	???	Beatties of London offering KM2 at 25s each.
3.81	80/1	Motorising the City of Truro
12.89	544	Plastic Surgery for Archaeologists - Stirling conversions.

[B] Model Railway News

Date	Page	Description
3.59	xxiii	Gamages ad featuring [2] [3] Press shots
	69/70	DEJ3 Intro foretold
4.59	iii	KMC1 full page ad
5.59		KMC2 full page ad for [6]
6.59	vii	KM2 full page ad for [6]
7.59	166/7	Review of [5] and [6]
9.59	xix	KMC3 half page ad for [9]
10.59	vii	SMRS motor ad for [5]
	ix	Peco announce Perf.(1) for [6]
	210	Reviews of [7] [9]
	xxvii	KMC4 for [7]
11.59	x	SMRS
	236	Review of [4] with pic
	242	Pug letters
	xxi	KMC? half page ad for [4]
12.59	xii	Peco ad inc (1)
	xxxiii	KMC6 half page for [8]
1.60	xvii	KC10 half page ad for [10]
2.60	xii	KC 11 for [11]
	xiii	SMRS
	73	Review of [11]
	74	pic of [11]
3.60	vi	KC12 half page ad for [12]
	95	Review of [10] with pic.
	118	Gamages ad for [13-16]
4.60	vii	Peco ad for interiors and (2)
	130	Brighton Fair - Kitmaster pavilion reviewed prototype of box van shown. Pics of 15/13 and interiors. Announce Croc and 1960 Catalogue
	xxiii	KC13 for [13/14/15]
5.60	XXV	J. N. Maskelyne biog
	X	KC14 half page ad for [16]
	XII	Half page ad for Perfecta (2) for [8]
	XIX	Bradshaws ad inc 1960 KM releases and pic of [14]
	176	The Last One by J. N. Maskelyne
6.60	iii	Southgate ad for Motorised Utility Van 'Southgate Special'
	xiii	KC15 half page ad for [16][17][18]
	xvi	K's ad for tender drive units
	225	Jennings introduce wheels for [2]
7.60	ix	Airfix intro of Cement/Oil wagons
	xi	KC 16 for [19]
	xiv	K's tender chassis
8.60	xi	KC 15 for [16-21]
	278	J. N. Maskelyne - An Appreciation
	300	pic [16] Reviews [16][17]
9.60	xiii	Perfecta (2) ad
	xiii	KC 17 for [22] half page
10.60	xvi	KC18 for [23] half page
11.60	xiv	KC 19 for 24
	410	pic of [19]
	xxiii	Peco ad for Perf. (4) for [11]
12.60	xviii	KC20 for [22] half page
1.61	9	Review of [22]
4.61	15	Review of [23] [24]
5.61	179	Review of [25] [26]
7.61	272	Review of [27] [28]
8.61	301	Review of [29]
9.61	XXV	Humbrol ad featuring J94
11.61	416	[30] picture only
12.61	455	[31] picture
	458	[31] [32] reviewed
1.62	22	Pic of [32][33]
5.62	xiv	K's Deltic chassis/sideframes ad
7.62	iv	W&H ad for wheel kits [6] [7] [30]
7.62	266	Airfix announce Interfrigo and Meat Van
8.62	xiii	H A Blunt ad for Romford [7]
9.62	361-4	An Approach to good kit construction -[4]
12.62	xi	Romford kits for [5] [25]
8.63	iii	Airfix ad for intro of Lowmac/JCB
		Airfix reintroduce Ariel Arrow
10.63	52	Airfix preview of Prairie [7] reintro
	56	Photograph of new Prairie [7]
1.64	175	Painting the Prairie
2.64	iii	reintro of J94 [26] Ad
	242	Review of J94 [26]
3.64	iii	reintro of Pug [6] Ad
	279/80	Review of Pug [6]
4.64	iii	Intro of Prestwin Silo wagon Ad
5.64	325	Airfix at Nürnberg Toy Fair

8.64	469	Airfix at Central Hall
12.64	iii	reintro of Rocket [1] Ad
	622	Rocket [1] and 9F [22] Reintro noted
10.67	475	New ad for Airfix Prairie
6.72	ins F/C	Humbrol ad featuring a Kitmaster 9F [22]
8.74	ins F/C	Humbrol ad featuring an Airfix Schools

[C] Model Railway Constructor

Date	Page	Description
3.59	69	Review and pic of [2]
4.59	76/7	Mechanising the Rosebud Kitmaster diesel
	90/1	Review and photos of [1] [2] [3]
3/4.59		Review of [2]
6.59	132/3	The General goes to town (with a Terrier motor)
	140/1	Reviews and photo of [5] [6]
7.59	162	Pugs motorised
8.59	174	Motorising the Schools
	183	Pic of [9]
9.59	ix	KMC3 ad for [9]
	194/5	A Stirling Loco (Motorising)
	208	Review of [7] and [9]
10.59	ix	SMRS
	216/7	Motorising the Kitmaster Prairie
	228	Review of Perfecta (1) for [6]
11.59		Review of [4]
12.59	ix	SMRS
	261	Fairlie Pug!
	271	Review of [6] with pic
1.60	viii	KC10 ad for [10]
2.60	vi	KC11 ad for [11]
	44	Review of [11]
	45	Fiddlers end - Pug to NG 0-4-2!
3.60	VI	KC12 half page ad for [12]
	52-53	Motorising the Deltic
	69	Kitmaster 1960 News pic of [12] [15]
4.60	iv	Half page ad KC13 for coaches
	96	Review of CK + [12] + pics
	97	Trade report- KM1 Perfecta and interiors
5.60	vi	Half page ad KC14 for [16]
	122	[14] noted
6.60	iv	KC15 half page ad for [16][17][18]
	134	Photo of [9]
	139	'From a Swedish Enthusiast' Comical text accompanies shot of motorised Pug and Shunter!
	146	Review and photo of [15]
7.60	IV	KC16 half page ad for [19]
	V	Airfix introduce Presflow Cement and Oil Tank
	170	Peco interior kits review with pic
8.60	192	Review of [16]
	193	Review of Tank and Presflow
	194	Review of [17]
9.60	vi	Half page ad KC17 for [22]
	198/9	Motorising the TT Scot
	215	Review of Peco BSK interior
	216	Review of Perfecta (2) for [7]
10.60	vi	Taylor & McKenna ad including P2 Set
	vii	KC18 half page ad for [23]
	226	Motorising the DB 23
	240	Review of [19]
11.60	251/2	A4 into Bulleid Light Pacific
	252	Kitmaster BR Standard Coaches
12.60	v	Airfix Railbus intro ad
	vi	Half page ad K20 for [22]
	287/8	Motorising the Railbus
	293	Review of Peco SO interior
	295	Mike Bryant letter on Perfectas
1.61	7-9 and FC	4-CEP unit from Kitmaster coaches I
	20	Review of [22]
2.61	47	Letters on Bryant motorising article
3.61	49	Photo of 241P
	56	Motorising the Kitmaster 2-10-0
	58	A Full Brake Van Kitmaster Conversion
	65	Review of City of Truro [24]
	68	Kitmaster 1961 Trade Fair report - review of range
	69	Airfix intro Booth Crane and Mineral wagon
	70	Peco Perfecta changes intro of (5) for [24] and (1a) for Railbus/XT60
4.61	vi	Airfix intro ad for Booth crane
	96	Kitmaster conversion 1 - SO to RMB
	87/8/9	Kitmaster conversion 2 - GW Mogul from Prairie and Truro
	100	Review of [23] and Booth
5.61	v	Airfix intro of Cattle wagon
	129	Review of Cattle and Brake
6.61	143/4	Kitmaster BCK conversion
	152	Review of [25]
	156	Letter on GW Mogul conv.
7.61	174	Finishing touches for Kitmaster Couplings
	180	Review of [26] with pic
	181	Review of [28] and [27] with pics
8.61	198/9	Motorising a Kitmaster Beyer-Garratt 2-6-6-2
	203	Review of [29]
9.61	218/9	City of Truro pics
	226	First Open conversions - FO, FK, BFK
	231	Duchess pic
10.61	iii	Airfix intro of Drewry
	239/40/1	Motorising the Kitmaster J94
	244	4-BEP conversion and MLV
	257	Review of [30] and Airfix 04 with pics
11.61	ix	Humbrol ad for [30]
	280/1	Motorising the Kitmaster 4MT Mogul
12.61	xi	Humbrol ad for [31]
	304	Motorising the Airfix Drewry Shunter
	311	Review of [31] [32] [33] [KM1]
1.62	F/C	[31] in action!
3.62		Review of [34]
5.62	135	Letter 'More Market Research'; bigoted reactionary bullshit!
7.62	iii	Airfix intro of Interfrigo and Meat
	vi	Romford kits for [7][26][30] in W&H ad
	165-7	Kitmaster catering vehicle conversion RB and RF
	182	Review of Interfrigo and Meat Van
8.62	III	Airfix introduce 10t Meat Van
	IV	[31] in Alan Brett Cannon ad
	197	A Kitmaster Open Brake Second BSO
10.62	249	A Kitmaster Unclassed Restaurant Car
	256	Kitmaster coach lighting
11.62	iii	Airfix intro of Scarab
	vii	Romford kits for [5] + [25] in W&H ad
	292	Review of Scarab
	293	Review of Airfix Old Bill Bus!
12.62		A Kitmaster Kitchen Buffet RKB/KB
6.63	?	Conversion of KM coaches and Airfix Railbus to Class 301 Clacton Set
7.63	?	Conversion of KM coaches and Airfix Railbus to Class 301 Clacton Set II
2.64	iii	Airfix J94 reissue ad
	242	Airfix J94 review
12.64	iii	Airfix 9F reissue ad
	321	'Maurice Onions - Designer' Pug Conversions
	70	A Kitmaster MLV conversion
4.65	106	Prototype pic of [27]
	108	Review of Airfix Truro noting tool changes
11.67	iv	W&H half page ad for reimported KM4/5/8/9/10/11/12/KM1

[D] Airfix Magazine

6.60	39	Review 13/14/15
7.60	78	Pic of KM Deltic
	84	Airfix intro of Tank/Presflo
8.60	127	Photo of Pug
9.60	191	The Kitmaster Story
11.60	258	TT reviews
	274/5	Motorising the Railbus
	276	Railbus review
12.60	302	Review of [22] with pic
3.61	466	Future production
	467	Review of [23] [24]
4.61	504	Breakdown Crane Conversion
5.61	572	Review of [26] with pic
	576	Motive Power photo
6.61	35	Reviews of [27] [28]
8.61	134	Review of [29]
10.61	232	Review of [30]
11.61	278	Review of [31] with pic
12.61	328	Review of [32] with pic
1.62	373	Review of [33] with pic.
2.62	417	Full page Humbrol Britfix/[31]/HMS Eagle ad
3.62	447	Review of [60] with pic
	448	Review of [34} with pic
6.62	10	Working dockside crane Pt1
7.62	42	Working dockside crane Pt2
8.62	88	Review of Romford motorising kits for [9] [22] [26]
12.62	206	Scarab variations
1.63	236	Variations on the Drewry Diesel motorisation
7.63	B/C	Full colour ad for XL5
8.63	74	Working Overhead Travelling Cranes Pt1
9.63	10	Working Overhead Travelling Cranes Pt2
10.63	40	Motorising Airfix Railbus
1.64	152	Motorising Airfix Prairie Tank
2.64	188	Modelling Airfix BR Scarabs
5.64	290	Pug narrow gauge conversion
6.64	308	Motorising the Pug
9.64	8	Motorising the J94
1.65	141	Motorising Evening Star Pt1
2.65	168	Motorising Evening Star Pt2
7.65	329	Motorising City of Truro
9.66	8	Making Plastic valve gear run smoothly
11.66	80	Motorising Drewry Shunter
2.67	200	Detailing City of Truro
5.67	320	GW Mogul from Truro + Prairie
6.67	366	Motorising 4MT Mogul
8.67	450	Variations on the Mogul
9.67	14	Truro to Aberdare 2-6-0
11.67	98	Truro to County
12.67	136	Truro to Bulldog
2.68	216	Truro to Curved-frame Bulldog
3.68	260	More Bulldog Bird variants
4.68	316	Dukedog from Truro + Prairie
5.68	342	Prairie to 2-8-0 42XX
6.68	384	Truro to Flowers and Atbaras
9.68	24	Prairie + Tri-ang 0-6-0 to 56XX
10.68	60	Pug to crane tank
1.69	212	Motorising Biggin Hill Pt1
2.69	254	Motorising and Detailing Biggin Hill Pt2
3.69	298	Tender detailing for Biggin Hill
5.69	410	Converting Pugs to narrow gauge
7.69	488	Fireless locos from Pugs
12.69	164	Schools to Thompson B1

[E] Model Maker

3.59	Publicity	H. A. Blunt ad for range [1] [2] [3] [5]
4.59	Publicity	H. A. Blunt ad for range [1] [2] [3] [5]
5.59	Publicity	H. A. Blunt ad for range [1] [2] [3] [5]
6.59	Publicity	Mail Order Models [1][2][3][5][6]
9.59	Publicity	H. A. Blunt [9[
12.59	Publicity	H. A. Blunt ad for [6][9] and Perfectas for [6]{4}
1.60	Publicity	KC10 half page ad for [10]
2.60	Publicity	KC11 half page ad for [11]
3.60	Publicity	KC12 half page ad for [12]
4.60	Publicity	KC13 half page ad for [13]
5.60	I.F.C	KC14 half page ad for [16]
6.60	Publicity	KC15 half page ad for [16][17][18]
8.60	Publicity	KC17 half page ad for [22]
12.60	Publicity	H. A. Blunt ad for [22[
8.61	441	Review of [29]
9.61	Publicity	Half page Humbrol/Kitmaster ad featuring [30]
1.62	45	Review of [31][32][33]

[F] Meccano Magazine

9.59	iv	KMC3 half page ad for [9]
10.59	viii	KMC4 half page ad for [7]
11.59	x	KMC5 half page ad for [4]
12.59	xiv	KMC6 half page ad for [8]
1.60	xv	KC10 full page ad for [10]
2.60	xi	KC11 full page ad for [11]
3.60	xvii	KC12 full page ad for [12]
4.60	xv	KC13 full page ad for [13][14][15]
5.60	xv	KC14 full page ad for [16]
6.60	xiii	KC15 full page ad for [16][17][18]
7.60	xv	KC16 full page ad for [19]
8.60	ix	KC15 full page ad for [16][17][18][20][21]
9.60	xv	KC17 full page ad for [22]
10.60	xiii	KC18 full page ad for [23]
11.60	xv	KC19 full page ad for [24]
12.60	xxi	KC18 full page ad for [22]
5.61	viii	Half page Humbrol/Kitmaster ad for J94
9.61	xvii	Half page Humbrol/Kitmaster ad for J94

[G] Boys' Own Paper

5.61	9	Humbrol/J94 half page ad
8.61	59	Humbrol/J94 Full page ad
7.63	B/C	Full page colour ad for XL5

[H] The Victor

29.6.63	No. 123	Half page b/w ad for Fireball XL5

[I] European Railways

No1 1960	22	Reviews of 1960 range
No3 1960	24	Reviews of [16] [19]
No2 1961	24	Reviews of [24][23] and 1961 range
No4 1961	23	Reviews of [25] [27]

[J] Ian Allan Publications

ABC British Railway Locomotives

Summer 1959 Editions

Parts 1-4	Ins B/C	Range ad featuring [1] full page

Winter 1959/60 Editions

Parts 1-4	B/C	KMC5 full page for [4]

The Ian Allan Book of Model Railways, by Mike Bryant.

1960	43	Full Page Kitmaster ad, no code, 'Improve your layout'.
	45-47	Full description of Kitmasters with many pics inc. motorising by author.

[K] Montezuma Magazine

November 1962	Reprint of Model Railroader review of [34]

[L] Model Aircraft

6.59	ix	KCM 2 (sic) for [6] full page
11.59	xiv	KMC5 for [4] half page
12.59	xiv	KMC 6 for [8] half page

[M] Hobbies Weekly

8.4.59	11	KMC1 for [1][2][3][5] full page
6.5.59	B/C	'KCM2', should be KMC2 for [6] full page
10.6.59	?	KMC2? *This should exist, but has not been checked/found yet.*
9.9.59	301	Half page ad for [9], no ref, but is KMC3.
7.10.59	13	KMC4 for [7] half page ad
11.11.59	105	KMC5 for [4] half page ad
9.12.59	184	KMC6 for [8] half page ad

[N] Aero Modeller

No data

[O] Trains Illustrated

04.59	b/c	KMC1 for [1][2][3][5] full page
05.59	III	KMC2 for [6] full page
06.59	b/c	KMC2 for [6] full page
09.59	ii	KMC3 for [9] half page
10.59	xi	KMC4 for [7] half page
11.59	iv	KMC5 for [4] half page
12.59	x	KMC6 for [8] half page

[P] The Eagle

4.4.59	14	KMC (1) Range ad half page
2.5.9	14	KMC 2 for [6]
6.6.59	4	KMC2 for [6]
5.9.59	7	KMC 3 for [9] half page
3.10.59	4	KMC 4 for [7]
7.11.59	19	(KMC 5) for [4]
12.12.59	16	(KMC 6) for [8]

[Q] Express Weekly

No Data

[R] Model Railway Collector

Issue 2	All Stuck Up - Collecting Kitmaster Scale Models
Issue 3	Deltic Doodlings - The Kitmaster Deltic
Issue 5	Pullman Pulling Power - The Kitmaster Pullmans
Issue 6	Getting the Presentation (Sets) Right

[S] British Railway Modelling

May 1993	Collecting Kitmaster Models
June 1993	Battle of Britain Class in Detail
Aug 1993	Kitmaster 3 mm Models in Detail
Oct 1993	Blue Movers - The Pullman Cars
Nov 1993	Deltic Details - The Prototype Deltic
Jan 1994	Diesel Shunters

[T] Collectors Gazette

12.90	Sean Rothman article on Gerry Anderson - XL5
03.91	Andrew Burford et al. photo of XL5 kit
07.91	Letter about XL5 boxes

[U] Model Railway Enthusiast

10.94	25-30	Profile of the L&Y Pug
	61	Models that might have been [34]
04.95	9-14	The Story of Kitmaster full colour pics
01.96		Kitmaster Spin-Offs 4 pages with pics
09.96		Kitmaster Continental prototypes 6 pages with colour

[V] Practical Model Trains

03.87	27-32	A Tale of Three Cities - motorising the Airfix/Kitmaster City of Truro

[W] Rosebud News

Vol 1	No. 1	Sept/Oct 1953
	No. 2	Nov/Dec 1953
	No. 3	Jan/Feb 1954
	No. 4	Summer 1954
	No. 5	Winter 1954
	No. 6	Winter 1955

[X] Model and Miniature Railways

Partworks	p.425-7	Plastic Kits Part 2: Locomotives and Rolling Stock, by Paul Towers.

[Y] Northamptonshire Evening Telegraph

June 16th 1964	Front Page Receiver Appointed for Rosebud Dolls

Appendix Two - A Short Chronology of Rosebud

1916 22nd April, Thomas Eric Smith born in London.
1934 T. Eric Smith takes over the family toy-making business in London.
1940 October Mrs Smith and Eric move to Raunds with Masks Ltd. and Nene Plastics Ltd. founded.
1946 12th June, T. Eric Smith marries Hazel.
1946 November, T. Eric Smith is demobilised and returns to Raunds, Northants.
1946 21st November Nene Plastics Ltd registered at Companies House, no. 424125.
1946 18th December Nene Plastics raises mortgage to buy part of site
1947 7th April larger mortgage (£6k) raised with Halifax to purchase the bulk of the site
1947 Nene Plastics Ltd. buys Masks Ltd., launches Starlight Dolls.
1947 20th March T. Eric Smith registers the 'Rosebud' trademark for dolls, No. 657461.
1949 Nene Plastics Ltd. appoints L. Rees and Co. as concessionaires for Rosebud Dolls.
1950 T. Eric Smith obtains two patents for doll manufacture by the injection moulding process using PVC. No. 667091 and 667906.
1953 Sept.,10000 sq ft of land is cleared to make way for new injection moulding shop.
1954 New PVC plant comes on line.
1954 'Neneware' kitchen utensils launched.
1954 1st January, T. Eric Smith awarded Knight of Dalcassian Order (Irish).
1954 1st February, new injection moulding plant goes on line.
1955 27th January, company name changed to Rosebud Dolls Ltd.
1955 Target to produce 5,000,000 dolls per year.
1955 Winter, 'Neneware' and 'Masks' dropped in favour of Rosebud as doll sales soar 63%.
1956 Wellingborough, Rock Street premises acquired for doll production.
1956 'Rosebud Walking Doll' launched.
1956 August, T. E. Smith has 'Broadfield House' constructed behind factory site and moves from Ashfield Hall.
1958 'Rosebud Teenage Dolls' introduced.
1958 Rosebud Kitmaster Ltd, Grove St., Raunds incorporated.
1958 13th November, Design Applications lodged with Patent Office.
1958 27th November Charge on assets agreed with Barclays Bank
1958 Association with L. Rees and Co terminated.
1959 A. A. Hales exclusive distributor.
1959 Doll production passes 4,800/day.
1959 27th April, Registered Design Nos. 891073-8 certified.
1959 March, Railway Modeller previews the Diesel Shunter kit.
1959 March-December, Rosebud Kitmaster introduce first kits, Nos. 1-12 and P1 set.
1959 December, T.E Smith announces relocation to Wellingborough.
1960 Rosebud Kitmaster introduce kits Nos. 13-24.
1960 E. Keil and Co. distributing in addition to A. A. Hales.
1960 Spring Rosebud Dolls Ltd. move to new factory in Westfield Rd, Wellingborough, freeing space at Raunds.
1960 March, Arby Perfecta Range introduced.
1960 8th September New finance package through Credit for Industry Ltd agreed to finance Wellingborough site.
1960 'Rosebud Big Dolls' launched.
1960 December, Kitmaster launch P2 set.
1961 June, Ashfield Hall destroyed by fire.
1961 Rosebud introduce kits Nos. 25-30.
1961 July, Author and Club Secretary Steve Knight born in Kingston!
1961 28th September 2nd Charge on assetts to Industrial Credit & Finance Corporation.
1962 Rosebud Kitmaster release kits Nos. 31-34, 60.
1962 July, Rosebud Kitmaster Ltd sold to Airfix.
1962 December, Airfix Ltd. announce purchase of moulds and stock.
1963 January, Hermes Supply Co issue first Nabisco kits.
1963 March, Rosebud Dolls sack 60 workers due to low demand.
1963 June, Hermes Supply Co. ships Fireball XL5 kits.
1963 July, Airfix commence reintroductions.
1963 December, switch from wholesalers to retailers.
1964 January, last 'Kitmaster' Nabisco kits despatched.
1964 Spring, J. R. Ashby leaves Rosebud Dolls.
1964 June, Hermes Supply Co. ships Stingray models.
1964 16th June, Rosebud Dolls Ltd. enters administrative receivership.
1966 7th July, Registered Design No. 927141 granted for a *Blank for making a box intended for holding and displaying dolls.*
1967 29th June, Rosebud Dolls Ltd. agreed merger with Mattel Inc.to form Rosebud - Mattel Ltd.
1967 26th July, End of receivership
1967 3rd August Name change to 'Rosebud-Mattel Ltd' approved by Board of Trade.
1967 21st December EGM agrees to change name to Bunker Huill Properties Ltd.
1968 T. Eric Smith resigns from board of Rosebud-Mattel Ltd., goes into retirement.
1969 T. Eric Smith buys back Raunds site from Rosebud-Mattel Ltd and clears Old Factory site.
1970 Production starts at Smith's Containers Ltd.
1971 'Rosebud' dropped from name of Mattel Ltd.
1971 November Airfix reissue the Mogul.
1980 Airfix sold to Palitoy subsidiary of General Mills Inc.
1980 9th December, Bunker Hill Properties Ltd dissolved by Companies House.
1982 Palitoy sell tools to Dapol Model Railways Ltd.
1985 T. Eric Smith awarded CBE in Honours List.
1989 T. Eric Smith retires from Smith's Containers/RPC Ltd.
1989 Kitmaster Collectors Club formed.
1990 Broadfield House demolished by RPC Ltd.
1997 Kitmaster Website goes live on the Internet.

Appendix Three
ABOUT THE KITMASTER COLLECTORS CLUB
'Actively Promoting Collection'

The Kitmaster Collectors Club was formed in 1990 by a small group of enthusiasts to document the history of the Kitmaster range and also to help and encourage collecting of the kits. The Club is a non-commercial organisation which aims to link collectors for the exchange of archive material, advice and information. Funds generated through kit sales are used for the day-to-day running of the Club, to expand and research the Kitmaster archive, to prepare and distribute promotional material, and to secure important kit collections for the Club when these come onto the market. Members receive first refusal on all kits in Club stock through the regular sales list. The Club also provides an exclusive forum for the buying, selling or swapping of the kits. The Club has over 150 members worldwide and many associates. During 1997, the Club launched a website - *http:\\www.kitmaster.mcmail.com.* The Club is administered by a Chairman and Permanent Secretary, drawn from the membership.

The Collectors Club publishes several works and holds copies of many documents referred to in the text of the forthcoming Collectors Handbook, all of which are available to Club members.

For further information, please write to:
Club Secretary Stephen Knight, *The Laurels,* 109 Head Street, Halstead, Essex CO9 2AZ

Appendix Four - Correspondence and References

SELECTED BIBLIOGRAPHY

Ian Allan - BR Fleet Survey No. 7 - The Diesel Shunters.
Ian Allan ABC Locomotives, 1960/61 Edition.
Ian Allan 'Profile' series No.10, Metropolitan-Cammell Pullman Multiple Units.
Raunds - Picturing the Past; D. Hall, R. Harding and C. Putt.
The Colour of British Rail - Vol. 1, The Diesel Pioneers.
Platform 5 Publications - BR Loco Hauled Rolling Stock, 1984 Edn.
New Cavendish Books - Hornby-Dublo Trains - Foster, Hornby Companion Series, Vol. 5.
New Cavendish Books - History of British Trix Trains - Matthewman.
New Cavendish Books - The Story of Rovex - Vol. 1 -Hammond.
New Cavendish Books - Frog Model Aircraft 1932-1976 - R. Lines and L. Hellström.
Rovex Publications - The Tri-ang Book of Trains, 1966 Edn.
Robert Hale and Co.- Pollock's Dictionary of English Dolls, Ed. Mary Hillier.
'Kitmaster Newsletter' Vol.1, Nos.1-3. Published by A.Burfiord 1988.
'Signal', house journal of KMCC.
TTRCA Gazette No. 73, January 1994.
Railway Modeller, Vols. 10/11/12/13/14/15.
Model Railway News, 1959/60/61/62/63/64.
Model Railway Constructor, 1959/60/61/62.
Boys' Own Paper, 1961.
Hobbies Weekly, Vols.128 and 129, 1959.
The Eagle, 1959.
Airfix Magazine, 1960/61/62/63/64/65/66/67.
Rosebud News, Vol . 1, Nos. 1-6.

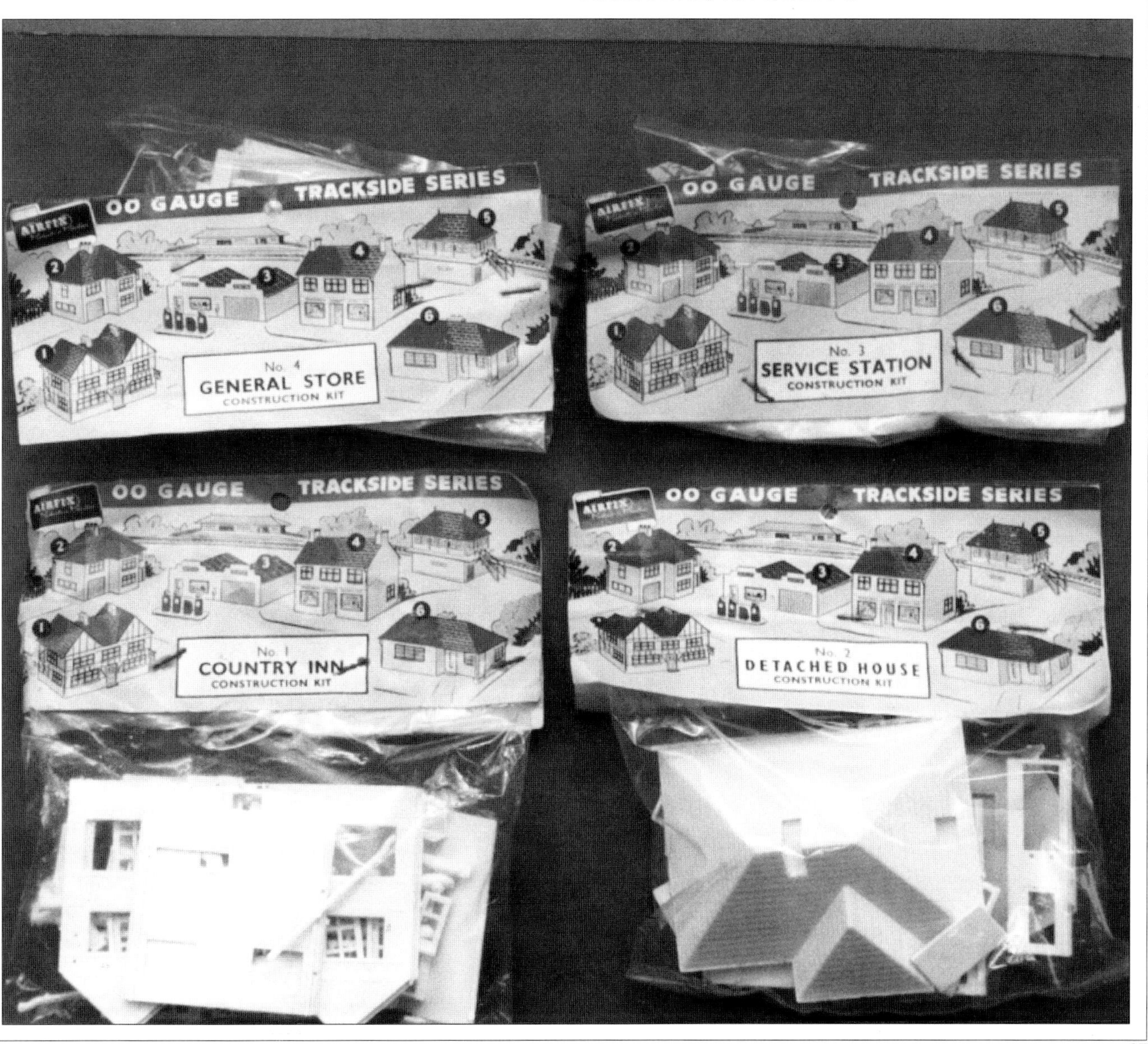

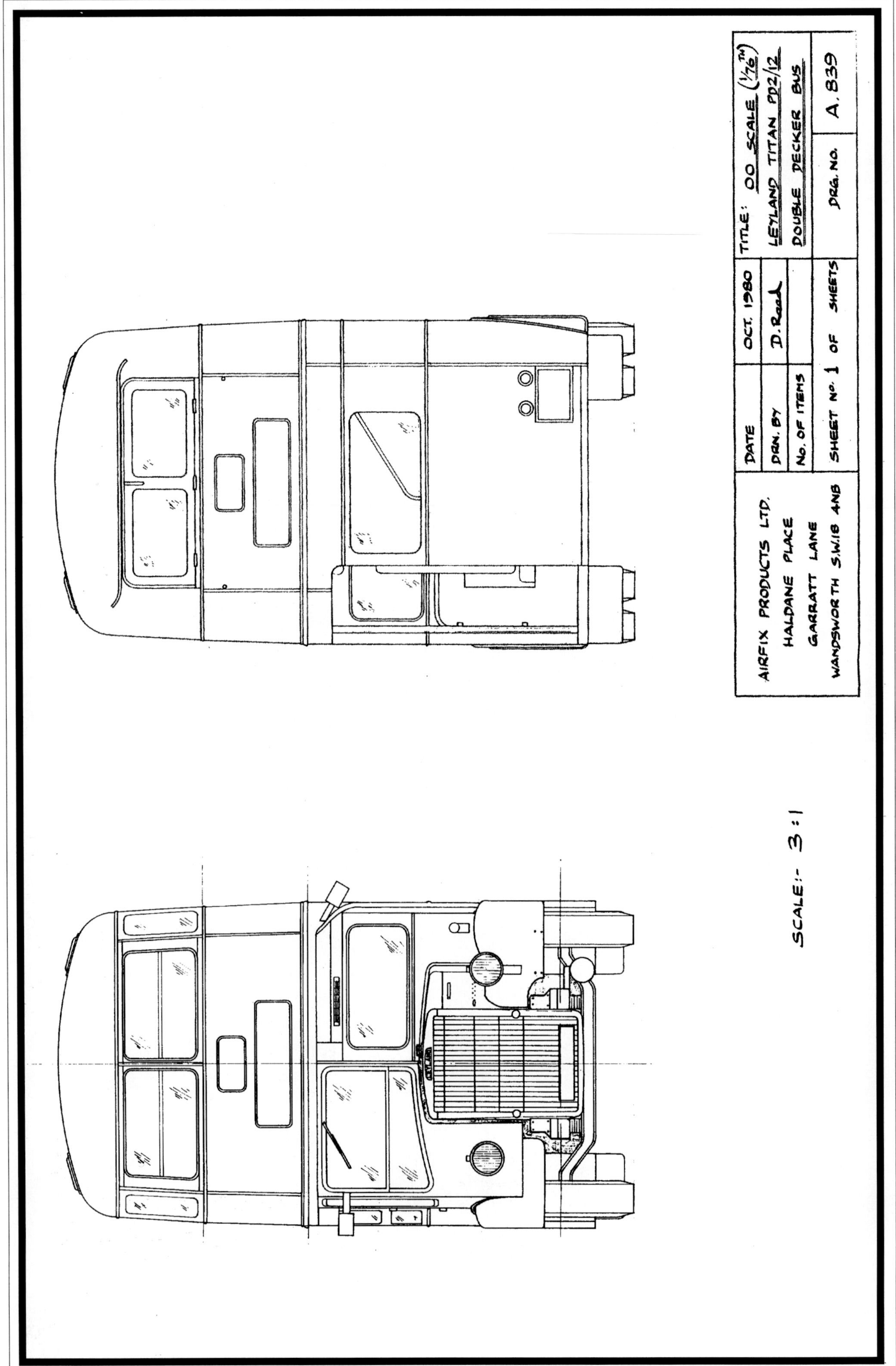
TITLE: OO SCALE (1/76TH)
LEYLAND TITAN PD2/12
DOUBLE DECKER BUS
DATE OCT. 1980
DRN. BY D. Read
No. OF ITEMS
SHEET No. 1 OF SHEETS
DRG. NO. A. 839
AIRFIX PRODUCTS LTD.
HALDANE PLACE
GARRATT LANE
WANDSWORTH S.W.18 4NB
SCALE:- 3:1

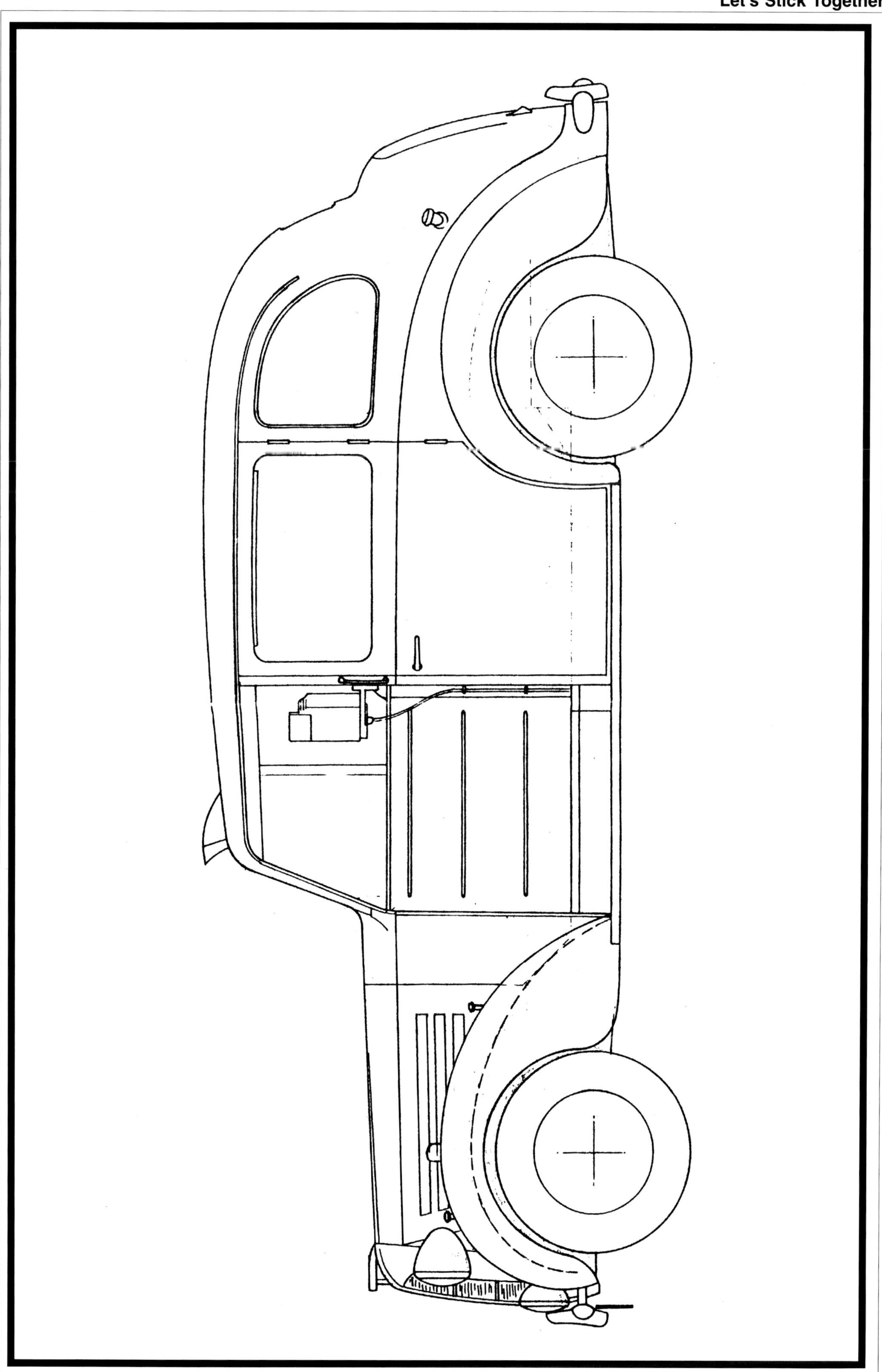